1/06

A Catholic in the White House?

Religion, Politics, and John F. Kennedy's Presidential Campaign

Thomas J. Carty

A Catholic in the White House?

Copyright © Thomas J. Carty, 2004.
All rights reserved. No part of this book may be used or reproduced in any manner whatsoever without written permission except in the case of brief quotations embodied in critical articles or reviews.

First published 2004 by
PALGRAVE MACMILLAN™
175 Fifth Avenue, New York, N.Y. 10010 and
Houndmills, Basingstoke, Hampshire, England RG21 6XS.
Companies and representatives throughout the world.

PALGRAVE MACMILLAN is the global academic imprint of the Palgrave Macmillan division of St. Martin's Press, LLC and of Palgrave Macmillan Ltd. Macmillan®is a registered trademark in the United States, United Kingdom and other countries. Palgrave is a registered trademark in the European Union and other countries.

ISBN 1-4039-6252-9 hardback

Library of Congress Cataloging-in-Publication Data

Carty, Thomas (Thomas Joseph)
   A Catholic in the White House? : religion, politics, and John F. Kennedy's presidential campaign / Thomas Carty.
      p. cm.
   Includes bibliographical references and index
   ISBN 1-4039-6252-9 (hc : alk. paper)
   1. Presidents—United States—Election—1960. 2. United States—Politics and government—1961-1963. 3. Kennedy, John F. (John Fitzgerald), 1917-1963. 4. Presidential candidates—United States—Biography. 5. Catholics—United States—Political activity—History—20th century. 6. Religion and politics—United States—History—20th century. 7. Anti-Catholicism—United States—History—20th century. I. Title.

E837.7C37 2004
324.973'0921--dc22   2004044578

A catalogue record for this book is available from the British Library.

Portions of chapter four were previously published as "The Catholic Question: Religious Liberty and JFK's Pursuit of the 1960 Democratic Presidential Nomination," *The Historian* 63, no. 3 (spring 2001), pp. 577-599. Reprinted with permission.

Design by Autobookcomp.

First edition: September 2004
10 9 8 7 6 5 4 3 2 1

Printed in the United States of America.

Contents

List of Illustrations	v
Acknowledgments	vii
Introduction: The Unresolved "Catholic Issue": The Debate about Religion's Role in the 1960 Presidential Campaign	1
Chapter One: Popish Plots, Religious Liberty, and the Emerging Face of American Catholicism before 1928	11
Chapter Two: Protestant America or a Nation of Immigrants?: Al Smith, Joe Kennedy, and Jim Farley Pursue the Nation's Highest Office	27
Chapter Three: Nativist Anti-Catholicism or Christian Evangelization?: Billy Graham, Norman Vincent Peale, and the Marginalization of Religion during the 1960 Presidential Campaign	49
Chapter Four: Religious Liberty or Religious Test? Debating the 1960 Campaign's "Catholic Issue" in Liberal Organizations and Media	67
Chapter Five: Defining Religious Bigotry: Pluralism and Political Strategy in the 1960 Presidential Election	83
Chapter Six: The Cold War and the Domestic Response to Kennedy's Catholicism	113
Chapter Seven: Testing the "Bailey Thesis": State-level Reactions to a Catholic Presidential Candidate in California, Georgia, Michigan, and New York	129

Epilogue: Catholics and Presidential Elections since 1960	159
Notes	173
Selected Bibliography	199
Index	211

List of Illustrations

1. "'The Promised Land,' As Seen From the Dome of Saint Peter's Rome," *Harper's Weekly* (1870)
2. "Church and State," *Harper's Weekly* (1870)
3. "Al Smith Express," *New York World-Telegram and Sun* (1921)
4a and b. Kennedy and Boston Archbishop Richard Cushing
5. New York Archbishop Francis Spellman and Senator Kennedy at the 1959 Alfred E. Smith Memorial Dinner
6. Kennedy and Protestant evangelical minister Billy Graham
7. "Change of Wardrobe," *Brooklyn Tablet* (1957)
8. Former President Truman and President Kennedy
9. Kennedy, Spellman, and Nixon at the 1960 Alfred E. Smith Memorial Dinner
10. President Kennedy and Michigan Governor G. Mennen Williams
11. California Governor Edmund "Pat" Brown and President Kennedy
12. Kennedy Speaking at the 1960 Alfred E. Smith Memorial Dinner

To Marisol Louise Carty, who carries our hope for the future

Acknowledgments

My maternal grandfather, James B. Murphy, discouraged me from discussing religion and politics in public. I hope the subject of this book does not show blatant disregard for this advice, especially because his memories of John F. Kennedy greatly inspired my study of the 1960 campaign's "Catholic issue." Mr. Murphy, known to me as "Fafa," sponsored Kennedy's admission into the third and fourth degrees of the Knights of Columbus, a lay Catholic fraternity organization. Fafa and his wife, Catherine Louise ("Gram"), attended the 1961 inaugural, and he told me some stories, although not enough (I should have asked more questions), of this experience.

Agnes Carty ("Nana") and Thomas J. Carty, my paternal grandparents, may have seen Fafa and Gram at that ceremony. As captain of the Ancient and Honorable Artillery Company of Massachusetts, Mr. Carty, who died prior to my birth, marched in the inaugural parade with this organization, within which Kennedy also held membership. Nana did not live long enough to engage a budding historian with stories of Kennedy's inauguration.

While my family did not have pictures of Kennedy in every room, these close links with the nation's first Catholic president made an impression on me. My grandparents and parents handed down to me a sincere and strong religious faith, and I have sought to imitate this example. Kennedy's Catholicism surely contributed to the fascination and admiration that my wife, a native of predominately Catholic Peru, and her family hold for the former U.S. chief executive.

This book reflects my effort to understand how the 1960 presidential election affected both my ancestors and the Catholic and American context in which they lived. John Kennedy and Richard Nixon proved most obviously significant, but I learned that many other U.S. citizens participated in defining religion's role in this campaign. I hope that future generations can benefit from my research and analysis of the complicated subjects, religion and politics, that Fafa warned me to approach with caution.

In preparing this work for publication, I incurred several economic, intellectual, professional, and personal debts. Financial support for this project came from many sources. Grants from the University of Connecticut, University of Michigan's Bentley Historical Library, Herbert C. Hoover Presidential Library, and John F. Kennedy Library facilitated my research. My parents provided me with the best education that I could seek without worrying about the cost. Several research librarians and professors promoted my efforts with enthusiasm and understanding. Dr. David J. O'Brien and Dr. Richard M. Fried extended generous advice and ideas at crucial early stages. Professors at the University of Connecticut nurtured me through the growing pains of graduate study. My advisor, Dr. Bruce M. Stave, offered me a model of professionalism, and inspired my efforts to produce worthy scholarship. The supportive comments of many individuals at Springfield College have furthered my ambition to reach this goal. I also thank the staff at Palgrave Macmillan, especially Debbie Gershenowitz and Brendan O'Malley, with whom I worked most closely.

Personally, I gained a lot during this period of my life. My wife granted me an international family in Lima, Peru, and I strengthened my bond with my extended family in the United States. My parents, Janice and Thomas Carty, have unfailingly supported my goals. I cannot express the joy of meeting and growing closer to my wife, Rosamaría, who has sacrificed both the comfort of family and the familiarity of her native country for a challenging role as my best friend, underappreciated advisor, and loving soulmate. Rosamaría's example and encouragement have challenged me to seek improvement as a teacher, scholar, and person. The unfolding miracle of our daughter's birth and development further defies words. We dedicate this book to her, Marisol Louise Carty. We pray that she will share our passion for learning, that she will understand our boundless love for her, and that she will find comfort in God. And I hope she listens when I tell her not to discuss religion and politics in public!

Springfield, MA
February 24, 2004

Introduction

The Unresolved "Catholic Issue"

The Debate about Religion's Role in the 1960 Presidential Campaign

Julie Nixon woke her father, vice president and Republican nominee for president Richard M. Nixon, on the morning after his defeat in the 1960 presidential election to ask, "Daddy, why did people vote against you because of religion?" The elder Nixon responded by repudiating this view of the election results, which Julie had heard reported on television. "Julie, people do not vote for one man or the other because they happen to be Jews or Catholics—or Protestants, as we are. They vote for a man because they believe in what he stands for or because they like him as a person." This story, recounted in Nixon's 1962 memoir, *Six Crises,* portrayed the religious issue as irrelevant to voters.

Yet Nixon strongly believed that Kennedy's Catholicism contributed significantly to the election results. Elsewhere in his account of one of the most closely contested presidential campaigns in the nation's history, Nixon complained that the religious issue actually caused himself greater political difficulties than Kennedy. "I was getting it from both ends: Republican Catholics were being urged to vote for Kennedy because he was of their religion; and Republican Protestants were being urged to vote for him to prove that they were not biased against Catholics!" Noting that Kennedy received support from large majorities of Catholic and Jewish voters, Nixon accused his opponents of consciously exploiting resentment of anti-Catholicism to attract voter sympathy. "At every possible juncture and on every possible occasion," Nixon wrote, "Kennedy's key associates were pushing the religious issue, seeing to it that it stayed squarely in the center of the campaign, and even accusing me of deliberate religious bigotry."[1] In a 1978 memoir, Nixon nearly exclusively blamed the election results on the Kennedy campaign's cynical management of the Democratic nominee's religious affiliation. "I was not prepared for the blatant and highly successful way the Kennedys repeatedly made religion an issue in the campaign even as they professed that is should not be one," Nixon charged. "Led by Robert Kennedy, they managed to turn the election partially into a referendum on tolerance versus bigotry."[2] Nixon presented the Catholic candidate's manipulation of religious sentiments as responsible for the 1960 election results.

Kennedy's chief counsel Theodore C. Sorensen disagreed strongly with Nixon's assessment. While conceding that the candidate's Catholicism "set him apart" and "helped attract a nucleus of followers," Sorensen insisted that the obstacles Kennedy faced because of his religion were much greater than Nixon's dilemmas.[3] Sorensen characterized anti-Catholicism as the Democratic nominee's most serious barrier to the White House. "Religious bias was the principal obstacle to election victory. It was always there, in every state."[4] By Sorensen's account, "life-long Democrats who were Protestant" abandoned the Democratic Party "in droves" due to Kennedy's Catholicism. To support this position further, Sorensen quoted political scientist V. O. Key, Jr., who concluded from election analysis that "Kennedy won in spite of rather than because of the fact that he was a Catholic."[5]

This book will analyze the elements that led to these dramatically different perspectives on religion's role in the 1960 presidential campaign. Fairness and equality have served as founding principles of the United States of America, and many American parents have taught their children that religious affiliation should not exclude an individual from becoming president of the United States. As the nation's first successful Catholic presidential candidate, John Kennedy appeared to embody and affirm this ideal in 1960. Kennedy's easy charm, patrician demeanor, and boyish good looks contributed to his victory—particularly in the age of television, which amplified these characteristics. By breaking the Protestant monopoly on the White House, however, Kennedy has come to symbolize the reality of equal opportunity in America, achieving iconic status among religious and ethnic minorities. "For millions of ethnic Americans, Kennedy remains more than a bright, promising young president whose life and time in office were prematurely snuffed out," Kennedy biographer and historian Robert Dallek recently wrote. "[Kennedy] is an enduring demonstration that ethnics and minorities, who, despite rhetoric to the contrary, did not feel fully accepted in America before 1960, have come into their own as first-class citizens."[6] By disproving the "unwritten law" that only a Protestant could win election to the presidency, Kennedy's achievement allowed Americans of every religion, race, and gender to maintain a genuine sense of his or her first-class citizenship and inclusion in American political culture.

Yet Kennedy's 1960 presidential election victory represents a unique moment in U.S. history. More than four decades passed, prior to John F. Kerry in 2004, before another Catholic received even the nomination by a major party for the presidency. Kennedy's campaign triggered numerous disputes about Catholicism and politics in American society on national, regional, and local levels. Mass-produced pamphlets, from extreme anti-Catholic organizations, recapitulated the centuries-old belief that the Roman Catholic pope ruled as a living antichrist. Theologians, academics, and politicians opined about the proper role of religion in public life. Jesuit priest John Courtney Murray graced the December 1960 cover of *Time* magazine as "Man of the Year" for his innovative reconciliations of Catholic teaching and the U.S. principle of church-state separation. Many Catholic politicians, such as California Governor Edmund "Pat" Brown, feared becoming caught up in the maelstrom of an anti-Catholic movement against Kennedy's campaign.

Much has been written about how socioeconomic status and ethnic identity contributed to American responses to Kennedy in the 1960 election, but religion also played a major role. While social class and ethnicity provide important perspectives for scholarly analysis, religious belief maintains a significant persuasive power in the political arena. Religion functions as a "cultural system" that conditions how faithful believers perceive political and social events.[7] Examining religion's impact on politics will inform discussion about American attitudes that economic and social analysis cannot fully explain. Political science research reveals that individuals form attitudes about religion and politics at an early age. Intensely personal opinions about Kennedy's Catholicism confronted both candidates in 1960. Institutional and philosophical differences among and within religious faiths offer novel perspectives for analyzing the events of this presidential campaign.

While high school and college history textbooks unfailingly recognize the significance of Kennedy's election, scholarly accounts of this campaign reflect continued divisions about Catholicism's place in U.S. society and culture. One group of scholars has portrayed the campaign as critical to creating a more egalitarian social order between Catholic and non-Catholic Americans. In this interpretation, Kennedy's individualistic, independent view of religion offered an image of a modern Catholicism to non-Catholics. According to historian Richard Polenberg, Kennedy's detached, cosmopolitan image defied stereotypes of Catholicism's conformist and parochial character.[8] Catholic academics have credited Kennedy's political success with encouraging Catholics to abandon self-segregated institutions and to enter mainstream U.S.

society. Catholic priest, author, and sociologist Andrew Greeley depicted Kennedy as a "doctor of the church" for teaching Catholics to engage with modern American social and political institutions. According to historian Philip Gleason, "[The 1960 election represented] the culmination of Catholic assimilation into American life and a climactic moment in the Catholic rapprochement with modernity."[9] Kennedy's victory profoundly changed American Catholicism, according to several accounts. Historian James Hennessey argued that the election of Kennedy decreased American Catholics' "psychological defensiveness."[10] Author Charles Morris even believed that the election of a skeptical, ironic, and secular Catholic, such as Kennedy, fractured the perception of a "rigorous, didactic, all-encompassing brand of Catholicism" and "heralded the final breakdown of the separatist American Catholic subculture."[11] These writers presented the post-1960 United States as a new era in Catholic relations with non-Catholic Americans.

In another perspective, however, Kennedy mischaracterized and even betrayed Catholic principles. For some individuals, Kennedy served as neither an apologist nor a reformer for American Catholicism. Senator Eugene McCarthy (MN), a former seminarian who consciously defended government assistance to needy citizens by referring to Catholic social teaching, asserted that he was "twice as Catholic as Kennedy." Robert F. Kennedy begrudgingly acknowledged McCarthy's perspective: "Gene McCarthy felt he should have been the first Catholic President just because he knew more [teachings of thirteenth-century Catholic theologian] St. Thomas Aquinas than my brother."[12] Others shared this view that Kennedy lacked profound identification with Catholicism. Kennedy's repeated declarations of both freedom from Vatican pressures and disassociation from Catholic dogma prompted journalist Murray Kempton to quip that the 1960 election produced the nation's "first anti-clerical President."[13] As historians uncovered more sordid details of Kennedy's personal and public life, several writers quoted a more cynical assessment, attributed to Jacqueline Kennedy: "I think it is unfair for Jack to be opposed because he is a Catholic. After all, he's such a poor Catholic. Now if it were [his brother] Bobby: he never misses mass and prays all the time."[14] These accounts questioned the assumption that Kennedy's election introduced a new era of equality and opportunity for U.S. Catholics.

More than forty years since Kennedy's election, this book seeks to reconcile these divergent opinions on the significance of Kennedy's election as a Catholic president. In 1987, historian Philip Gleason noted the absence of any "notable publications" on the 1960 campaign's religious issue. Until recently, historians have accepted the standard narrative that Americans rejected bigotry by electing Kennedy. Yet the facts reveal a much more complicated story that academics such as John McGreevy and Mark Massa, and authors such as Charles Morris and Thomas Maier, have outlined. McGreevy's research demonstrated that significant liberal opposition to Kennedy derived from the writings of mid-twentieth-century, non-Catholic American intellectuals who defined themselves in opposition to American Catholics. Portraying Catholicism as rooted in authoritarian, absolutist traditions from medieval times, intellectual liberals advocated democratic, experimental evaluation of truth based on the scientific method.[15] McGreevey's thesis suggested that opposition to Kennedy in the 1960 campaign did not merely reflect fundamentalist Protestant anti-Catholicism.

Mark Massa has also challenged the assumption that Kennedy's victory reconciled Catholic and non-Catholic Americans. In Massa's perspective, anti-Catholicism pressured Kennedy to "secularize" the presidency by marginalizing religious language in the campaign. By advocating an absolute separation of church and state, and dealing with the "Catholic issue" in a strictly secular manner, Kennedy relegated religion to the private, personal sphere. Citing Kennedy's heralded September 1960 address to Houston's Protestant ministers, Massa perceived the Catholic candidate's words as consciously nonsectarian and even nonreligious. According to Massa, the Catholic candidate needed to profess support for an absolute separation of church and state in order to achieve election as president: "Kennedy's Houston Speech can be fruitfully seen as a key moment, not only in American Catholicism's 'coming of age,' but also of the articulation of the *terms* of that rite of passage."[16] In other words, Kennedy compromised Catholic and religious principles to secure the secular goal of the presidency. Massa views the 1960 campaign as a pivotal event in the removal of religion from public discourse: "Kennedy's razor-thin victory ushered in the end of ideology—religious ideology included."[17] Massa's recent book, *Anti-Catholicism in America: The Last Acceptable Prejudice*, adds to a flurry of works echoing the theme that the Roman Catholic Church has not received full acceptance in U.S. political culture.[18]

An exceptional combination of circumstances, sometimes unique to particular geographic regions, conditioned Americans to vote for a Catholic president in 1960. Non-Catholics constructed a case against the prospect of a Catholic in the White House by attempting to marginalize Catholic religious beliefs and cultural practices as "foreign," authoritarian, and thus incompatible with U.S. traditions and ideals of religious liberty. Some Protestant ministers argued that Catholics, including Kennedy, would inevitably choose loyalty to the pope above allegiance to the United States. In this perspective, clerical pressure to align his decisions with the Holy See's religious dogma would prevent a Catholic president from governing independently and objectively in pursuit of the ideals and security of diverse U.S. citizens. Several U.S. intellectuals also portrayed Catholicism as incompatible with liberal democratic traditions. Many Protestants, Catholics, and Jews, however, unified against intolerance of racial and religious minorities. Interfaith opposition to communism also discouraged U.S. citizens from viewing Catholics, who fought for America in World War II and the Korean War, as un-American.

This book examines Catholicism's impact on the 1960 presidential campaign in seven chapters. The first chapter examines the history of American Catholics in U.S. politics prior to 1928, when U.S. Senator Thomas J. Walsh from Montana and New York Governor Alfred E. Smith became the first Catholics to contend realistically for the presidency. Anti-Catholicism helped unite and define the subjects of England's monarchs in Europe and America as Englishmen. The American Revolution inspired an egalitarian ethic that generated tolerance for Catholics, especially since Catholic France and Spain had aided the patriots against England. Although Catholic Americans assimilated easily during the new nation's first forty years, some native-born Protestants created anti-Catholic conspiracy theories and organizations from the 1830s through the 1850s. In response to an influx of Catholic immigrants in the nineteenth century, the Native American Party and the American Protective Association alleged clerical conspiracies to seduce and violate women and to undermine American liberty. Portraying Catholicism as a menacing, alien threat to U.S. ideals, these groups sought to ban Catholics from political office. The Ku Klux Klan revived this message in the 1920s, and evangelicals within various Protestant denominations, such as the Southern Baptists, echoed these arguments. Al Smith's appeal to religious and racial minorities, however, revealed the potential for unity among non-Protestant, nonwhite Americans.

Chapter Two examines how Catholicism proved an obstacle to the presidential ambitions of Al Smith, Tom Walsh, Postmaster General James Farley, and Ambassador Joseph P. Kennedy in the years 1928 to 1956. While Walsh's rural roots and support for Prohibition made this Catholic acceptable to some Protestants, Smith's urban, immigrant past and opposition to Protestant hegemony, exemplified in the banning of alcohol, attracted religious and racial minorities. Anti-Catholicism undermined both these candidates. Smith's landslide defeat in 1928 discouraged both parties from nominating another Catholic, although President Franklin D. Roosevelt aided many Catholics through appointments to federal offices. Roosevelt's opposition to Catholic presidential candidates Farley and Joe Kennedy fostered a sense of victimization among these Catholics. Increasing tensions between Catholics and liberals regarding church-state separation complicated the prospect of a Catholic presidential candidacy. Despite suspicions about the militancy of Catholic anticommunism, Senator John Kennedy (MA) pursued the vice presidency in 1956. Kennedy's failure did not proscribe this politician's pursuit of the presidency four years later.

The third chapter addresses the responses of politically powerful conservative Protestant ministers, such as Billy Graham and Norman Vincent Peale, to Kennedy's Catholicism in 1960. In private and public comments, Graham and Peale suggested that Kennedy would face irresistible pressures to favor the Roman Catholic Church in public policy. While denying that religious bias motivated opposition to a Catholic president, the Southern Baptist Convention and National Association of Evangelicals argued that the Roman Catholic Church consistently opposed religious liberty. As Kennedy directly challenged these doubts about a Catholic president by addressing the Houston Ministerial Association in September 1960, Peale and Graham terminated efforts to mobilize opposition to Kennedy on religious grounds.

Chapter Four discusses how liberals debated the proper response to Kennedy's candidacy. During the 1960 campaign, American liberals promoted religious freedom among an array of social justice issues, yet Kennedy's Catholicism divided the liberal camp. In the view of Protestants and Other Americans United for Separation of Church and State (POAU), American Catholic politicians and the church's hierarchy presented a threat to religious liberty by violating the principle of church-state separation. Lawyer Paul B. Blanshard and other POAU officials persistently demanded that Catholic presidential candidates renounce their church's advocacy of a U.S. ambassador to the Vatican, federal aid to parochial schools, and all partnership between religious and political organizations. These disputes led several organizations, such as the Americans for Democratic Action and the American Civil Liberties Union, to withhold endorsement of the Catholic candidate. Within these organizations, liberal theologian Reinhold Niebuhr and historian Arthur Schlesinger, Jr., defended Kennedy from a litmus test that could deny Catholics free and equal access to the highest office in American politics. Kennedy attempted to persuade skeptical liberals by opposing the nomination of an emissary to the Holy See, government assistance to Catholic schools, and any breach in the absolute wall of separation between spiritual and secular life.

Chapter Five discusses how Kennedy's candidacy, despite these challenges, encouraged solidarity among distinct religious and ethnic communities. In the 1930s, the Democratic Party united Protestant, Catholic, Jewish, and African Americans behind common economic and social goals. The 1960 campaign's "Catholic issue" threatened to divide this fragile coalition. Many members of the Masonic Order, such as former President Harry S. Truman, initially expressed opposition to a Catholic president. Some American Jews feared another Inquisition, and Baptist minister Martin Luther King, Sr., symbolized widespread African American suspicion of Catholics by publicly repudiating Kennedy's candidacy on religious grounds. After Kennedy managed the Catholic issue well enough to secure the Democratic nomination, however, Truman campaigned actively against anti-Catholicism. When Truman's speeches included accusations that Nixon promoted anti-Catholic bigotry, Republican Catholics protested. But Nixon's policy of avoiding discussion of Kennedy's religion suppressed these responses to Truman. Kennedy's late October maneuvers in support of Martin Luther King, Jr., inspired the majority of African Americans to endorse the Catholic candidate in November.

The sixth chapter reviews the Cold War's affect on the campaign's "Catholic issue." Only years after the Korean War and the Soviet launch of the Sputnik satellite, the Roman Catholic Church's reputation for uncompromising anticommunism threatened to detract from Kennedy's candidacy. The anticommunist militancy of New York Archbishop Francis Cardinal Spellman and Republican Senator Joseph R. McCarthy (WI) persuaded some Americans to predict that a Catholic president would provoke a third world war with the Soviet Union and People's Republic of China. Kennedy's past decisions and personal relationship to McCarthy generated special mistrust among liberal Democrats, such as Eleanor Roosevelt and theologian John C. Bennett. By advocating a liberal critique of both the hunt for internal subversives and President Dwight D. Eisenhower's Cold War policies, however, Kennedy attracted Democratic support. Yet these statements also alienated Catholics and non-Catholics who had supported McCarthy's search for subversives and rejected peaceful coexistence with communist nations. Conservative anticommunists, such as Gerald L. K. Smith and William F. Buckley, charged Kennedy with disloyalty to Catholic teachings about communism. Kennedy's Catholicism and anticommunist rhetoric nonetheless insulated the Democratic nominee from charges of being "soft" on communism.

In four states—California, Michigan, New York, and Georgia—the Kennedy campaign managed the religious issue's diverse manifestations, which Chapter Seven examines. Kennedy's ability to win each of these states except California, which had a Catholic governor in 1960, demonstrated religion's complex role in this election. California Governor Edmund Brown, who harbored ambitions for the presidency or vice presidency, perceived the Democrats as likely to nominate only one Catholic to the national ticket and thus withheld early endorsement of Kennedy, a competitor. Despite the state's Democratic majority of registered voters, Nixon won this state in November. Michigan Democratic leaders, including Protestant Governor G. Mennen Williams, worked tirelessly to unite liberals and labor leaders to secure Kennedy's close victory, which seemed critical to their personal and political ambitions. Republican occupation of New York's two senate seats and the governor's office did not prevent the Democrats from effectively mobilizing liberals, urban Catholics and Jews, and rural Protestants behind Kennedy. In Georgia, a state of less than 5 percent Catholics, party loyalty and economic motives allowed Kennedy to secure the votes of many Methodists and Baptists. Demonstrating confidence in this state's support for Kennedy in the campaign's final weeks, Democratic Senator Richard Russell (GA) campaigned on Kennedy's behalf in Texas. Kennedy's ability to win many northeastern, midwestern, and southern states compensated for the loss of some votes due to Catholicism.

The epilogue reviews the attempts by several Catholics to become the nation's second Catholic president. Prior to John F. Kerry's (MA) nomination in 2004, no Catholic had seriously contested for the presidency since 1960. The Democrats nominated two Catholics, Peace Corps Director R. Sargent Shriver and Congresswoman Geraldine Ferraro (NY), for vice president, but Republicans won landslide victories in both years. In 1972, President Richard Nixon secured support from many Catholics, who responded well to his endorsement of federal aid to parochial schools, opposition to abortion, and uncompromising anticommunism. Abortion's increasing relevance for voters affected Catholic responses to Ferraro and New York Governor Mario Cuomo, who briefly considered running for president in 1988. New York Archbishop John O'Connor challenged both these politicians to oppose the legal right to abortion. This clerical pressure may have discouraged other Catholic Democratic presidential candidates because of the party's strong lobby for abortion rights. In the 1990s, anti-abortion Catholics, such as Reform Party candidate Patrick J. Buchanan and Republican hopeful Alan Keyes, appeared more frequently than Catholic Democrats, such as Jerry Brown.

Demographic changes, not moral issues such as abortion, may dramatically and permanently alter Catholicism's status within U.S. political culture. The two most recognizable Catholic politicians in the United States—John Kerry and California Governor Arnold Schwarzenegger (husband of John Kennedy's niece), both defend the legal right to abortion. Yet other analysts, such as political scientist Samuel P. Huntington, warn against the potentially divisive impact of Latin American immigration. Hispanic-Catholic immigrants could ultimately undermine Anglo-Protestant culture—essential to America's strength, in Huntington's interpretation—because of the disproportionate rate of Mexican immigrants and the high fertility rates of Latin Americans. These nonwhite Catholics have successfully maintained cultural and even linguistic traditions despite the assimilating power of the United States.[19] John Kerry's consideration of New Mexico's Governor Bill Richardson, also a Catholic, for the vice presidency revealed the growing significance of this voting bloc. If the Republican Party does not adjust to this challenge, Democrats may attract the Latin American population in the United States with the same fierce party loyalty that another Catholic bloc, Irish Americans, consistently demonstrated for many years.

This Irish Catholic loyalty to the Democratic Party largely derived from the hostile reception with which native-born Protestant Americans greeted immigrants from Ireland. Chapter One recounts the origins of anti-Catholic nativism and the political consequences for U.S. Catholics.

Chapter One

Popish Plots, Religious Liberty, and the Emerging Face of American Catholicism before 1928

Massachusetts Senator John F. Kennedy "conveyed an intangible feeling of depression" on the night of January 2, 1960, according to historian Arthur Schlesinger, Jr. Earlier that day, Kennedy had officially announced his intention to run for president. As an advisor to Kennedy's campaign, Schlesinger enjoyed intimate access to the Catholic candidate. In Schlesinger's view, Kennedy's uncharacteristically sullen mood derived from the Catholic candidate's fear of religious opposition. "I had the sense," Schlesinger recalled, "that he feels himself increasingly hemmed in as a result of a circumstance over which he has no control—his religion; and he inevitably tends toward gloom and irritation when he considers how the circumstance may deny him what he thinks his talent and efforts have earned."[1]

This historian's acute awareness of America's anti-Catholic past may have sensitized Schlesinger to Kennedy's inner preoccupation with the campaign's looming "Catholic issue." As a student of American political culture, Schlesinger recognized Kennedy's profound religious challenge in the 1960 campaign. Schlesinger's father called opposition to Catholics the "deepest bias in the history of the American people."[2] Only years earlier, historian John Higham had written that "[n]o other xenophobia functioned in so highly organized a way as anti-Romanism."[3] No Catholic had received nomination for the presidency by a major political party prior to 1928. In that year, Catholic New York Governor Alfred E. Smith suffered a landslide defeat.

In order to understand the nature of U.S. responses to Kennedy's Catholicism in 1960, this chapter examines the complex, changing attitudes toward Catholics in American politics prior to Al Smith's 1928 campaign. To the majority of seventeenth- and eighteenth-century English settlers in North America, Catholicism threatened England's survival as a political and cultural community. The contribution of Catholic France and Spain to the American Revolution decreased Protestant-Catholic tensions. Although Catholics in the early American republic adapted well to the new nation's rational, Enlightenment principles, some native-born Protestant Americans, such as congregationalist minister Lyman Beecher and inventor Samuel F. B. Morse, defined American culture in opposition to the Roman Catholic Church by the 1830s. During periods of high Catholic immigration, formal political organizations—such as the Native American Party, the American Protective Association, and the Ku Klux Klan—mobilized resistance to Catholics.

Despite the profound, bitter roots of anti-Catholic attitudes in the United States, the twentieth century revealed signs of increasing tolerance for Catholic Americans, since Catholics had demonstrated loyalty to the U.S. government in several wars, and Catholic organizations contributed substantially to support American efforts in World War I. Following this war, a spirit of inclusiveness, known as pluralism, gained momentum in the 1920s. This philosophical idea took concrete form in the consideration of two Catholics—Al Smith and Senator Thomas J. Walsh (MT)—for the Democratic Party presidential nomination in 1924.

Al Smith and Tom Walsh competed to define Catholicism's best role in U.S. politics. As a governor of diverse racial and religious minorities in New York State, Smith inspired many Catholic, Jewish, and African Americans to believe in the nation's commitment to equal opportunity. Tom Walsh's rural, western roots attracted many Protestant progressives who sought to demonstrate tolerance toward a Catholic candidate. Walsh offered an alternative to Smith, whose urban, immigrant characteristics matched negative anti-Catholic stereotypes. The raucous, inordinately long 1924 Democratic National Convention left a mixed legacy for future Catholic presidential candidates.

"Popish Leviathan": The Roman Catholic Threat to Anglo-America, Sixteenth to Eighteenth Centuries

Prior to the American Revolution, anti-Catholicism provided one of the strongest bonds between the Protestant majorities in both England and England's colonies in North America. Domestic and foreign struggles against Catholics afforded Protestants a mythology around which to construct a distinct English identity. Powerful memories, such as "Bloody" Catholic Queen Mary's murder of Protestant dissenters and

England's miraculous naval victory against Catholic Spain's "invincible" armada in the sixteenth century, symbolized the religious character of an embryonic English nationalism.[4] Historian David H. Bennett traced the roots of English anti-Catholicism to the "rival imperial ambitions of Catholic Spain and France."[5] This threat of Catholicism arose within England also. On November 5, 1605, the failure of a conspiracy of thirteen Catholics to kill King James I and other national leaders by exploding barrels of gunpowder in England's Parliament inspired an annual memorial known as Guy Fawkes Day. Named after the organizer of this "Gunpowder Plot," the yearly event featured ritual burning of the conspirators and the pope in effigy.[6] According to historian Ray A. Billington, "Popery was feared, not so much as a religion alone, but as an instrument through which England itself was to be overthrown."[7] These anxieties traveled with England's American colonists. Seventeenth-century English settlers, in northern and southern colonies alike, organized public singing and alcohol consumption on Guy Fawkes Day—also known as Pope Day—to commemorate English liberty from Catholic religious and political authority.[8] In the words of historian Philip Jenkins, "English (and American) freedom was defined against the feared alien force of Catholicism."[9]

Although dominant denominations may have varied from colony to colony, anti-Catholic actions and sentiments appeared in each. Virginians worshipped within the Church of England. Massachusetts Bay settlers espoused Puritanism and perceived Virginia's Anglicans as dangerously akin to Roman Catholics.[10] Both colonies restricted Catholic liberties. Massachusetts expelled a member of the Bay Colony in 1631 for allegedly adhering to papal decrees, while Virginia disenfranchised all Catholics in 1642. Even the colony of Maryland, founded by Roman Catholic Sir George Calvert (Lord Baltimore), became unfriendly to Catholics by the mid-seventeenth century. Maryland's rising Protestant majority replaced the colony's Toleration Act in 1654 with a law declaring "none who profess to exercise the Popish religion, commonly known by the name of Roman Catholic religion, can be protected in this province."[11] After the 1689 Glorious Revolution, England's joint monarchs William and Mary revoked Maryland's charter to impose royal authority and an established Anglican church in that colony. Only Rhode Island granted full legal equality to Catholics, but this colony's founder, Roger Williams—who left Massachusetts in pursuit of religious freedom—characterized the Roman Catholic Church as a "wolf" and a "popish leviathan."[12]

Anti-Catholicism continued to dominate Anglo-American political culture until the American Revolution. The English philosopher John

Locke—whose contract theory of government defended the Bill of Rights that limited royal authority following the Glorious Revolution in England—excluded Catholics from the liberties entitled to Protestant Englishmen. In North America, the Great Awakening revival of Protestant fundamentalism and evangelicalism inspired anti-Catholic sentiments in the 1740s. Evangelical minister George Whitfield warned against "swarms of monks . . . and friars like so many locusts . . . overspreading and plaguing the nation." Public schools and fireside games often reinforced contempt of the Roman Catholic Church—"that arrant Whore of Rome." Fears about Catholic France conspiring with Indians and African slaves during the Seven Years' War in the 1750s and 1760s perpetuated the anti-Catholic bond between England and her North American colonies.[13]

The search for European allies against England's colonial rule, as well as the egalitarian ideal of the American Revolution, helped dissolve some Protestant distrust toward Catholics in the late eighteenth century. Resistance to English rule provided the North American colonies with a common bond beyond Protestantism. In the face of English tyranny, "the real test of loyalty was whether a person supported the new government or the crown, not whether he or she practiced Catholicism or some other religion," noted historian David Bennett.[14] The need for intercolonial unity, as well as support from Catholic France and Spain, encouraged General George Washington to denounce Guy Fawkes Day as a "ridiculous and childish custom." The Declaration of Independence's rhetoric of equality inspired a spirit of toleration. The U.S. Constitution's provision against a religious test for public office and the disestablishment of religion in the First Amendment provided a vision of religious tolerance that emerging states would eventually follow. These documents helped to form an intellectual basis for twentieth-century pluralist ideology.[15]

"Awful Disclosures": Nativist Conspiracy Theories about Catholicism, 1790s to 1850s

In the decades prior to the Civil War, however, some native-born Protestant Americans revived anti-Catholic arguments to unify Protestants of diverse denominations and social class. From the 1790s to the 1820s, Catholics easily adjusted to the new republican establishment. By the 1830s, however, nativists characterized Catholicism as politically authoritarian and sexually subversive. Lyman Beecher and Samuel Morse publicized these theories to mobilize various Protestant sects and socioeconomic groups against Catholicism. Industrialization in the 1840s attracted Irish Catholic immigrants, whose lack of skills and education confirmed Protestant stereotypes about Catholics' incompatibility with political independence and freedom of conscience. The Know-Nothing movement and Native American Party enjoyed brief success in the 1850s by appealing to northeastern Protestants, who feared an unholy alliance between a southern oligarchy of slaveowners and the American Catholic Church.

After the American Revolution, Catholics in the United States benefited from the postwar spirit of political and religious toleration. Although Catholic Americans remained a small minority, they shared with non-Catholics an Enlightenment view of religion as rational and practical. Symbolizing the common goals of U.S. politics and American Catholicism in the early republic, John Carroll, the first bishop in the United States, modeled the nation's first cathedral, in Baltimore, on the capitol building in Washington, D.C. Other Catholic Americans participated openly in the interfaith spirit of republican ideology and tolerance. This bishop's cousin, Charles Carroll, served as a delegate to the Continental Congress and signed the Declaration of Independence. Another Catholic, Mathew Carey, immigrated to Philadelphia from Ireland in 1784, and became the nation's most prominent publisher. Carey's Catholicism did not prevent him from coordinating the city's civic services with Protestant evangelical and medical doctor Benjamin Rush, as well as American founding father Benjamin Franklin.[16] At this time, few Americans perceived a contradiction between the Catholic religion and American politics.

Nativist anti-Catholicism emerged as many Protestants feared a loss of authority in U.S. political culture. Massachusetts had removed New England Congregationalists' official status as the establishment religion by 1833, and denounced the Roman Catholic Church as the "anti-Christ" in an effort to decrease factionalism among Methodists, Baptists, and Unitarians.[17] Congregationalist ministers, such as Lyman Beecher, feared that Roman Catholic clerics sought to displace the Protestant faith through a network of parochial schools. Catholicism suppressed freedom of conscience through a global, clerical hierarchy, Beecher argued in three Boston sermons that inspired the burning of a Catholic convent in Charleston, Massachusetts, in 1834.[18] Beecher's 1835 book *A Plea for the West* similarly sounded an alarm that the founding of Catholic schools in Ohio and other western states threatened America's tradition of educating youth through public institutions.[19]

Criticism of Roman Catholicism also united American Protestants from all socioeconomic levels. Samuel Morse portrayed Catholic immigrants as "human priest-controlled machines" that conspired with the Holy See and European monarchies to colonize the United States.[20] Educated professionals read Morse's opinions in the *New York Observer* and the *New York Journal of Commerce* in the 1830s. Morse published this argument in a book, *Foreign Conspiracy*, which sold well enough to justify five editions by 1841.[21]

Salacious novels attracted a more popular audience to anti-Catholicism. Several published works accused the Catholic Church of perverse sexual practices and reckless disregard for human life within cloistered orders. In 1836, a woman adopting the pseudonym Maria Monk published a book, *Awful Disclosures of the Hotel Dieu Nunnery of Montreal*, which described Catholic priests who raped nuns and subsequently murdered the children produced by these violent sexual encounters. The author's mother soon contradicted this account, and two Protestant clergymen proved unable to substantiate these accusations after an investigation of the convent. Maria Monk's book nonetheless earned a place with *Uncle Tom's Cabin* (written by Lyman Beecher's daughter Harriet Beecher Stowe) as a best-selling novel in the pre–Civil War United States. The financial success of *Awful Disclosures* also inspired imitations, such as *Six Months in a Convent* and *The Testimony of an Escaped Novice*. Several urban committees soon emerged to investigate the internal affairs of Catholic convents.[22]

Beginning in the late 1840s, Catholic immigration to the United States confirmed nativist theories for some Americans. Although industrial growth in the United States created new jobs, some native-born Americans resented the economic competition from impoverished Irish immigrants who willingly worked for lower wages. Ethnic differences and economic competition fostered mistrust and resentment among native-born U.S. citizens. In the eyes of some Protestants, Catholic refugees from Ireland's potato famine seemed ignorant and unable to assimilate to U.S. culture. In addition to the Irish, German-speaking Catholic migrants from Central Europe's Palatinate region sometimes clashed violently with American Protestants, especially in U.S. cities. According to Protestant nativists, Catholicism failed to nurture individual conscience among these immigrants, who became pawns of the priestly class. Many Anglo-Saxon Protestant Americans favored the wealthy Protestant German political refugees, who entered the country after the failed European revolutions of 1848. Since these Protestant immigrants often fled the German principalities for ideological reasons, American nativists accepted them as genuine republicans who rejected the European monarchies.[23] The German Protestant, nativists believed, assimilated more easily into U.S. political culture than did the Irish Catholic, who was believed to value dependence and obedience to monarchs and bishops.[24]

Organized political anti-Catholicism appeared in response to these social and economic changes in the mid-nineteenth century. Some native-born Protestants assumed that Catholics, unable to exercise independent judgment, would choose representatives based on crass self-interest rather than elect intelligent, independent leaders. A secret society, the Know-Nothings, formed in the 1840s to resist this increasing Catholic immigration, and many of these nativists created the Native American Party in 1854.[25] Alleging that the Roman Catholic Church conspired with the southern slaveholding aristocracy against the expansion of liberty in the United States, nativist candidates won both the Massachusetts governorship and 376 of 378 seats in the state house of representatives.[26]

At this time, Protestant evangelicals and antislavery reformers perpetuated the notion that American Catholics shared the tyrannical spirit of southern slaveowners. In *Uncle Tom's Cabin,* Harriett Beecher Stowe portrayed the Roman Catholic St. Clare family as oppressing not only the African American slave Uncle Tom but also the young, innocent Eva. When Uncle Tom converts the child Eva St. Clare to Methodism, Stowe encourages the reader to equate her religious liberation with the prospect of black emancipation. Former slave and abolitionist Frederick Douglass more explicitly criticized the "cunning illusions" of American Catholics. Comparing southern slaveholding to the Spanish Inquisition, evangelical Protestant George Cheever credited Supreme Court Chief Justice Roger Taney's Catholicism as inspiration for the 1857 *Dred Scott* decision. The majority decision, written by Taney, denied all constitutional rights to African Americans in the United States.[27]

The Know-Nothing movement, however, enjoyed a very brief success. In the attempt to attract national support, in 1856 party members chose a presidential candidate, Millard Fillmore, who had slave-owning friends and had enrolled his daughter in Catholic schools. Although the Native American Party elected five U.S. senators and won 20 percent of the popular vote for president, the issue of slavery and state's rights distracted Americans from fears of Catholicism, and Catholic contributions to the nation during the Civil War undermined nativist anti-Catholicism for several years.[28]

"Menace to Our Liberties": Catholic Success and Nativist Resistance, 1860s to 1910s

From the Civil War through World War I, anti-Catholicism survived, principally due to the increasing visibility of Catholics in U.S. political life. Nativist mistrust of Catholicism persisted despite Catholic participation in northern suppression of the Confederate rebellion. Irish Catholics employed existing institutions, such as New York City's Tammany Hall political machine, to gain access to governmental offices. Postwar industrial expansion during this period prompted another boom in Catholic immigration, church attendance, and parochial school construction, which contributed to Catholicism's increased visibility in the United States. Organized nativism reemerged in the form of the American Protective Association (APA), whose members vowed to combat the political and economic ascent of Catholics in 1890s America. An early twentieth-century revival of 1850s nativist fraternities, such as the Ku Klux Klan and the Junior Order of United American Mechanics, linked the new, southern European Catholic immigrants with African Americans as racially impure and inferior.

In the wake of the American Civil War, nativists maintained suspicions of Catholicism. The presence of two Catholics among the accomplices in President Abraham Lincoln's assassination fostered theories of Catholic conspiracy and disloyalty.[29] Thomas Nast's cartoons in the late 1860s and early 1870s symbolized the continued authority of anti-Catholic assumptions in U.S. culture. Nast immortalized nativist images of Irish immigrants as an indoctrinated and inebriated electorate, Catholic clerics as saboteurs of independent public schools, and the pope as a conquering invader sailing across the Atlantic to colonize America for the Catholic Church. Some Protestants viewed Catholic priests as uncooperative with the temperance movement, as well as supportive of radical Catholic labor organizations. Only days before the 1884 presidential election, New York City Presbyterian minister Samuel D. Burchard called the Democratic Party the home of "rum, Romanism, and rebellion." Although present at Burchard's speech, Republican nominee James G. Blaine—who had a

Catholic mother—neglected to repudiate the attack on the Roman Catholic Church.[30]

The political success of Irish Catholics in America fostered these late-nineteenth-century expressions of anti-Catholicism. Several analysts credited Blaine's defeat in 1884 to electoral votes in heavily Catholic Connecticut, New Jersey, and New York, where Democrats publicized Burchard's anti-Catholic statement.[31] Catholics utilized New York City's Tammany Hall, which Aaron Burr and Martin Van Buren had employed to help elect presidents Thomas Jefferson and Andrew Jackson, in 1800 and 1828 respectively. From 1862 to 1871, Tammany's leader, William M. "Boss" Tweed, expedited the naturalization of new immigrants, including many Catholics, to gain electoral support from these grateful voters. After "Honest" John Kelly assumed leadership of Tammany in 1871, Catholics monopolized this post until 1962.[32] Irish Catholic mayors earned election in Boston and New York City for the first time during this period.[33] A Catholic, New York lawyer Charles O'Conor, mounted a third-party candidacy for president in 1872, and the Knights of Columbus formed in 1882 to resist nativist anti-Catholicism.[34]

Postwar industrial expansion also attracted further Catholic immigration, especially from eastern and southern Europe. Around twelve million immigrants, often illiterate and unskilled, arrived from 1870 to 1900. Although Irish and Germans constituted the largest migrant groups prior to the late 1880s, Italians and Slavs represented the substantial majority of immigrants by 1901.[35] The prohibition of immigration from Asia in this period demonstrated that Catholics were not the most feared foreigners. Yet this new wave of immigration corresponded with mounting evidence that the Catholic Church was planting deep roots in the United States. Catholic religious publications expanded, and parochial school construction proceeded surprisingly quickly as Catholics proudly commemorated the four-hundredth anniversary of Christopher Columbus' expedition, sponsored by Catholic Spain's monarchs, to the Americas.[36]

In response to these public displays of Catholicism in the United States, nativist organizations reconstituted the spirit of Beecher, Morse, and the Know-Nothings. The American Protective Association formed in 1887 to counter Catholic electoral power. Requiring that members pledge never to vote a Catholic candidate to political office, the APA defined "true Americanism" as resistance to foreign "ecclesiastical power," endorsement of "nonsectarian" public schools, and repudiation of "preferential legislation" toward any religious denomination.[37] This organization gained popularity among farmers, railroad men, and laborers who often opposed Irish-dominated unions and Irish competition for jobs. Membership reached about 500,000 in 1893.[38] A future U.S. senator from Georgia, Thomas Watson, published a 1910 article with the apocalyptic title "The Roman Catholic Hierarchy: The Deadliest Menace to Our Liberties and Our Civilization." A Missouri publication, *The Menace,* echoed these ideas and achieved a weekly national circulation of 1.5 million by 1915.[39]

Racial theories of Anglo-Saxon superiority merged with anti-Catholicism in the early twentieth century. Nativists began to argue that Catholic nations in southern Europe and Latin America failed to foster the racial evolution described by social Darwinists. The Junior Order of United American Mechanics, whose 224,000 members in 1914 lived predominately in the South and West, viewed Catholic Latin America as a model of miscegenation's folly. Citing intermarriage between people of European and African descent in Latin American nations, such as Brazil and Cuba, this fraternity warned that sexual unions between southern European immigrants and African Americans in the United States would undermine America's racial purity.[40] The Ku Klux Klan (KKK), a covert terrorist organization of white supremacists in the nineteenth-century South, reemerged in 1915 with a national commitment to resisting Catholic political power.[41] Defining Americanism by geographical origin, race, and religion, the Klan's slogan praised "native, white, Protestant supremacy."[42]

Despite this resurgence of anti-Catholic movements, signs appeared that Catholic institutions had established themselves in U.S. politics and culture. A national committee to investigate anti-Catholicism formed in 1915. During the First World War, the National Catholic War Council (NCWC) formed under the leadership of Catholic clerics, editors, and politicians, such as past U.S. Commissioner of Labor Charles P. Neill. Later known as the National Catholic Welfare Conference, the NCWC worked with the War Department and other service organizations, such as the Federal Council of Churches and the Young Men's Christian Association (YMCA), to coordinate American Catholic assistance to the war effort. By establishing an institutional organization to confront national and international challenges, American Catholics gained unprecedented public exposure and status as participants in U.S. society and politics.[43]

"Religious Freedom": The Emerging Catholic Faces in Presidential Politics, 1919–1927

In the decade following World War I, nativists targeted communism, which American Catholics also rejected. In the 1920s, however, American Catholics disagreed profoundly on the progressive reforms. Tom Walsh promoted child labor laws, for example, which some preeminent members of the American Catholic hierarchy, such as Boston Cardinal William O'Connell, opposed. Failing to appreciate this institutional diversity, Ku Klux Klansmen appealed to liberals, as well as nativists, by portraying Catholicism as reactionary and sympathetic with fascism. At the 1924 Democratic National Convention, Walsh and Al Smith offered two distinct faces of American Catholicism. Smith's urban, northeastern roots and opposition to Prohibition appealed to Catholic, Jewish, and African Americans who resisted rural, white, Protestant social and political hegemony. Walsh's rural, western background and support for Prohibition appeared independent of New York City's Tammany Hall political machine. The convention's debate about religious liberty proved bitterly divisive, and neither Smith nor Walsh could secure support for the party's presidential nomination.

Although some Americans linked Catholicism and communism rhetorically, most contemporary Catholics would have seen this association as ludicrous. American Catholics received strong anticommunist messages from the Holy See during this era. Communism's atheistic and antireligious attitudes threatened the Roman Catholic Church. Upon seizing power in Russia, Soviet leaders closed most churches, nationalized church lands and buildings, and outlawed religious instruction to individuals younger than age eighteen.[44] The Soviet secret police, the Cheka, killed multiple thousands of Catholic clerics, nuns, and laity.[45] This bitter hostility between Catholicism and communism complicated attempts to portray these two groups as aligned against American freedom.

Although Catholicism's repudiation of communism appeared clear, Catholics disagreed about liberal, governmental activism in the United States. Some members of the American Catholic hierarchy perceived communist impulses in progressive reforms. Baltimore Archbishop Michael J. Curley opposed a proposed constitutional amendment to ban child labor. Tom Walsh, a Catholic, had produced this initiative with the assistance of Catholic priest John A. Ryan. Boston's Cardinal O'Connell dismissed the proposal as "Socialistic as it puts the State above the Parents." In O'Connell's opinion, Ryan proposed "radical," "queer crooked," and "bolshevik" ideas, but most Catholics supported restrictions on child labor.[46] This exchange revealed substantial diversity in American Catholic views of liberalism and communism.

As nativism declined in popularity, Ku Klux Klansmen surprisingly advanced liberal arguments to challenge Catholicism in the 1920s. Some Klansmen continued to criticize the Roman Catholic Church for "appealing to the polyglot peoples who threatened the good and pure society." At the same time, however, the Klan also characterized the pope as an authoritarian monarch who harbored reactionary, fascist sympathies. Citing Roman Catholic support for autocratic monarchs in earlier centuries, Klansmen portrayed Catholicism as inherently opposed to liberal, democratic principles. Alerting Americans to the "Papacy's campaign against liberalism and freedom," the Klan described the Holy See as a natural "ally of [Italian dictator Benito] Mussolini's fascism." This traditionally nativist organization sounded more like liberal, Social Gospel reformers—who viewed Christ's teachings as inspiration for promoting political equality—than conservative fundamentalists when accusing Catholics of resisting both progressive taxation and governmental protection of workers. Charging Catholic Americans with routine tax evasion, Klan publications also accused the pope of endorsing child labor. Yet nativist assumptions underlay this liberal rhetoric. Even when insisting that such criticisms did not represent anti-Catholicism, Klansmen betrayed a belief that Catholics carried alien values to America. One publication asserted that the Klan was "no more aimed at Roman Catholics than it would be aimed at Buddhists, Confucianists or Mohammedans, or anybody else who owes allegiance to any foreign person and/or religion."[47] Confronted with decreasing support for nativist anti-Catholicism, the Klan encouraged liberal doubts about the Catholic Church's support for modern reform.

The rise of Catholic New York Governor Al Smith symbolized the new mood of the nation's growing dissatisfaction with nativism. Philosopher Horace Kallen defined this attitude as cultural pluralism, which celebrated the contribution of America's diverse ethnic population. In Kallen's interpretation, a successful democratic system required an acceptance and accommodation of different cultures.[48] Smith's political magnetism partially derived from his immigrant characteristics. Liberal pundit Walter Lippmann recalled the appeal of Al Smith for religious and racial minorities as unique in U.S. politics: "He holds these crowds as no man can hold them[,] . . . without the promise of a millennium, without a radical program, without appeal to their hatreds, without bribes and doles and circuses." For Catholics, Jews, and

African Americans, Smith embodied "the incarnation of their own hope and pride; he is the man who has gone, as they would like but do not quite dare to go, out into the great world to lift from them the secret sense of inferiority."[49] In the face of nativist anti-Catholicism, Smith had risen from humble circumstances to the governor's mansion. This accomplishment earned the respect of those groups that nativists had labeled alien and un-American.

This reputation as a crusader against racist, nativist anti-Catholicism made Smith the ideal presidential candidate for many racial and religious minorities in 1924. Smith's defense of Catholic and Jewish immigrants inspired an African American journalist from Baltimore to declare, "Governor Smith is the colored man's hope in America."[50] The Democratic National Convention in multiethnic New York City promised to attract intensely loyal supporters of the Catholic governor. The opportunity to challenge the white, Protestant monopoly on the White House excited the passions of many Americans. For example, one woman wrote to Smith in July 1924, "If we do not have a test at this election, a Catholic, a Jew, or a colored man will not have a chance again."[51] Smith's proximity to the immigrant experience politically animated nonwhite, non-Protestant Americans like no other previous candidate.

While Montana Senator Thomas Walsh believed that a Catholic could win election to the presidency in 1924, he insisted that only a particular kind of candidate would secure the West and South. In Walsh's opinion, Smith's attraction for racial and religious minorities was insufficient to secure the presidency. Outside of Catholic, Jewish, and African American communities, suspicion of an urban, anti-Prohibition, machine politician such as Smith reinforced negative stereotypes of Catholicism.

The 1924 Democratic National Convention witnessed a confrontation of these two faces of American Catholicism. Although some Democrats believed that former Treasury Secretary William G. McAdoo was most qualified to unite these various religions and regions, his unwillingness to denounce the Ku Klux Klan encouraged many Catholics to support Smith as a defender of pluralism. Walsh viewed himself as a compromise candidate, because of his ability to attract western and southern Protestants as well as Catholics. Coming from a rural western state without political machines and supporting prohibition, Walsh might attract Catholic voters without alienating Protestants especially in the South and West. Walsh's position as chairman of the national convention offered this western Catholic national exposure, and events initially appeared to make his nomination possible.[52]

A "religious liberty" resolution at the Democratic National Convention further polarized nativist anti-Catholicism and pluralist support for a Catholic president.[53] Smith's supporters promoted a clear repudiation of religious bigotry and the Klan, which boasted an official membership of four million in 1924 and had helped elect governors and state legislators in the South, Midwest, and Pacific Northwest. McAdoo refused to repudiate the Klan. Despite Walsh's opposition to the Klan, the Montana Senator did not disagree with McAdoo's position. Prior to the convention, Walsh had stated, "I would vote for a very strong, straight religious freedom plank, and think we should adopt one, but would not name the Ku Klux Klan."[54] In the convention, Walsh lobbied for compromise between supporters of Smith and McAdoo. Walsh sought to lead the Democrats away from this prospect of mutually assured destruction.

The convention's outcome left both Catholics with hope for future success. One vote prevented the passage of a religious liberty resolution that criticized the Klan. After ten days of voting and an unprecedented 103 ballots, Smith's supporters blocked McAdoo, the "Klan candidate," from the nomination. Although Smith had not secured the party's endorsement, many Democrats believed that the party owed the 1928 nomination to the New York governor in compensation for the 1924 convention's failure to repudiate religious bigotry. The Democrats selected a Protestant compromise candidate, New York attorney and former solicitor general John W. Davis of West Virginia. However, Walsh's name immediately emerged as the ideal vice-presidential nominee for religious ticket balancing. On the convention floor, the chant of "Walsh" for vice president immediately followed Davis' nomination. This spontaneous and apparently unanimous support of convention delegates for Walsh made a profound impression on contemporary observers and historians alike. Historian Robert Murray noted, "how ironic it was that this convention, after suffering through ten days of acrimonious controversy based in part on religious grounds, should have literally begged a Catholic to be vice president, with only his refusal preventing it."[55] Walsh's rejection of Davis' personal request seemed a fitting, if paradoxical, conclusion to an unprecedented two-week convention that witnessed sixty different individuals receiving votes for president at various periods.[56] Walsh had emerged as a potential compromise presidential candidate for 1928.

Despite the fact that two Catholics received consideration for the nation's highest office in 1924, Kennedy still found reasons for pessimism in 1960. Although the prospect of two Catholic presidential candidates suggested that tolerance toward this religious minority had triumphed, political conditions changed drastically for U.S. Catholics in the intervening thirty-six years. Smith's landslide defeat in the 1928 presidential campaign revealed the persistence of nativist and liberal anti-Catholicism. While President Franklin D. Roosevelt's New Deal coalition opened unprecedented political opportunities to American Catholics, subsequent Democratic Catholic presidential aspirants—such as Postmaster General James Farley and Ambassador to the Court of Saint James Joseph Kennedy—continued to encounter religious skepticism. After World War II and the Cold War initiated an interfaith alliance against atheistic totalitarian regimes, some political analysts even suggested that Catholicism could help a presidential ticket in 1956. Yet rising liberal-Catholic tensions continued to threaten John Kennedy's pursuit of the highest office.

Chapter Two

Protestant America or a Nation of Immigrants?

Al Smith, Joe Kennedy, and Jim Farley Pursue the Nation's Highest Office

"[American Catholics] don't deserve to have a President," Joseph P. Kennedy said in response to a deluge of criticism that the Catholic public and press heaped upon his son John Kennedy in 1959.[1] Seeking to dispel suspicion of a Catholic presidential candidate, the younger Kennedy agreed with Supreme Court decisions that limited federal aid to Catholic schools, opposed official recognition of the Holy See through the appointment of a U.S. ambassador to the Vatican, and asserted that "nothing takes precedence over [one's] oath to uphold the Constitution."[2] After Kennedy's quotations appeared in the March 1959 *Look* magazine, many ordinary Catholics and editors of Catholic publications denounced such strong assertions that Catholicism would not significantly affect his political decisions. Kennedy received numerous letters critical of his apparent absolute separation of church and state, and the *Indiana Catholic and Record* summarized the view of the general Catholic press by writing, "Young Senator Kennedy had better watch his language."

Having experienced three decades of American politics from the vantage point of an American Catholic, Joe Kennedy believed that these Catholics failed to recognize his son's delicate political position regarding the religious issue. The elder Kennedy viewed these criticisms as self-defeating: "The only result of it can be to knock a Catholic out of the chance of getting the big job." Anger even clouded the father's all-encompassing ambition to see his son become president. Although Joe Kennedy dedicated an entire life to seeking political and economic power as an Irish Catholic in an Anglo Protestant nation, he momentarily expressed a willingness to abandon these ambitions: "I myself am thoroughly disgusted and if I were Jack, I would tell them all to go jump in the lake and call it quits."[3]

This chapter examines how doubts about a Catholic president proved an insurmountable obstacle to several Catholics who pursued the nation's highest office from 1928 to 1956. In 1928, two Catholics—U.S. Senator Thomas J. Walsh (MT) and New York Governor Alfred E. Smith—competed for the presidency. Smith's attraction to religious and racial minorities surpassed Walsh's appeal in the Democratic presidential primaries. Yet Smith could not overcome nativist and liberal allegations of Catholic conspiracy and disloyalty. In the 1930s, President Franklin D. Roosevelt appointed several Catholics to high-level federal offices, but Al Smith and Father Charles Coughlin attacked Roosevelt's New Deal as "socialistic." Both Postmaster General James Farley and Joe Kennedy, who served as both Securities and Exchange commissioner and U.S. ambassador to the Court of Saint James, also blamed Roosevelt for using suspicion of Catholicism to block the presidential ambitions of these two Catholics in the 1940s. The militant anticommunism of New York Archbishop Francis Spellman and Catholic Senator Joseph R. McCarthy (WI) heightened Protestant and liberal fears of Catholic power in the 1950s. Despite these suspicions, Joe Kennedy's son, John, pursued the vice presidency in 1956 based on the belief that a Catholic bloc, especially in northeastern states, would counterbalance the anti-Catholic vote in the South and West.

Rum, Romanism, and Respectability: Smith and Walsh in the 1928 Campaign

Al Smith's religion surely contributed to the high emotions surrounding the 1928 campaign. Although Americans had long abandoned the practice of burning effigies of the pope and Catholic conspirator Guy Fawkes on November 5, the Alabama Ku Klux Klan staged a dramatic display of mock political violence at the Houston Democratic National Convention in 1928. After Smith received the party's presidential nomination, several Klansmen dragged a life-size representation of the Catholic candidate into the convention hall, slit the effigy's throat, and splashed false blood on its chest. As the mob chanted "Lynch him!", others fired bullets into the tattered figure. The spectacle concluded with a mock lynching of the "Smith" carcass.[4]

Religious tensions were not always contained in symbolic violence. The Klan's icon, a burning cross, appeared through the windows of Smith's campaign railcar in Oklahoma and Montana. Dynamite exploded when Smith arrived in Billings, Montana.[5] Election Day provoked even more powerful passions. Four New England residents died of heart attacks due to the excitement, and a Hoover loyalist killed a Smith devotee in Kentucky. When a Georgia judge knifed a deputy, who had accused him of supporting Smith's candidacy, the wounded deputy fatally shot the judge twice in the stomach.[6]

The 1928 campaign's "Catholic issue" exposed powerful negative and positive implications of Catholicism in presidential elections. Smith's candidacy encouraged nativists to revive anti-Catholic arguments based on racial and religious prejudice. Klansmen, such as U.S. Senator J. Thomas Heflin (AL), unapologetically sought to inspire a national resistance to Smith on religious grounds. Most southern politicians, such as U.S. Senator Theodore Bilbo (MS) and Senate Majority Leader Joseph Robinson (AK), demonstrated loyalty to the Democratic Party. While Smith's opponent, Republican nominee Herbert C. Hoover, refused to exploit anti-Catholic attitudes for political gain, several Republicans—including Hoover's wife—publicly and privately justified religious opposition to the Catholic candidate.

The 1928 campaign also challenged Americans to consider the impact of a Catholic president on liberal and pluralist ideals. Non-Catholic liberals debated the political significance of Smith's Catholicism. Episcopalian lawyer Charles Marshall, the *Christian Century*, and the *New Republic* challenged Smith to explain Catholic dogma that contradicted the separation of church and state. Most prominent liberals, such as columnist Walter Lippmann and philosopher John Dewey, endorsed Smith's independence from clerical dictate. These liberals considered support for Smith a sign of tolerance and repudiation of religious bigotry. Many racial and religious minorities viewed Smith's candidacy as a symbol of the nation's diversity.

Some Protestants initially seemed more willing to support the Catholic Senator Walsh, who favored Prohibition and challenged Smith in the Democratic primaries. Smith's reputation as a defender of non-native, nonwhite, non–Anglo Saxon, and non-Protestant Americans, however, prompted Catholics to view Walsh's candidacy as a front for nativist anti-Catholicism. In the general election, Smith showed broad support from African, Jewish, and Catholic Americans.

Smith's candidacy inspired a powerful revival of nativist anti-Catholicism in 1928. Smith ally and future president Franklin Roosevelt estimated that the Ku Klux Klan spent as much as five million dollars to publish and distribute the *Fellowship Forum* from Washington, D.C. With a staff of 125 individuals, this Klan organ spread vicious anti-Catholic propaganda that depicted Smith as a drunkard and a pawn of Catholic clerics who sought to repress American freedoms. The publication's political cartoons mimicked nineteenth-century illustrator Thomas Nast's graphic depictions of Catholic bishops menacing innocent Americans through manipulation of public schools and Irish politicians.[7] The publishers claimed a circulation of 360,000. Michael Williams, editor of the lay Catholic magazine *Commonweal,* estimated that one hundred anti-Catholic newspapers published three to five million copies weekly during the 1920s. In small-town parks and courthouses, hundreds of itinerant preachers and lecturers repeated and revised the discredited stories—popularized by charlatan "ex-nun" Maria Monk and nativist Protestant minister Lyman Beecher in the nineteenth century—of Catholic priests who impregnated nuns and papal plots for Jesuit missionaries to conquer America by seizing public schools and corrupting the youth.[8]

Nativist anti-Catholicism had limited support among national politicians in 1928. Senator Thomas Heflin stood apart in rallying Klansmen across the nation against a Catholic president. In January 1928, the Alabama senator exploited a baseless rumor that the Mexican government had bribed several U.S. senators and suggested that the pope had coerced Mexicans and Nicaraguans into plotting preemptive war on the United States. Smith's presidential ambitions served as Heflin's primary target. Heflin compelled Americans to "gird your loans for political battle" against Smith lest "the heavy hand of a Catholic state . . . crush the life out of Protestantism in America."[9] Other southern senators, however, defended Smith. Senate Majority Leader Joseph Robinson, who Smith would choose as a running mate, immediately repudiated Heflin's appeal on the senate floor. Even white supremacists in the Democratic Party dismissed anti-Catholicism to demonstrate party loyalty and protect local autonomy. In the general election, Senator Theodore Bilbo of Mississippi spread rumors that Republican nominee Herbert Hoover had danced with a black woman. For some southerners, Smith's election became essential for the preservation of white rule in the South. In Bilbo's interpretation, racial segregation preceded Protestant-Catholic divisions in political significance: "I would swallow the Pope and the whole dern Vatican than vote for Herbert Hoover and negro supremacy in the South."[10]

Smith's personal and political decisions fueled nativist propaganda and conspiracy theories. Some historians, such as David Burner, have credited Smith's parochialism with Hoover's 1928 victory. Smith alienated rural, Protestant Americans by drinking in defiance of Prohibition, exaggerating his New York roots and accent, and taking excessive pride in "outward tokens of his faith," according to Burner. The New York governor had publicly kissed the ring of papal ambassador Giovanni Bonzano in 1926. When New York Cardinal Patrick Hayes conducted the wedding service of Smith's daughter in that year, Franklin Roosevelt's political mentor, New York newspaperman Louis Howe, expressed fear of such open display of religious loyalty. "I hope the young couple won't have to kiss the Cardinal's toe as part of the ceremony."[11] During the campaign, Smith volunteered to serve as an acolyte—an assistant to the clerical celebrant of a Catholic service—in New Jersey. Such "public" Catholicism created problems for the Democratic nominee in 1928, and Burner concluded that another kind of Catholic might have responded to the issue more shrewdly: "Smith was at once a victim of prejudice and of his own clinging loyalty to his special environment."[12]

Smith's selection of a Catholic, General Motors executive John J. Raskob, as Democratic National chairman also alarmed nativists. Raskob's wealth, financial connections, and management skills probably motivated Smith's decision. Yet many Democrats bristled at the choice of Raskob, who had worked for the wealthy Catholic Du Pont family, actively opposed Prohibition, and voted for Republican presidential nominee Calvin Coolidge in 1924. Nativists focused particularly on Raskob's religion. As a Catholic who had donated more than a million dollars to his church, Raskob received several high honors from the Holy See. Raskob's selection as a private chamberlain in the papal household, as well as knighthood in the orders of both Saint Gregory the Great and Malta, suggested that this particular Catholic held strong loyalties to the Vatican.[13] Raskob's immediate ascent to Democratic Party leadership through political patronage appeared typical of the undemocratic, secret dealings of Smith's Catholic New York City political machine, Tammany Hall. Anti-Catholic nativists perceived such decisions as indicative that Smith would favor co-religionists in the White House.

Smith's opposition to Prohibition reinforced the anti-Catholicism of many Protestant Americans. Temperance and anti-liquor campaigns arose partly out of evangelical Protestant reforms. According to Edmund Moore, a historian of the 1928 campaign, "To millions of evangelical Protestants, [Prohibition] was a *de facto* point of religious orthodoxy."[14] Methodist Bishop Edwin Mouzon called upon his followers to study "the historic protest of Evangelical Christianity against the errors of Rome."[15] Many Protestants perceived Catholic clerics as excessively tolerant of alcohol consumption, and urban, Irish immigrants became known for abuse of this substance. In Mouzon's view, "the nomination of Smith . . . signalized the uprise of the unassimilated elements in our great cities against the ideals of our American fathers."[16] A 1927 article in the *Nation* buttressed charges that Smith illegally consumed alcohol: "I am reliably informed . . . that ['Al'] drinks every day, and the number of his cocktails and highballs is variously estimated at from four to eight."[17]

Some Southern Baptist and Methodist ministers bolted the Democratic Party on the Prohibition issue, which was intimately linked to Smith's Catholicism. Methodist Bishop James Cannon and Reverend Arthur J. Barton, a leader of the Southern Baptist Convention, organized an alternative "dry" Democratic convention to protest the party's selection of a "wet" anti-Prohibition candidate.[18] Cannon's claim to oppose Smith "altogether apart from his religion" lacks credibility in light of his subsequent reflection, "I knew that he was the intolerant, bigoted type characteristic of the Irish Roman Catholic hierarchy of New York City."[19] The defense of Prohibition and the opposition to a Catholic candidate worked hand in hand.

Some Republican officials promoted this nativist anti-Catholicism, both publicly and privately, against Smith. Assistant Attorney General for Prohibition Enforcement Mabel Walker Willebrandt publicly asked a meeting of 2,500 Methodist ministers in Ohio to campaign for Hoover: "You have in your churches more than six hundred thousand members . . . in Ohio alone. That is enough to swing the election."[20] When the Republican National Committee (RNC) repudiated Willebrandt's remarks, she protested that RNC officials had pre-approved her speeches.[21] A Virginia National Committeewoman, Willie W. Caldwell, distributed a letter that asked the state's women to "save the United States from being Romanized and rum-ridden." Recalling the 1884 campaign—when Catholic voters mobilized against the Republican nominee after a Protestant minister labeled the Democrats as the party of "rum, Romanism, and rebellion"—Republicans quickly denounced this letter for fear of a Catholic backlash against Hoover.[22]

Yet Hoover's wife Lou also defended opposition to Smith on religious grounds. Despite repudiating the use of rumor and innuendo, Mrs. Hoover wrote to close family friend Edgar Rickard, "there are many people of intense Protestant faith to whom Catholicism is a grievous sin." In the future first lady's opinion, "they have as much right to vote against a man for public office because of that belief." She denied that such political behavior signified "persecution."[23]

Some American liberals agreed with Lou Hoover's assessment that suspicion of a Catholic presidential candidate did not violate the political rights of that religion's membership. Secular liberal publications, such as the *Atlantic Monthly* and the *New Republic,* even raised doubts about a Catholic president's ability to protect the separation of church and state. Despite the magazine's sympathy with Smith's political program, a March 1927 *New Republic* editorial questioned a Catholic's ability to demonstrate independence from clerical authority on two issues: government aid to public schools and U.S. relations with Mexico.[24] In April, the *Atlantic Monthly* published an "open letter to Al Smith" by New York lawyer Charles C. Marshall, who asserted that Catholic teaching also undermined the cause of liberty in U.S. marriage law. Although Smith answered these questions in a subsequent issue, these liberals had identified critical points of interfaith disagreement.[25]

When the Mexican government seized Catholic Church property and attacked priests, American Catholic pressure groups advocated an aggressive response by the U.S. government. The Knights of Columbus lobbied for military intervention. According to pundit Walter Lippmann, such belligerency proved more effective than nativist propaganda at alarming "moderate, tolerant and liberal people . . . about the effect of making Al Smith president." Despite supporting Smith's candidacy in 1928, Lippmann warned that war with Mexico would instantly destroy the Catholic candidate's presidential ambitions.[26]

Advocates of contraceptive devices perpetuated liberal suspicions of Smith by portraying the Catholic Church's opposition to artificial birth control as emblematic of Catholicism's antipathy toward personal, individual freedom. Field Secretary of the Birth Control League Edith Pierce opposed Smith's candidacy because of the Catholic Church's alleged pressure on state legislatures to oppose legalized contraception. Recognizing that such religious-based opposition to Smith aligned her with nativist Klansmen and Protestant fundamentalists, Pierce nonetheless blamed the Catholic Church's male hierarchy for aggressive resistance to artificial birth control. In a 1927 letter to Charles Marshall, Pierce cited this justification for opposing Smith in the presidential campaign: "I was never bigoted till I had this experience."[27] Birth control activist Margaret Sanger exploited anti-Catholicism to argue that Catholic clerics and politicians sought to enforce church dogma through legislation that violated political liberty.[28] Sanger held Smith responsible for Catholic dogma.[29] Calling Catholic Church opposition to birth control a "menace of intolerant tyranny," Sanger viewed Smith as leading the movement to frustrate the spread of birth control clinics: "If such power is to be given national scope, through a Presidential aspirant, its disastrous effect on the future of American civilization will be incalculable."[30]

Smith's Catholicism became the most important issue for many liberal Protestants. In *Current History*, a Unitarian minister argued that Protestants should not deny Smith's election "on account of religious grounds," but rather "because the Catholic Church is opposed to the principles of democracy." Editors at the nation's most prominent Protestant publication, *Christian Century*, denied that Smith's Protestant detractors expressed prejudice or bigotry. Protestants should legitimately worry, the editors suggested, about a "real issue between Catholicism and American institutions," and "the seating of a representative of an alien culture, of a medieval Latin mentality, of an undemocratic hierarchy and of a foreign potentate in the great office of President of the United States."[31]

Despite these caveats, most mainstream Protestants ultimately repudiated a blanket ban on Roman Catholic presidential candidates. Protestant and secular liberals generally expressed satisfaction that Smith's Catholicism would not compromise American freedom. Theologian Reinhold Niebuhr chastised those Protestants who opposed Smith's Catholicism. In the *New Republic*, philosopher John Dewey endorsed Smith while repudiating "narrow bigotry." Future Supreme Court Justice Felix Frankfurter pledged support, in the same publication, for Smith. These endorsements nonetheless subtly acknowledged liberal fears about Catholicism's dogmatic rigidity. "Happily," wrote Frankfurter, "Smith has not set, doctrinaire 'principles' but possesses a mind free for new experience and responsive to its directions." Also in the *New Republic*, philosopher E. C. Lindeman assured readers that Smith employed a "pragmatist" political philosophy, rather than a moralistic program: "His mind is not encumbered with *a priori* generalizations."

A desire to respect the pluralist ideal of inclusiveness also encouraged these liberals to accept a Catholic for president. The liberal magazine *Nation* portrayed Smith as a model "of tolerance in American life—racial, religious, and social tolerance, accepting into the American family the city-dwellers who have come to us within the last century."[32] Smith's unique appeal for urban immigrants made the Catholic candidate particularly attractive to those Americans who sought social harmony between native-born and non-native citizens.

Catholic rejection of Senator Walsh's pursuit of the Democratic Party's presidential nomination demonstrated how strongly Smith represented this religious group's pluralist political ideals. Some Protestants viewed Walsh as a Catholic who could create an interfaith consensus. Most Democrats believed that the nativist anti-Catholicism that prevented Smith's presidential nomination in 1924 made a Catholic nominee essential for the party's survival in 1928. The *New York Times* initially presented Smith's nomination as necessary to avoid losing the "Roman Catholic vote which is essential to Democratic success and harmony."[33] Recognizing the social and political need for Democrats to nominate a Catholic, the liberal Protestant editors at *Christian Century* nonetheless distinguished Walsh's Catholicism from Smith's. The writers presented a Walsh candidacy as most likely to slay "the specter of religious bigotry in his party."[34] Claiming to speak for the "ordinary American voter," the editors argued that nonreligious issues explained the nation's willingness to accept the rural, advocate of Prohibition Walsh, but not the urban, anti-Prohibition Smith. Walsh's religious affiliation lacked the "popular connotations that make the Catholicism of Governor Smith such an issue." While admitting that this distinction "may elude theological definition," the editors claimed that Smith's "city-mindedness" offended the majority of U.S. citizens.[35] Protestant liberals, the magazine suggested, could thus oppose Smith without violating the liberal principle of religious liberty.

Although historian Paul Carter suggested that Americans would have accepted Walsh as a Catholic opposed to Prohibition, anti-Catholicism blocked Walsh's pursuit of the Democratic nomination. Senator Heflin rejected the appeals of Democratic delegate and Walsh advocate Patrick Callahan to endorse Walsh's candidacy as a Catholic who supported Prohibition.[36] Walsh-For-President supporter J. T. Carroll of Los Angeles perceived widespread anti-Catholic attitudes among California Democrats, who gave Walsh less than 20 percent of the state's primary votes. "'Twas easy enough to line up the ministers, but when it came to casting a vote for a 'horrible catholic' many of the laity rebelled."[37] Despite assurances that a rural Catholic would not face anti-Catholic opposition, evidence indicated otherwise.

Yet Catholic resistance to Walsh proved most damaging to the Montana senator. Many Catholics argued that anti-Catholic nativists manipulated the rural Catholic. *The Tidings,* a Catholic paper published in Los Angeles, decried Walsh's entry into the contest for the Democratic nomination: "Now we have two candidates who are Catholics, or, rather, one candidate and a decoy."[38] Walsh represented the latter to those who believed that Smith defended the sincere interest of Catholic Americans. According to many Catholic writers, the same nativist anti-Catholic forces that blocked Smith's nomination in 1924 had reconstituted in 1928. Catholics especially viewed Walsh's candidacy as a plot by former Treasury Secretary William G. McAdoo, who refused to support a "religious liberty" clause that would have repudiated the Klan four years earlier at the Democratic National Convention. After placing a distant third to Smith in the California primary, Walsh received many appeals to concede the nomination to his fellow Catholic. Al Smith's Hollywood campaign coordinator P. W. Corake warned Walsh that Californians viewed him as "a stalking horse for McAdoo and by a strange paradox your votes were principally Ku Klux."[39] Many other Catholics expressed the same sentiment in letters to Walsh.[40] While Walsh's candidacy may have attracted southern and western Protestants, Smith proved immensely popular with Catholic voters.

This strong Catholic loyalty to Smith, who embodied the yearnings of immigrants for inclusion in a pluralist political community, extended to African and Jewish Americans. Although the Democratic Party traditionally supported or tolerated white supremacy in the South, anti-Catholicism endeared religious and racial minorities to Smith's candidacy. According to Smith biographer Robert Slayton, "it was the attacks by the Klan, by the bigots and the hate-mongers, that drew blacks to Al Smith. . . . They understood that his enemies were their own, and that by standing against these forces, he was taking on the people and ideas that oppressed them as well." Founder of the four million member United Negro Improvement Association Marcus Garvey endorsed Smith. Bayard Rustin, future organizer of a major civil rights rally—the 1963 March on Washington—distributed Smith's campaign material with a young Jewish friend. Jews on Manhattan's Lower East Side voted for Smith in higher percentages than did some Irish districts.[41]

Although nativist and liberal anti-Catholicism certainly damaged Smith's presidential hopes in 1928, the attraction of a New York City Catholic proved powerful for religious and racial minorities. Smith refused to accept the rules of a majority Protestant society and culture. Smith's opposition to Prohibition symbolized the pride of immigrant and urban Americans. The persistence of nativism in the Protestant clergy and the Klan further perpetuated Catholic, Jewish, and African American sympathy and sincere love for Smith. In the words of Robert Slayton, "Immigrants and city dwellers recognized that he was someone in higher politics who stood up for them, accepted them as equals, and above all, who gave them respectability."[42] Despite Tom Walsh's potential to attract more southern and western non-Catholic support, he could not rival Smith's reputation among Catholic, Jewish, and African Americans, who viewed Smith as the embodiment of a pluralist ideal that would replace Protestant hegemony. The White House head cook, an Irish American, voted for Smith and felt compelled to confess this fact to First Lady Lou Hoover, even though she feared that it might cost her the job (it didn't).[43]

"The Established Halls of Washington and Rome": James Farley and Joe Kennedy in the 1930s and 1940s

One American Catholic, Joe Kennedy, did not proudly boast of loyalty to Al Smith. In an April 1929 letter to Hoover's secretary of the navy Charles Francis Adams, Kennedy claimed to have voted Republican in 1928. Adams' appointment, Kennedy wrote, "was reason enough for President Hoover's election and sufficient justification for a good Democrat like myself to vote for him again." This shocking admission that a prominent Catholic Democrat voted against Smith's presidential bid may merely demonstrate Kennedy's penchant for using blandishments to secure political allies in government. Yet when Smith contested for the party's nomination in 1932, Kennedy again rebuffed the Catholic candidate by actively supporting the front-runner, Protestant New York Governor Franklin Roosevelt. This decision clashed with Joe's father-in-law, John F. Fitzgerald, who wanted the Catholic Smith to represent the party in 1932, a year that seemed destined for Democratic success in the wake of the 1929 stock market crash.[44] Kennedy's two defections from Smith demonstrate his belief that Catholic politicians needed to work within the Protestant system to succeed at the national level.

Having suffered from anti-Catholic prejudice parallel to Smith's experience, Kennedy's refusal to challenge the rules of a Protestant-dominated political world distinguished him from Smith. According to Kennedy family biographer Thomas Maier, "[Joe Kennedy and his family] avoided the brassy, political machine methods of Al Smith, the unpolished Democratic Party candidate, whom a bigoted nation viewed as leading a horde of unwashed foreigners into the White House." Unlike Smith, who proudly boasted of his New York City origins, the Kennedys "maneuvered smartly though the established corridors of Washington and Rome to make their own mark."[45] Joe Kennedy donated $25,000 to Roosevelt's successful 1932 candidacy, and secured another $100,000 in anonymous gifts for FDR's campaign.[46] In the years following Smith's 1928 defeat, Kennedy persisted in his vision of upward political mobility despite continued challenges to Catholics in American politics.

From 1928 to 1959, Catholic politicians reached the highest levels of U.S. government, but consistently fell short in trying to repeat Smith's achievement of receiving a major party presidential nomination. In the 1930s, Franklin Roosevelt established political alliances with some Catholics, such as Kennedy and George Cardinal Mundelein, although others, including Al Smith and Father Charles Coughlin, berated his policies as socialistic. Kennedy and Postmaster General James Farley received consideration for the presidency in the 1940s, but both perceived religion as a limitation to this goal. Despite the pluralist cooperation of Protestant, Catholic, and Jewish Americans in the face of Nazi racist ambitions for world domination during World War II, John F. Kennedy encountered heightened religious controversy as Protestants and liberals increasingly shared fears of rising Catholic power.

In the 1930s, Franklin Roosevelt demonstrated sympathy toward Catholics, who felt rejected by Smith's 1928 defeat. Roosevelt's rhetoric emphasized an attitude of inclusiveness toward this immigrant church. Addressing the nativist Daughters of the American Revolution, Roosevelt cautioned nativists, "Remember, remember always, that all of us, and you and I especially, are descended from immigrants and revolutionists."[47] While campaigning for the presidency in 1932, Roosevelt quoted a papal encyclical to criticize economic oligarchy and to defend his progressive economic program of expanded federal assistance to the underprivileged.[48]

Roosevelt used the power of presidential appointments to advance the political careers of many Catholics. New York Catholic Jim Farley served as Roosevelt's campaign manager in the 1932 presidential race, and became postmaster general. Roosevelt selected Senator Thomas Walsh to serve as attorney general, but his premature death allowed the president to appoint another Catholic, future Supreme Court Justice Frank Murphy, as the nation's highest law enforcement officer. Catholics represented 25 percent of FDR's judicial appointments compared with previous presidents, who appointed Catholics at a rate of one in twenty-five.[49]

By the mid-1930s, potential divisions in this political coalition emerged when prominent Catholics accused Roosevelt of communist sympathies. Former Democratic Party standard-bearer Al Smith had accused Roosevelt of class warfare in the 1932 campaign. Smith's 1936 rhetoric, however, represented a dramatic departure from the standard political disagreements between these two men. Speaking to a meeting of the American Liberty League—a conservative organization founded by wealthy Catholic businessman John Raskob to defend property rights against Roosevelt's "New Deal" expansion of federal authority—Smith denounced the similarity of the Democratic Party and the Socialist Party platforms. In Smith's opinion, representative democracy could not tolerate communism: "There can be only one flag, the Stars and Stripes, or the red flag of the godless union of the Soviet."[50] Catholic-liberal clashes about communism arose again in response to anticlerical regimes in Mexico and the Soviet Union. Radio priest Charles Coughlin also turned against Roosevelt after initially praising the Democratic president. Coughlin's broadcasts attracted an audience more than twice the size of today's most popular radio programs.[51] Berating Roosevelt's alleged support of "communistic Jews," Coughlin backed a third-party presidential candidate in 1936.[52]

Joe Kennedy and Jim Farley, Roosevelt's Catholic allies, rallied to reconcile the president and the Catholic hierarchy. Kennedy arranged a secret meeting between FDR and New York Auxiliary Bishop Francis Spellman, who had close ties to the Vatican Secretary of State Cardinal Eugenio Pacelli. Kennedy's role proved critical because Pacelli preferred Spellman as a liaison to the president instead of Boston Cardinal William O'Connell. Kennedy's intervention also overcame Roosevelt's suspicion of Spellman. As assistant secretary of war in World War I, Roosevelt refused to appoint Spellman as a chaplain in the armed forces because he perceived the young Boston priest as impetuous.[53] Farley also intervened in response to the accusations of Coughlin and Smith by advising Roosevelt to secure Cardinal Mundelein's affirmation that the administration had "no communistic tendencies." While avoiding instructions on how to vote, Mundelein called Roosevelt "his friend" and asked Americans to appreciate "the prosperity, the happiness, and the freedom now abroad in our land."[54] Roosevelt further placated Catholics by adopting neutrality toward the Spanish Civil War, which began in 1936, despite liberal calls for intervention against the fascist, Catholic dictator Francisco Franco. Burnings of Catholic churches and murders of Catholic priests served as Franco's justification for violent resistance to a leftist government in Spain.[55] Roosevelt's attention to Catholic voters facilitated his 1936 landslide, which substantially exceeded his 1932 margin of victory.

As Roosevelt's second term came to a close, Joe Kennedy and Jim Farley both received consideration for the presidency in 1940. Kennedy's plan to evacuate German Jews, who faced violent attacks in 1938, to the United States prompted *Life* magazine to propose that success would "add luster to a reputation that may well carry Joseph Patrick Kennedy into the White House." Although many American

Jews rejected this proposal, which contradicted Zionist plans to settle in Palestine, *Liberty* magazine similarly speculated optimistically about Kennedy's presidential prospects. According to the *Washington Post,* Kennedy held "an excellent chance to be the first Catholic President." When Farley actively challenged Roosevelt for the Democratic Party nomination in 1940, Interior Secretary Harold Ickes considered Kennedy's nomination as FDR's vice president as essential to "match a Roman Catholic against a Roman Catholic."

Twelve years after Al Smith's defeat, however, Catholicism proved just as sensitive a political issue. When Kennedy encouraged U.S. Senator James F. Byrnes of South Carolina to run for president, a Roosevelt aide dismissed the idea on religious grounds. Byrnes' baptism as a Catholic, and subsequent conversion to Episcopalianism, created "a double-disadvantage politically; for not only would anti-Catholic bigots oppose him, but Catholics themselves might resent his change of religion."[56]

Farley accused FDR of knowingly exploiting the Catholic issue to eliminate him as an opponent. As Farley considered a presidential bid, *Washington Post* reporter Ernest K. Lindley claimed that Roosevelt warned "one of the elderly stalwarts of the Democratic Party" that a Catholic would impair the party ticket. Lindley's source quoted Roosevelt as saying that Farley's presence on the Democratic slate—even as a vice-presidential candidate—would make the party's presidential nominee appear as a proxy—a "stalking horse" in the article's words—for the pope.[57] Although FDR did not repudiate the *Post* story until more than a week later, the president claimed that a chief executive could not respond to every inaccurate story published in the newspapers. Farley claimed, however, that Lindley's position as FDR's "official biographer" validated the report.[58]

According to Farley, even Cardinal Mundelein raised the specter of anti-Catholicism to prevent a challenge to Roosevelt's pursuit of a third term. Farley's memoirs recount that Mundelein personally discouraged him from opposing FDR: "It is my sincere feeling that a Roman Catholic could not be elected President of the United States at this time or for many years to come." Mundelein even implied that Farley's candidacy might injure Catholic America: "I hope, therefore, that you will do nothing to involve the Catholics of this country in another debate such as we experienced in 1928." This heavy-handed political advice from a religious figure bothered Farley, who told the cardinal, "You are the first person in the Church who has ever attempted to influence me on a political matter and I have been in politics for thirty years."[59] Mundelein's argument, as described by Farley, echoed Democratic fears of nativist anti-Catholicism. This Catholic official similarly advocated a policy of retreat or surrender in the face of nativism.

For some Democrats, Farley's candidacy tested how well Catholics had achieved acceptance into the American pluralist ideal. While managing Roosevelt's presidential victories in 1932 and 1936 and serving as Democratic national chairman during FDR's two terms, Farley established a personal network of political alliances across the country. In Farley's estimation, these efforts "had broken down a great deal of the prejudice against a Roman Catholic."[60] Nominating Farley at the convention, Senator Carter Glass (VA) denounced interference with a Catholic candidate's right to pursue the presidency: "While I have been sitting on the platform, I have received two communications objecting to the nomination of Jim Farley because he is a Catholic." A co-author of the Volstead Act establishing Prohibition, Glass cited "a few spiritual reasons" for this endorsement of Farley: "I rejoice that among the achievements of Thomas Jefferson is the Virginia statute of religious freedom."[61] Glass challenged the Democrats to honor a spirit of inclusiveness that Roosevelt had earlier encouraged. Joe Kennedy did not openly endorse either candidate. In Kennedy's opinion, however, anti-Catholicism was "firmly imbedded in the Roosevelt family." Joseph P. Kennedy, Jr., a Democratic delegate in 1940, voted for Farley instead of Roosevelt at the national convention.[62]

Jim Farley and Joe Kennedy operated in "the established corridors of Washington and Rome" by maintaining political ties within the U.S. and Vatican hierarchies, but they did not secure America's highest office. President Roosevelt's patronage opened many doors to Catholic politicians even though Al Smith and Father Coughlin actively opposed his domestic policies. The consideration of Catholics for the presidency might have been regarded as a substantial achievement for Farley and Kennedy, but the experience of 1940 taught these two politicians that anti-Catholicism remained a powerful barrier to the White House.

"A Nation of Immigrants": John F. Kennedy and Joseph R. McCarthy in the Postwar Era

By the 1950s, fears of rising Catholic power in the United States threatened to erect another barrier against Catholics who pursued the presidency. Liberal focus on economic reforms had dissipated by the late 1930s, and individual freedom became the centerpiece of mid-twentieth-century U.S. liberalism. As European fascism and communism competed for power, the Catholic Church viewed the latter as a greater threat while liberals feared the former. In this context, liberals looked with suspicion on Catholicism's promotion of parochial education in contrast to public schools, as well as Catholic attempts to censor sexually explicit and anti-Catholic Hollywood movies and popular novels.[63]

Although the common purpose of war against fascism and militarism eased these tensions during World War II, consciousness of Catholic threats to Protestant and liberal authority in America prompted strong responses during the postwar era. Philosopher John Dewey, who advocated tolerance toward Al Smith's Catholicism in 1928, now characterized the Roman Catholic Church as a "reactionary world organization." In 1947, leading Protestant ministers and teachers formed Protestants and Other Americans United for Separation of Church and State (POAU) to protest the Supreme Court's *Everson v. Board of Education* ruling that New Jersey could legally pay transportation expenses for children in parochial schools. Civil libertarian Paul B. Blanshard published a best-selling book, *American Freedom and Catholic Power,* which advocated a "resistance movement" against "the antidemocratic social policies of the hierarchy." Selling 100,000 copies and meriting 10 printings in less than a year, the book received high praise from John Dewey for "exemplary scholarship, good judgment, and tact," and physicist Albert Einstein concurred.[64] Many Protestant clergy and secular academics agreed on Catholicism's threat to religious liberty.

John Kennedy, as a Massachusetts congressman, directly confronted Protestant and secular liberal fears of Catholic power during a 1947 House subcommittee hearing. Kennedy protested the testimony of Elmer E. Rogers, assistant to the Sovereign Grand Commander of the Freemasons in the South. Rogers told congressmen that the Catholic Church plotted "to destroy our liberties and further expand their theocracy as a world government." When Rogers asserted that the Holy See would excommunicate Catholic parents who did not send children to parochial schools, Kennedy protested, "I never went to a parochial school. I am a Catholic and yet my parents were never debarred from the sacrament, so the statement is wrong." Rogers claimed that Kennedy benefited from his family's close connections to the very Catholic hierarchy that secretly worked to undermine American freedom: "You are prominent people up there in Massachusetts. I know something of the prominence of your father, and the bishops are pretty diplomatic and have good judgment about such things." Thirteen years prior to pursuing the presidency, Kennedy confronted the same challenge that Charles Marshall had issued to Al Smith in 1927. "I do not want to get in an argument about Catholic theology," Kennedy insisted, "but you do not want to make statements that are inaccurate." While not mentioning his recognition for heroism by saving several members of his PT-109 crew in the Pacific, Kennedy nonetheless defended the patriotism of U.S. Catholics: "Now you don't mean the Catholics in America are legal subjects of the Pope? I am not a legal subject of the Pope."[65]

John Kennedy's denials notwithstanding, this Catholic congressman worked on behalf of his church's educational institutions by lobbying for financial assistance to parochial school students. In 1950 federal aid-to-education legislation, several proposals provided government support for public schools alone. The Boston archdiocese newspaper, the *Pilot*, blamed anti-Catholic "prejudice" for this refusal to fund Catholic alternatives to public schooling. John Kennedy fought to include federal aid for bus transportation and health services of parochial school students. Catholic publications glowingly praised Kennedy's efforts. The *Pilot* described Kennedy as "a white knight against the crepuscular haze." Kennedy's "adroit intra-committee maneuvering" encouraged the *Sign* to praise this "Galahad in the House."[66]

In the 1950s, Catholic unity behind anticommunism appeared particularly militant and excessive to many Protestants and secular liberals. Catholic Senator Joseph R. McCarthy (WI) obtained national recognition for attacking liberals with alleged communist sympathies. The alignment of American and Catholic anticommunism allowed many Catholics to feel liberated from aspersions of dual loyalty. According to historian Patrick Allitt, "Aware that anti-Catholic nativists had often regarded them as un-American, some Catholics now took pleasure in declaring themselves champions of a 'one hundred percent American' campaign against political leftists, rarely Catholic by birth, whose Americanism was now open to question."[67] Senator Daniel Patrick Moynihan (NY) later recalled, "To be an Irish Catholic became *prima facie* evidence of loyalty. Harvard men were to be checked; Fordham men would do the checking." Yet the Catholic media and hierarchy, most notably New York Francis Cardinal Spellman, promoted a stringent anticommunism that alienated many liberals.[68] The strong Catholic consensus against communism created suspicion that this religion's members would emerge as a powerful, united voting bloc.

In 1956, John Kennedy's aide Theodore Sorensen attempted to counter lingering nativist reservations about a Catholic presidential candidate by arguing, in a widely circulated memorandum, that Al Smith's landslide defeat, which haunted the Democratic Party for decades, nonetheless brought many Catholics voters into the Democratic fold.[69] Citing journalist Samuel Lubell's conclusion that Smith initiated a political "revolution" by mobilizing immigrant voters from religious and racial minority groups, Sorensen suggested that a Catholic vice-presidential candidate could help secure many Catholics, and thus many important electoral votes, in the 1956 campaign. Since Catholics represented 20 percent of the population of fourteen large states, with substantial electoral votes, Sorensen stressed the Democrats' need to win these "Catholic states." While Democratic majorities among Catholic voters had consistently topped 65 percent, Republican President Dwight D. Eisenhower's support among Catholics reached 53 percent in the 1952 presidential election.[70] The memorandum did not mention Kennedy by name, and this strategy risked arousing widespread anti-Catholicism among Protestants and secular liberals. Kennedy took pains to avoid responsibility for the memo, and Sorensen asked Connecticut Democratic Chairman John Bailey to take credit for the document, which became known as the "Bailey Memorandum."[71]

In response to the Bailey Memo, an alternative argument emphasized the persistence of anti-Catholicism in U.S. politics. Intending to discredit Kennedy and promote Senator Hubert H. Humphrey's (MN) vice-presidential ambitions, political scientist Louis Bean suggested that a Catholic candidate might harm the party in fourteen predominately Protestant southern and border states. Seeking primarily to assist Humphrey, Bean did not disguise the purpose of discrediting Kennedy's candidacy on religious grounds: "Hard to see John (Kennedy) making an appeal to rural populists as an urban Boston Irish Catholic." Bean unabashedly revived fears of the nativist anti-Catholicism that undermined Al Smith by asking rhetorically, "How will the candidacy of an Irish Catholic for Vice-President affect the party in Protestant areas . . . , a host of states of rural non- (or even anti-) Catholic orientation."[72] Bean's memo blatantly encouraged Democrats to consider religious bigotry when endorsing a vice-presidential candidate.

Liberal Protestant resistance to a Catholic president, however, presented the most difficult obstacle for Kennedy. Liberals represented an important financial and electoral base of the Democratic Party. The liberal Protestant magazine *Christian Century* viewed Kennedy and other Catholic contestants for the vice presidency as too heavily compromised by loyalty to the Vatican. Only months previous, Kennedy secured $1 million in federal aid as reparations for destruction of Vatican property during the U.S. bombing of Rome in World War II.

This legislation also provided $8 million for education in the predominately Catholic Philippines. In the same issue in which the editors rejected Kennedy's candidacy on religious grounds, *Christian Century* denounced the Vatican for accepting this grant, which violated church-state separation in their opinion.[73] The editors called U.S. House Majority Leader John W. McCormack (MA) "the papal knight" for his role in passing this law.

The magazine's language revived the nineteenth-century fear of papal designs on U.S. political power: "None of those [candidates] suggested has demonstrated sufficient independence so that he can be trusted to stand against the unceasing drive of the Roman Catholic Church for access to public funds." These writers rephrased *Time* magazine's question, "Can a Catholic win?" to ask, "*Should* any of the public figures who hold that faith and who have so far been suggested as possibilities for vice-president be nominated, and if they are nominated, *do they deserve to be elected?*"[74] *Christian Century* asserted that Kennedy and other prominent Catholics had not proven themselves worthy of such an honor.

Despite these liberal Protestant fears, several Catholic politicians agreed that a Catholic should not yet pursue the nation's highest office. Jim Farley ironically repeated the arguments used against his own pursuit of the White House in the 1940s by telling Democratic presidential nominee Adlai Stevenson: "America is not ready for a Catholic." Other Catholics, such as Stevenson's campaign manager James Finnegan and Democratic National Chairman Frank McKinney, also discouraged the choice of Kennedy because of the potential for an anti-Catholic backlash. Even Joe Kennedy discouraged his son from the vice presidency because he feared Democrats would blame a defeat in 1956 on the choice of a Catholic vice-presidential nominee. The elder Kennedy hoped that John would instead pursue the presidency in the future. Joe Kennedy expressed relief when the Democratic convention did not choose his son for the vice presidency.[75]

As the 1960 presidential campaign approached, therefore, the Kennedys appealed specifically to the religious and ethnic groups who had supported Al Smith so fervently in 1928. Rose Kennedy recalled that her husband viewed JFK's prospects for higher office more optimistically after 1956. Joseph Kennedy believed that religious and racial minorities would propel his son into the presidency: "There's a whole new generation out there and it's filled with the sons and daughters of immigrants from all over the world and those people are going to be mighty proud that one of their own is running for President." John Kennedy's 1958 book *A Nation of Immigrants* consciously praised

America's pluralistic ideal. Having worked in the Congress against immigration legislation that privileged white Europeans at the expense of Asians and Latin Americans, Kennedy now targeted the nativist roots of this religious and racial discrimination. Kennedy's book, distributed by the Anti-Defamation Society of B'nai B'rith, failed to duplicate the sales of his earlier book, *Profiles in Courage*, but allowed the Massachusetts senator to express sympathy and understanding for the experiences of Al Smith's most loyal supporters. While many Americans challenged the Catholic candidate's stance toward religious liberty, John Kennedy linked the idea of freedom with the struggle of religious and racial minorities. In a 1957 speech to the Irish Institute in New York, Kennedy asserted, "we will recognize that whether a man be Hungarian or Irish, Catholic or Jew, white or black, there forever burns within his breast the unquenchable desire to be free."[76]

The barrage of criticism of John Kennedy's 1959 *Look* magazine interview and Joe's hotheaded response revealed the extent of the Kennedy family's sense of betrayal by Catholics. When Boston archbishop Richard Cardinal Cushing agreed to advocate John's candidacy in March 1959, therefore, Joe Kennedy offered gushing gratitude. Joe greatly valued Cushing's appeal for the support of Pennsylvania's David Lawrence, a Catholic governor who believed that a Catholic could not win the presidency. Joe assured Cushing that this favor "gave me confidence that there was somebody left in high places in the Catholic Church who saw something in this battle that Jack is making." Furthermore, Joe insisted, "if Jack stays in this fight, it will be you who has kept him in."[77]

Catholic politicians must have viewed the presidency as visible, but just beyond their reach, from 1928 to 1956. Just as Jewish and African Americans, as well as women, look forward to the opportunity to break a barrier to the White House, Catholics at that time hoped that one of their own would soon become president. Al Smith's overwhelming defeat, however, raised serious doubts. The widespread, vicious anti-Catholicism of that campaign instilled a fear among both Democrats and Republicans that a Catholic could be fatal to a party's national ticket. Although President Roosevelt facilitated the rise of Joe Kennedy and Jim Farley, he groomed neither Catholic politician as a successor and even impeded their presidential ambitions. Rising liberal-Catholic tensions over issues of church-state separation and anticommunism in the 1930s further discouraged Democrats from promoting Catholics in national politics. Even Catholic politicians discouraged John Kennedy, one of their own, from pursuing the vice presidency in 1956. Al Smith's heroic status among many Catholics, Jews, and African Americans, however, revealed the untapped potential for a Catholic presidential candidate to attract extreme loyalty from minority groups. The Kennedys appealed to this pluralistic ideal in the 1960 presidential campaign.

Chapter Three

Nativist Anti-Catholicism or Christian Evangelization?

Billy Graham, Norman Vincent Peale, and the Marginalization of Religion during the 1960 Presidential Campaign

Less than ten days prior to the 1961 presidential inauguration, evangelical minister Billy Graham arrived at the Kennedy family's Palm Beach mansion. Democratic Senator George A. Smathers (FL) arranged this meeting for President-elect John F. Kennedy, who recognized that this popular Protestant minister could sway the opinions of many Americans. Graham's acceptance might have indicated a hope that he would continue to enjoy the contact with the nation's political establishment that President Dwight D. Eisenhower had facilitated for him in the 1950s.[1]

Having just showered, Kennedy extended his head from the bathroom to direct Graham: "My father's out by the pool. He wants to talk to you." Former ambassador to the Court of Saint James Joseph P. Kennedy dispensed with a few pleasantries, and abruptly turned to politics: "When Jack was elected ... I told him you could be a great asset to the country, helping heal the division over the religious problem in the campaign." Although the minister found this discussion disagreeable, Graham agreed to perform any service that would improve interfaith relations.

After a day of golf, John Kennedy surprised Graham by stopping to meet reporters, and then shocked the minister by announcing to the assembled media, "I want to present to you Dr. Billy Graham, who's going to answer some questions." For a half hour, reporters accosted Graham about the campaign's Catholic issue. The evangelical's words encouraged interfaith cooperation: "I don't think Mr. Kennedy's being a Catholic should be held against him by any Protestant." The following day's *New York Times* headline read, "Dr. Graham Hails Kennedy Victory."[2] Kennedy had maneuvered Graham into an implicit endorsement of the nation's first Catholic president. In his 1997 autobiography, Graham recalled feeling callously manipulated by the newly elected Catholic president: "Mr. Kennedy was using me for his own purposes."[3]

Graham's comments, however, revealed the Protestant minister's acute ability to assess and act upon political realities. Graham could have mentioned Kennedy's insincere tactics in the press conference, but chose not to do so. Rather than using this stage to warn Kennedy publicly against favoring American Catholics and violating the rights of Protestants, Graham advocated cooperation and healing between the various religious faiths. Graham's strategy avoided his being labeled as anti-Catholic or nativist, despite the fact that he had expressed nativist assumptions about Kennedy's candidacy privately. Graham was careful to avoid any statement that would confirm, or even imply, that he held anti-Catholic attitudes.

This chapter explains how Kennedy's candidacy challenged politically powerful conservative Protestant ministers, such as Graham, to choose between anti-Catholic nativism and interfaith cooperation. Graham and best-selling author Reverend Norman Vincent Peale, pastor of the Marble Collegiate Church in New York City, inspired popular, middle-class religious evangelism in the 1950s. Although these men did not confront intellectual issues of theology or moral philosophy, such as the work of Jesuit priest John Courtney Murray and Protestant theologian Reinhold Niebuhr, Graham and Peale defined Christian ideals for millions of Americans. Most importantly, these preachers offered an interfaith appeal. Rather than appealing to sectarian prejudices, Graham and Peale presented an inclusive message known, respectively, as the "new evangelism" and "the power of positive thinking."[4]

When John Kennedy pursued the presidency in 1960, however, some native-born Protestant Americans continued to portray Catholicism as an alien religion that threatened U.S. traditional values. These nativists still perceived Catholics as ignorant immigrants who could never fully assimilate into mainstream Protestant American culture, holding on to a vague belief that Protestantism molded the national traits of independence and individualism. In the nativist interpretation, Catholics could not resist clerical authority on fear of banishment from the religious community, and thus could not truly act as independent decision makers.

Since the first major wave of Catholic immigrants in the first half of the nineteenth century, many Protestant ministers gained prominence by promoting nativist anti-Catholicism. During the influx of five million Irish Catholic migrants from the 1830s to the 1850s, Hartford's Congregational minister Horace Bushnell, called by one scholar "the father of American theological liberalism," mobilized anti-Catholicism with aggressive rhetoric: "[O]ur first danger is barbarism [from immigration], Romanism next."[5] In the 1884 election, Reverend Lyman Burchard sought to stigmatize the Democratic Party at a GOP rally by challenging Catholic loyalty: "We are Republicans, and don't propose to leave our party and identify ourselves with the party whose antecedents have been rum, Romanism, and rebellion. We are loyal to our flag, we are loyal to you."[6] Encouraged by 1921 and 1924 federal legislation establishing quota limits on predominately Catholic immigrants, Protestant fundamentalists, such as Reverend Bob Jones of Florida, worked with a revived Ku Klux Klan to undermine Catholic New York Governor Alfred E. Smith's 1928 presidential bid through nativist publications, anti-Catholic itinerant preachers, and weekly sermons from the pulpit.[7]

Conservative Protestants particularly identified with nativism during the Great Depression and World War II, as Catholics gained political and cultural authority. In the 1930s and early 1940s, President Franklin D. Roosevelt assigned numerous Catholics to public office, provided Catholic bishops with unprecedented access to the White House, and appointed a personal representative to the Vatican.[8] Reacting against increased Catholic participation in U.S. politics and culture, the National Association of Evangelicals (NAE) formed in 1942. NAE leaders viewed Catholics as competitors in the global quest for converts, and often found common cause with nativist attempts to thwart Catholic power in American politics. In the 1940s and 1950s, NAE leaders decried the overrepresentation of Catholic priests as U.S. military chaplains.[9] The NAE passed numerous resolutions in 1950 attacking the Catholic hierarchy's political goals, such as federal aid to parochial schools, and contributed to Protestant pressure that encouraged President Harry S. Truman to withdraw the nomination of an official ambassador to the Vatican in 1951. Protestant evangelicals lobbied the U.S. government to employ diplomatic pressure against several majority Catholic countries, such as Spain and Colombia, that thwarted the efforts of evangelical Protestant missionaries.[10] These conservative ministers lobbied to keep the Roman Catholic Church subordinate to the Protestant majority.

Despite this evangelical Protestant competition with Catholicism, social forces undermined anti-Catholicism and nativism in the mid-twentieth century. Falling immigration rates, due to the 1920s quotas, decreased the fear of social disorder from the influx of new citizens. The Great Depression and World War II fostered interfaith cooperation through the federal government's collective efforts to promote economic growth and national security. Wartime propaganda against Nazi theories of Aryan racial supremacy contributed to the decline of nativist organizations, such as the Klan, which portrayed America as a nation first and foremost for white, Anglo-Saxon Protestants. Political insecurity during the Cold War and atomic age prompted Americans to place faith in religious authorities.[11]

Recognizing these demographic and cultural trends, Norman Vincent Peale blurred denominational distinctions. Peale's earliest public statements expressed the traditional evangelical warnings that Catholicism threatened individual freedom. Evangelical Protestants and Catholics particularly clashed in the 1920s over Prohibition. In 1928, Peale opposed Catholic presidential candidate Al Smith, who sought to legalize alcohol consumption, and preached a 1929 sermon that suggested papal sinister designs on Protestant churches, "The Pope Looks at Protestantism—Is It Exhausted?"[12] By the 1940s, however, Peale's image of Catholicism appeared more tolerant. After World War II, Americans held deep anxieties about the dangers of a world with unprecedented destructive power through atomic weapons. Such common fears encouraged Peale to deemphasize sectarian theological differences while preaching trust in a good and benevolent God.[13] Peale's 1948 self-help book, *A Guide to Confident Living*, discouraged sectarian differences: "It is not important what church you attend—Protestant, Catholic, or Jewish."[14] This postwar passion for cooperation and consensus contributed to this book's sales, which continued to reach one thousand copies weekly in 1951.[15] Peale's 1952 book, *The Power of Positive Thinking*, spent two years on the best-seller list, and made the author a national celebrity.[16]

In this same decade, Billy Graham offered Protestant evangelicalism a tolerant message that challenged nativism. During the 1950s, Graham gained popularity through leadership of "New Evangelical" Christians who avoided the anti-Catholic nativism characteristic of the "Old Fundamentalism."[17] These "new" evangelical Protestants constituted a significant American demographic. According to Grant Wacker, University of North Carolina professor of religious studies, "Arguably, [popular American artist] Norman Rockwell's middle America found its fullest expression—sociologically, culturally, perhaps even theologically—in post–World War II evangelicalism." In Wacker's interpretation, Graham's leadership held great importance for many Americans: "When Graham spoke, middle America heard itself." Despite attending Bob Jones College in Florida, a school named after a fundamentalist minister and one of 1928 presidential candidate Al Smith's most vocal anti-Catholic critics, Graham freely associated with both liberal Protestants and Catholics.[18] In 1953, Graham's desegregation of religious meetings also challenged white supremacy.[19] Graham recognized that mainstream white Protestants decreasingly supported nativist views.

Adopting a platform of religious tolerance allowed Graham to reach beyond parochial, rural communities to a national audience. Democratic Representative John W. McCormack (MA), a Catholic, introduced the preacher to President Harry S. Truman, a Southern Baptist like Graham, in 1952. Graham's impulsive decision to kneel in prayer before cameras in the White House's Rose Garden repulsed Truman. Yet Graham continued to enjoy access to national political leaders. Graham encouraged the presidential ambitions of General Dwight D. Eisenhower, who then sought his counsel about adopting formal church membership. Believing that Americans would require a president to belong to a formal religious organization, Eisenhower accepted Graham's recommendation to join the Presbyterian Church.[20] Although many of Eisenhower's religious statements echoed evangelical themes, the president advocated religious tolerance, viewing any kind of spiritual faith as a means of buttressing democracy: "Our form of government makes no sense unless it is founded in a deeply felt religious faith, and I don't care what it is. With us of course it is the Judeo-Christian concept but it must be a religion that all men are created equal."[21] Eisenhower also reached out to Catholics, speaking at the Notre Dame graduation in 1959, for example. By associating closely with the president, Graham came to embody an interfaith message.

Despite the efforts of prominent conservative ministers such as Graham and Peale, nativist anti-Catholicism remained strong in 1960. Polling data in the late 1950s demonstrated that many Americans would not support any Catholic for the presidency. Most opponents of a Catholic president mentioned the religion's "alien" nature. In Gallup Poll surveys, respondents echoed themes from nineteenth-century nativist anti-Catholicism. Conservative Protestants in the NAE and the Southern Baptist Convention (SBC) challenged Kennedy's candidacy on religious grounds. To justify rejection of a Catholic candidate in 1960, nativists characterized Catholics as foreign and culturally unfit for office.[22] These individuals insisted that Roman Catholics owed primary loyalty to religious authorities and thus could not act entirely with U.S. national goals at heart. Graham and Peale shared these suspicions, but feared alienating the broad base of Americans who supported their interfaith message.

Early in 1960, Kennedy's staff challenged Peale and Graham to denounce religious bias in the campaign. Having entered all Democratic primaries to provide evidence that a Catholic candidate would not alienate Protestant voters, Kennedy asked these ministers to sign an open letter that criticized opposition to a Catholic president on religious grounds alone. The letter advised Americans to employ "reasoned balance of judgment" regarding the religious issue. Both Peale and Graham refused to sign the statement.

Nativist assumptions partially explain Peale's clear and direct rejection of this request. On Kennedy's behalf, dean of the Episcopal Cathedral in Washington, D.C., Frank Sayre, approached Peale, who indicated an unwillingness to support Kennedy on religious grounds. Peale's refusal to assist a Democrat appeared consistent with his political conservatism. Peale opposed Franklin Roosevelt's New Deal reforms, encouraged General Douglas MacArthur to pursue the presidency in 1952, and enthusiastically supported the Eisenhower-Nixon administration. Peale's uncharacteristic alignment with liberal Protestants to oppose Spain's Catholic General Francisco Franco, however, revealed a deeper, anti-Catholic impulse.[23] Peale's mistrust of Catholicism surfaced again in response to Sayre's appeal. Writing to Sayre, Peale claimed to have "gotten very tired of the power hungry and contemptuous attitude of the Roman Catholic Church." To sign a call for tolerance "would give the impression to thousands of Protestants that I am for Kennedy or at least openminded toward him, and that would be a falsehood." Peale even echoed nativist arguments about Catholicism's threat to Protestant American traditions: "I am sorry, Frank, but I think it time to restrengthen the oldtime, if somewhat narrow, loyalties of Protestantism, or else we shall deteriorate altogether."[24] Peale's claim to defend Protestant loyalties appeared hypocritical in light of the nativist assumption that Catholics held allegiance to religious leaders, which thus undermined their national duties. Confronted with the prospect of a Catholic president, Peale jettisoned the interfaith inclusiveness characteristic of his popular books.

Graham's rejection of Kennedy's request contained none of Peale's nativist rhetoric, and revealed his reluctance to burn political bridges. Kennedy campaign spokesman Pierre Salinger initially obtained a verbal acceptance from Graham, who changed his mind only days later.[25] In a conversation with Kennedy aide Theodore Sorensen,

Graham explained that religion would remain a legitimate issue "whether we like it or not."[26] Graham claimed later to fear that the letter might suggest partisan support for Kennedy. In a 1997 autobiography, Graham recalled, "I was afraid some might interpret anything I said on the subject as an implied political endorsement."[27] Salinger and Sorensen believed that Graham wanted to avoid any action that would have helped Kennedy and hurt Nixon. Yet Graham's wavering reflected his political savvy, as well as concern not to be perceived as nativist or anti-Catholic.

As the media highlighted religious divisions among voters in the Democratic Party primaries, Peale promulgated nativist charges about Catholic disloyalty. In Wisconsin's April primary, predominately Catholic districts tended to favor Kennedy while Protestant regions supported Senator Hubert H. Humphrey (MN). West Virginia's May primary became critical to Kennedy as its population was less than 5 percent Catholic, thus providing an important test of Kennedy's popularity among non-Catholics. In this context, Peale personally wrote a West Virginia friend to encourage support for Humphrey's candidacy. Echoing the argument that Catholics owed primary political allegiance to the pope, Peale implied doubts about Catholic loyalty. "I don't care a bit who of the candidates is chosen," Peale wrote, "except that he be an American who takes orders from no one but the American people."

Just as nativists characterized immigrant ethnic groups as foreign to U.S. values, Peale privately portrayed Kennedy as culturally unsuited to become chief executive. In the same letter to his West Virginia friend, who supported Kennedy, Peale implied that Catholics lacked sufficient pedigree to serve as president. "[I cannot understand] how a dedicated Protestant such as yourself could so enthusiastically favor an Irish Catholic for President of our country which was founded by Calvinistic Christians." Peale's comment identified a nativist hierarchy of religious and ethnic groups in the United States. Since more "Calvinistic" Christians participated in the nation's political origins, Peale argued, this group deserved greater consideration for the executive office than an "Irish" Catholic, whose ancestors arrived in America chronologically much later. Peale's implication that Irish Catholics deserved lower status than—even second-class citizenship to—Calvinistic Christians had origins in the nativist belief that immigrants threatened America's Protestant civilization.

If the reader of this letter failed to perceive Kennedy as the object of these remarks, Peale's subsequent public statements clarified his meaning. With the primary mere days away, Peale addressed the subject of Kennedy's political independence even more directly while speaking in

Charleston, West Virginia. Peale asked rhetorically whether Kennedy was as "free as any other American to give 'his first loyalty to the United States.'"[28]

Billy Graham privately revealed similar fears of Catholic power. Kennedy's May victory in the West Virginia primary indicated the strong likelihood for a Catholic Democratic presidential nominee in 1960. A few weeks later, Graham wrote Vice President Richard M. Nixon. As the Republican Party's national convention approached, Nixon's presidential nomination seemed ensured. Writing in late June, Graham discouraged Nixon from choosing a Catholic running mate, such as Eisenhower's labor secretary, James P. Mitchell, to court Catholic voters. In Graham's opinion, Catholics would vote as a bloc for Kennedy regardless of Nixon's appeals to this religious constituency. "[Kennedy] will capture the Catholic vote—almost 100 percent of it—no matter what concessions you make to the Catholic church or how you play up to them," Graham argued. He assumed, just as nativists traditionally did, that American Catholics would unquestioningly support a fellow Catholic rather than choose the best-qualified candidate.

Despite criticizing Catholic support for Kennedy as motivated by religious sectarianism, Graham ironically encouraged Nixon to pursue a Protestant bloc vote. Counseling Nixon to preserve the loyalty of Protestants by avoiding any special favors to Catholic voters, Graham noted that Protestant voters exceeded the Catholic voter base by a three to one margin. In Graham's interpretation, Nixon's choice of a Catholic running mate might "divide the Protestant vote." Graham proposed a Protestant, medical missionary to China and U.S. congressman Walter H. Judd (MN), for the vice presidency. Characterizing Judd's nomination as essential—"almost a *must*"—Graham argued that a Nixon-Judd ticket "would put much of the South and border states in the Republican column and bring about a dedicated Protestant vote to counteract the Catholic vote."[29] Graham justified the strategy of appealing to Protestants on religious grounds by claiming that Catholics would unquestionably vote for Kennedy.

While he may not have perceived himself as espousing nativist anti-Catholicism, Graham understood the controversial nature of these remarks. If Nixon had honored Graham's postscript request, neither the public nor posterity would have access to this appeal on Judd's behalf: "You would do me a favor by destroying this letter after reading it."[30] Graham's letter revealed neither the ethnic hierarchy nor the accusations of Catholic disloyalty that Peale advanced.[31] Graham never made a public call for Protestants to unite against Kennedy, nor did he campaign openly against the dangers of Catholic power. But Graham's view of Catholics as a threat to Republican and Protestant evangelical goals ignored the fact that more than 50 percent of Catholic voters supported Eisenhower in 1956, and that conservative Catholics, such as *National Review* editor William F. Buckley, often shared this group's mission to promote traditional values and uncompromising resistance to communism. Despite these realities, Graham's words and actions outside the public eye revealed an unwillingness to consider that Catholics might express political opinions independent of religious loyalty in the coming election.

Although Nixon chose a Protestant vice-presidential running mate—Henry Cabot Lodge of Massachusetts—Graham still privately lobbied Republican leaders to generate a Protestant bloc vote against Kennedy. In August, Graham encouraged President Eisenhower to campaign for Nixon in regions where few Catholics resided. "With the religious issue growing deeper," Graham advised, "I believe you could tip the scales in a number of key states from Kentucky to Texas." Graham called on Eisenhower to exploit nativist anti-Catholicism in the so-called southern Bible Belt, where Protestant fundamentalism had flourished. In Graham's opinion, Eisenhower's political stature would attract attention to the Catholic issue and thus turn voters to the Republican candidate.[32] Graham also counseled Nixon to exploit the suspicion of a Catholic presidential candidate among conservatives in these southern and border states. Nixon could "dramatize the religious issue, without mentioning it publicly," the minister proposed, by visiting Graham's North Carolina home.[33] Obsessed with the potential for Catholics to support Kennedy's candidacy because of religious loyalties, Graham failed to acknowledge the hypocrisy in attempting to manipulate Protestant fears of a Catholic president.

Despite his previous advocacy of interfaith cooperation, Graham reacted with alarm when confronted with the possibility of Catholics assuming major governmental offices in 1961. Graham seemed to believe in the old nativist trope that American Catholic public officials promoted political goals incompatible with U.S. national interest. Convinced that Catholic Church leaders exercised absolute authority over American Catholic politicians, Graham feared the potential for a Catholic president, a Catholic majority leader in the Senate, and a Catholic speaker of the House. Since Kennedy chose Senate Majority Leader Lyndon B. Johnson as a running-mate, Graham calculated that Johnson's rise to the vice presidency would allow the ranking Democrat, Catholic Senator Mike Mansfield (MT), to assume the majority leader position—the Senate's most powerful office. In the House of

Representatives, Catholic Majority Leader John W. McCormack (MA) would soon succeed House Speaker Sam Rayburn (TX). Graham believed that this scenario would allow the Holy See an unprecedented opportunity to manipulate both the executive and legislative branches of government: "The Roman Catholic Church will take advantage of this."[34]

While Graham privately lobbied the Republican administration to exploit nativist anti-Catholicism, other evangelical Protestants prepared to mobilize national opposition to a Catholic president. Encouraged by Norman Vincent Peale to endorse Nixon publicly, Graham invited this author and Protestant minister to meet with 25 to 30 Protestant evangelical leaders on August 18 in Montreaux, Switzerland. Although Graham recalled the meeting's purpose as an "evangelism strategy conference," fear of Kennedy's Catholicism constituted the major theme of these discussions.[35] As Peale's wife explained in an August letter to a friend, "they were unanimous in feeling that the Protestants in America must be aroused in some way, or the solid block [sic] Catholic voting, plus money, will take the election."[36] The NAE agreed to sponsor a conference to generate opposition to the prospect of a Catholic president. According to Graham's most recent account, secretary of the World Evangelical Fellowship, Clyde Taylor, encouraged Peale to attend and act as chairperson for a September 7 meeting entitled, "Study Conference on the Relationship of Religion and Freedom," in Washington, D.C.

Having fostered a national image distinct from nativism, Graham refused to risk his public reputation through public opposition to Kennedy. Sensing that the public would rebuff such religious-based resistance to Kennedy's candidacy, Graham excused himself from attending by continuing a European vacation that conflicted with the conference date.[37] In a September 1 letter to Nixon, Graham expressed embarrassment about anti-Catholic spokesmen. Announcing that he was "detaching myself from some of the cheap religious bigotry and diabolical whisperings that are going on," Graham advised Nixon "to stay a million miles from the religious issue at this time."[38] While not dismissing the possibility of future discussion of Kennedy's Catholicism, Graham perceived a popular consensus against nativist anti-Catholicism in September.

The organizers of the September conference adopted particular measures to avoid the appearance of nativist bias while seeking a broad and favorable reception of their message. By choosing the nation's capitol, the organizers sought national media attention. Washington correspondents for newspapers, such as the *New York Times,* and news magazines, such as *Time,* would cover the proceedings and distribute the story to a nationwide audience. The conference's title, National Conference of Citizens for Religious Freedom (NCCRF), reflected a desire to appear in a positive context. Rather than fashioning a negative theme such as "against Catholic power" or "countering papal oppression," the group's name promoted the image of members of a democratic society supporting the free exercise of religion. In the statement released by NCCRF, the authors insisted that individual Catholics deserved tolerance, fairness, and religious liberty. "We further believe that persons of the Roman Catholic faith can be just as honest, patriotic, and public spirited as those of any other faith," the statement read. These words emphasized that the conference did not seek to ostracize all members of this particular religious faith. NCCRF's organizers wanted to appear as defenders of freedom rather than as opponents of equal opportunity.

These attempts to advance a positive image for the conference had limited success. While the meeting received substantial media attention, the coverage produced different, and more negative, messages than the organizers intended. Although several Protestant evangelicals officially organized this weekend conference, Peale provided the event's most recognizable name. Rather than use the cumbersome seven-word title, National Conference of Citizens for Religious Freedom, reporters often identified the meeting as the National Conference or the Peale Group. The *New York Times* used Peale's name, since he served as chairman and no other ministers in attendance rivaled his popularity. This paper's front page headline on the day following the conference read, "Protestant Unit Wary on Kennedy: Statement by Peale Group Sees Vatican 'Pressure' on Democratic Nominee." In the context of a presidential campaign, Kennedy's Catholicism and Peale's participation overshadowed the theme of religious freedom.

NCCRF sought to keep the idea of religious liberty as a central thrust of the proceedings, but the group's official statement revealed fear of only one threat to this concept—the Roman Catholic Church. Nativist assumptions that Catholic power dictated the political decisions of church members stood at the center of this meeting's discussions. "The key question is whether it is in the best interest of our society for any church organization to attempt to exercise control over its members in political and civic affairs," the official conference statement read. By focusing primarily on the question of freedom, NCCRF's participants avoided characterization of all Catholics as alien or un-American. The Catholic hierarchy's ambitions for political authority—not the individual Catholic—created their doubts about Kennedy's ability to exercise independence as president: "While the current Roman Catholic contender for the Presidency states specifically that he would not be so influenced, his church insists that he is duty-bound to admit to its discretion."[39] Criticizing the Roman Catholic hierarchy for seeking a U.S. ambassador to the Vatican and federal aid to Catholic schools, and for suppressing freedom of worship in Spain and Colombia, the NCCRF statement warned of the gradual Catholic domination of U.S. institutions. "In various areas where they predominate, Catholics have seized control of the public schools, staffed them with nun teachers wearing their church garb, and introduced the catechism and practices of their church." The image of Catholic nuns in dark habits may have inspired subconscious nativist fears of the foreign.

In an effort to demonstrate the group's distance from anti-Catholic nativism, however, NCCRF included pluralist and liberal language in its arguments against Catholic political power. NCCRF took care to convey an overtly tolerant and inclusive message: "Brotherhood in a pluralistic society like ours depends on a firm wall of separation between church and state." By emphasizing the need for an absolute barrier between religious and political issues, the conference participants expressed arguments in terms of defending constitutional principles.

Despite these attempts to distinguish criticism of Catholicism from religious bias, Peale's comments particularly suggested that NCCRF's essential message did not differ much from nativists of the past. In a post-meeting press conference, a reporter asked Peale what impact the election of Kennedy would have on the United States. In response, Peale implied that a Catholic president would impose alien elements on U.S. civilization: "Our American culture is at stake. I don't say it won't survive, but it won't be what it was."[40]

In the wake of this conference's portrayal of a Roman Catholic threat to religious liberty, several Americans countered this accusation. On September 9, Jesuit priest and theology professor John Courtney Murray traced a direct link between Peale's accusations about the Roman Catholic Church and nativist anti-Catholicism. Murray's response to Peale equated the old nativism with NCCRF's charges. "The brutal fact becomes increasingly clear," Murray wrote, "The 'oldest American prejudice,' as anti-Catholicism has rightly been called, is as poisonously alive today as it was in 1928, or in the Eighteen Nineties, or even the Eighteen Forties." In Murray's interpretation, critics of the Roman Catholic Church used footnote citations to appear more scholarly and rational. "The footnotes, of course, prove none of the time-worn anti-Catholic charges in the text"; Murray argued, "they merely serve to cloak the prejudice that long ago wrote the text."[41] According to Murray, Peale belonged in the same grouping as nineteenth-century nativists.

Murray's comments were soon followed by other important statements that rejected NCCRF's opinions. On September 11, 100 religious leaders of several faiths released a joint statement that religion should not serve as a basis for choosing public officials. Bishops of the Protestant and Methodist churches, Jewish rabbis, Greek Orthodox archbishops, and Roman Catholic archbishops, as well as several independent scholars, signed this denunciation of voting on religious grounds.[42] Many reports of NCCRF published negative responses to Peale's comments. *Time* magazine suggested a mean-spiritedness to Peale's comments about Catholicism. In a sub-headline about the NCCRF, the editors playfully—but meaningfully—altered the title of Peale's book to read "The Power of Negative Thinking."[43] A San Francisco *Chronicle* cartoon lampooned Peale as an oppressive Roman emperor sending a helpless Christian, John F. Kennedy, to a Coliseum full of lions. Similarly, a Lou Grant cartoon, "The Power of Positive Sinking," depicted a well-dressed arm hoisting a sign, above garbage and sludge, which read "Religion is an Issue."[44] Many national media perceived Peale's comments as unfair and intolerable.

On September 12, John Kennedy used the platform of an invitation by the Greater Houston Ministerial Association to confront NCCRF's charges. Kennedy's staff viewed the speech as a potential turning-point in the campaign, according to aide Theodore Sorensen, who confided to a friend, "we can win or lose the election right there in Houston on Monday night."[45] Kennedy presented a statement of political faith. Attempting to highlight hypocrisy within nativist assumptions, Kennedy drew parallels between a Catholic priest and a Protestant minister who might advocate public policies or political candidates: "I believe in an America . . . where no Catholic prelate would tell the President—should he be Catholic—how to act, and no Protestant minister would tell his parishioners for whom to vote." Kennedy equated Catholics who showed favoritism to a Catholic presidential candidate with Protestants who advocated anti-Catholic voting: "I believe in an America . . . where there is no Catholic vote, no anti-Catholic vote, no bloc voting of any kind." If some warned that the presidency might become "humbled by making it the instrument of any religious group," Kennedy asked for the same vigilance against allowing the office to be "tarnished by arbitrarily withholding its occupancy from the members of any one religious group." While NCCRF criticized Catholic nations for denying equal rights to Protestant missionaries, Kennedy also opposed such intolerance by Protestant nations: "I hope that you and I condemn with equal fervor those nations which deny their Presidency to Protestants, and those which deny it to Catholics."[46] The NCCRF claimed to defend pluralism and religious liberty, but Kennedy succeeded in portraying this rhetoric as empty.

In this context, Peale faced public consequences for participating in NCCRF. Two-time Democratic Party presidential nominee Adlai Stevenson quipped that he found Christian missionary Saint Paul "appealing" and Peale "appalling."[47] Beyond the public embarrassment, Peale suffered financial losses for these comments. The *Philadelphia Inquirer* and several other papers ceased syndication of Peale's national column.[48] Peale's public comments lacked the ethnic distinctions of traditional nativism, yet this fact did not prevent the widespread backlash. Americans in leading national institutions perceived Peale's criticism of Catholicism as inconsistent with the pluralist, interfaith postwar consensus that Peale himself had helped create.

After a week of silence, Peale denied both anti-Catholicism and any intention of preserving the presidency as a Protestant monopoly. Rejecting any responsibility for the meeting's origins, Peale announced that he had immediately broken with NCCRF upon realizing that the religious dialogue had political consequences. "I am strongly opposed to any admixture of religious discussion and political partisanship," Peale asserted. In Peale's interpretation, his "thirty years of interfaith activity" discredited those who attempted to portray him as anti-Catholic. "I have never relinquished my convictions on the question of harmonious relationships among the faithful for one instant and I do not intend to begin doing so now." Peale even endorsed the right of Americans to elect a person of any religious affiliation, or none at all, to the presidency: "Each of us must vote according to the dictates of his own conscience."[49] Uncomfortable with the controversy surrounding this conference, Peale repudiated nativist and anti-Catholic beliefs.

While Peale expressed contrition about participating in the weekend conference, he ultimately refused to disavow suspicions about Kennedy's Catholicism. Blaming the media for misleading the public about his comments, Peale wrote in a form letter to critics, "The meeting was invaded by reporters who distorted its purpose and gave a very false and distressing picture of my own personal relationship to this matter." Peale's letter recanted his earlier regrets about participating in the conference. "I do not feel that I was wrong in attending this meeting," Peale asserted, "but it may have been unwise under the circumstances." Despite this reluctant admission of indiscretion, Peale insisted upon the right to investigate the political significance of Kennedy's religious affiliation: "I felt a sense of concern about the matter of religious freedom and believe it is proper at any time for a Protestant to meet with fellow Protestants to discuss matters relating to our faith."[50] Ignoring the original intention of warning Protestants about the potential dangers of a Catholic president to U.S. traditions, Peale now portrayed the conference as strictly theological in content. Retreating from public resistance to Kennedy's candidacy, Peale regretted the conference results rather than the meeting's goals.

In response to these attacks on Peale, some Protestants defended NCCRF and insisted that Kennedy's Catholicism invited legitimate skepticism. More than a week after the conference, Dr. Daniel Poling, Peale's close friend, asserted that neither he nor Peale repudiated NCCRF's statement that questioned Kennedy's ability to resist Vatican pressure. Others endorsed Peale's comments that expanded doubts about a Catholic president beyond the topic of religious liberty. A member of Peale's church, described by the *New York Times* as an "active member" of the congregation, asserted, "I insist on the right of a Protestant to say that there is something in our Protestant background and ethic that makes a Protestant better equipped to be President of the United States."[51] Despite the NCCRF's attempts to focus on Catholic threats to religious freedom, such individuals based opposition to Kennedy on the belief in Protestant culture's superiority.

The National Association of Evangelicals (NAE) also continued to oppose Kennedy publicly on religious grounds. After the September conference, the NAE refused to limit discussion of Kennedy's Catholicism to the topic of religious liberty. Asserting Protestantism as America's official religion, this group lobbied to turn Reformation Sunday, October 30—a week before the election—into a day for rallying opposition to the prospect of a Catholic president.[52] A NAE bulletin for Christian Conviction Sunday—October 23—rejected the prospect that pluralism had replaced Protestant ascendancy. Raising fears of the potential for decline in Protestant hegemony, this publication appealed to nativist belief in Protestantism's essential place in U.S. history and institutions. "Some suggest that America is now in a post-Protestant era," the NAE advertisement read, "They say the dynamic is gone from Protestantism and the emphasis of our nation has shifted away from the traditions of our Protestant heritage." The NAE called upon Protestants to prevent this potentiality despite rising Catholic power. "Public opinion is changing in favor of the Church of Rome. It is time for us to stand up and be counted as Protestants."[53] NAE leaders believed that a Protestant president would better preserve that religion's position as defining U.S. culture.

In the final week of the presidential campaign, NAE publications continued to portray Kennedy's candidacy as a threat to U.S. political culture. A full-page advertisement, sponsored by the NAE's Minneapolis chapter, in the *Minneapolis Tribune* raised a series of questions detailing clerical pressures a Catholic would encounter as the nation's chief executive. An "Open Letter to the Voter" asserted that the Vatican's "declared opposition to American institutions is well known and has been fully documented."[54] A *New York Times* article reported that, on this same day, a New York City church distributed a NAE pamphlet entitled "There IS a Religious Issue."[55] This organization offered the most persistent, widespread, and unapologetic nationwide resistance to Kennedy on religious grounds.

While the NAE highlighted the election's Catholic issue, Billy Graham wrestled with the question of what role to play in the campaign's final days. Delivering the invocation at a Nixon rally in South Carolina only two days prior to the election, Graham joined the vice president and President Eisenhower in Pittsburgh the following day.[56] These meetings belatedly fulfilled Graham's call for a visit from one or both of these men to "dramatize the religious issue." Graham continued to avoid public comment on Kennedy's religion, however. After submitting an article praising Nixon for *Life* magazine, Graham received criticism from the Democratic governors of North Carolina and Tennessee. Kennedy himself protested to *Life* editor Henry Luce, who asked Graham for an alternative article that merely encouraged Christians to vote. This compromise also satisfied Graham's wife, who feared the public backlash that might follow the evangelical minister's open endorsement of Nixon.[57]

Graham's ambiguous response to Kennedy's Catholicism reflected complex motives. Never describing a Catholic as unfit for the executive office, Graham refused to lead a late-twentieth-century nativist campaign against a Catholic president, as was done by the Ku Klux Klan and Senator J. Thomas Heflin (AL) in 1928. Sociologist William Martin has suggested that Graham primarily supported Nixon to ensure continued access to the White House and political power.[58] In the 1950s, President Eisenhower frequently consulted Graham's advice on religious and political issues, and many evangelical Protestants viewed this president as sympathetic to their spiritual mission. Nixon's presidency would presumably continue the close personal, professional, and spiritual relationship Graham enjoyed with America's most powerful public official.

Nativist assumptions nonetheless conditioned Graham to conspire against Kennedy in 1960. If the Republicans openly appealed to conservative Protestant voters, Graham believed, this constituency would unite against the Catholic candidate. Many evangelical Protestants shared Graham's fear that the Roman Catholic Church would manipulate Kennedy and other Catholic politicians in positions of national power. While reluctant to express these beliefs publicly, Graham actively encouraged Nixon and Eisenhower to exploit nativism to undermine Kennedy's candidacy.

Norman Vincent Peale also viewed a Catholic president as fatal for U.S. religious and cultural traditions, yet his willingness to retreat from the campaign discussion suggests a shallow commitment to Kennedy's defeat. While Peale's public opposition to a Catholic president ended in September, this Protestant minister still perceived Kennedy as a threat to an American civilization that required Protestant leadership. Peale's private comments—and even his earlier public statements—revealed strong anxiety about the fading of Protestant cultural power. Upon learning of Kennedy's election, Peale counseled a friend to record the date as a historical turning point: "Protestant America got its death blow on November 8th."[59] Despite NCCRF's expressions of support for religious liberty and diversity, discomfort with religious pluralism and distress about Vatican power remained prominent in Peale's mind.

Graham's spontaneous endorsement of President-elect Kennedy in Florida constituted a short-term victory for the evangelical minister. Graham benefited when John Kennedy disingenuously told reporters that the evangelical Protestant minister wanted to address the media on the campaign's religious issue. By avoiding public opposition to Kennedy's Catholicism, Graham preserved a reputation as a nationally respected religious figure.

Opposition to a Catholic president in 1960, however, resulted in both short- and long-term defeat for conservative Protestants. Graham, Peale, and other conservatives perceived the immediate goal of Nixon's victory as essential to strengthen traditional and evangelical Christian values in the United States. Yet Graham's private encouragement of open resistance to Kennedy by Peale and other evangelical Protestants unintentionally mobilized liberal Protestants and Catholics to defend the election of a Catholic president. Kennedy's ability to attract Protestant liberals proved significant in the Democratic Party's November victory.

A lasting consequence accompanied this direct, unintended result of conservative Protestant ministers' resistance to Kennedy's Catholicism. Peale and the NCCRF defended religious liberty and pluralism to justify skepticism toward a Catholic president. When Kennedy demonstrated full commitment to these principles, many liberal and conservative

Protestants jettisoned the nativist argument that a Catholic could not preserve Protestant American cultural traditions. Kennedy's pledge to maintain rigid distinctions between the sacred and the secular marginalized meaningful religious discourse in American public life. In future years, conservative Protestants regretted this political precedent that required American public figures to endorse the absolute separation of church and state.

Chapter Four

Religious Liberty or Religious Test?

Debating the 1960 Campaign's "Catholic Issue" in Liberal Organizations and Media

Author James A. Michener recalled feeling quite startled when guests at publisher Bennett Cerf's early 1960 dinner party challenged John F. Kennedy's presidential candidacy on religious grounds. In this highly educated and intellectually sophisticated crowd, Michener was surprised to encounter "American liberals [who] . . . had the most serious and deep-seated fears of a Catholic in the Presidency." One individual called the Vatican "dictatorial, savage[,] . . . reactionary . . . [and] brutal in its lust for power." Others feared that clerical pressures would determine Kennedy's political decisions. Another declared that "Irish priests" would manipulate a Catholic president "as if he were their toy." A Catholic at Michener's table characterized her church as antidemocratic and incompatible with church-state separation and religious liberty. According to Michener, these fellow guests claimed to know many other ideological liberals who also mistrusted Catholic presidential candidates.[1]

Essayist Clifton Fadiman, who perceived the religious controversy as a civil rights issue, raised his voice in disagreement with the general, anti-Catholic consensus. Chastising the others for denying Catholics the equal opportunity to occupy the presidency, Fadiman countered, "I am unwilling to proscribe an entire body of people from high office merely because of their religion, which history has proved is a reasonably good religion that yields reasonably good results."[2] Recounting this event in a 1961 book on the campaign, Michener recalled thinking, "I've fought to defend every civil right that has come under attack in my lifetime. . . . I've tried to write as if all men were my brothers." Michener's reflections became very personal as he recalled confronting racial intolerance in his travels: "In Hawaii I've stood for absolute equality, and it would be ridiculous for a man like me to be against a

Catholic for President."³ Fadiman and Michener saw Catholics as a minority group that suffered prejudicial discrimination and intolerance. These liberals determined that Kennedy should not encounter unequal treatment, or exceptional skepticism, due to religious affiliation alone.

In college textbooks and classroom lectures, historians have described how the 1960 election ended the Protestant monopoly on the presidency. Most, however, have focused mainly on Republican, fundamentalist Protestant anti-Catholicism, which they explain with the theory of nativism—the movement to promote white, Anglo-Saxon Protestant individuals and institutions.⁴ By portraying the issue as merely a Protestant-Catholic divide, scholars have failed to address the divisions within the liberal community that Kennedy's candidacy exposed. Even prior to the election year, a critical internal debate between two subgroups of liberalism appeared. Libertarians believed that Catholic candidates would be subject to pressure from their church hierarchy, and they feared that Catholic Church intervention in U.S. politics would undermine the religious liberty of non-Catholic Americans. They insisted on absolute separation of church and state, which they considered impossible under a Catholic president. Accommodationists, on the other hand, believed that an active partnership between government and religious institutions would extend individual freedom and civil rights. In order to defend citizens who sought to promote religious values, these liberals portrayed opposition to Kennedy or other Catholic Americans on religious grounds as intolerant and biased. Exposure of liberalism's disagreements regarding Catholicism and church-state separation threatened permanent fragmentation of the ideological and political liberal coalition.

This chapter explains how Kennedy's 1960 campaign prompted liberals to extend the principle of religious liberty to American Catholics. Despite strong opposition within self-described liberal organizations and publications, Kennedy was able to win the Democratic presidential nomination by successfully distancing himself from unpopular Catholic political positions and strongly asserting his commitment to separation of church and state, thus allaying libertarian concerns. Once the nomination was secured, party solidarity silenced most remaining liberal critics in order to ensure a Democratic victory.

Anti-Catholicism had long permeated twentieth-century U.S. liberalism. Indeed, according to historian Robert Moats Miller, allegedly tolerant, "'enlightened' liberal Protestantism" proved more critical of the Roman Catholic Church than anti-alien, native-born Protestants.⁵ Seven years before Kennedy's candidacy, author Peter Viereck attracted widespread attention by describing "Catholic-baiting" as "the anti-Semitism of the liberals."[6] Mid-twentieth-century American liberals rejected Catholic dogma, contrasting their supposed experimental, scientific method of empirical observation and discovery with the Vatican's hierarchical, authoritarian tradition.[7] Former First Lady Eleanor Roosevelt openly opposed federal aid to Catholic schools in the late 1940s and publicly clashed with New York Archbishop Francis Spellman regarding this issue.[8] During interviews in 1959 for a biography, *Mr. Citizen,* former President Harry S. Truman suggested that Catholics could not respect church-state separation because they pledged primary devotion to religious leaders: "[Catholics] have a loyalty to a church hierarchy that I don't believe in. . . . You don't want to have anyone in control of the government of the United States who has another loyalty, religious or otherwise."[9]

While the terms "libertarian absolutist" and "accommodationist" did not characterize all liberal reactions to Kennedy's Catholicism, these two subgroups catalyzed the debates within liberal circles. Libertarians frequently charged the Roman Catholic Church with seeking state support, which they believed subverted the First Amendment's principle of absolute government neutrality toward religious organizations. This absolutism received clearest articulation in the American Civil Liberties Union (ACLU) and Protestant and Other Americans United for Separation of Church and State (POAU). During the 1950s, ACLU Executive Director Patrick Murphy Malin and Associate Director Alan Reitman criticized Catholic pursuit of censorship in attempts to restrict access to anti-Catholic and pornographic books and movies and resistance to birth control.[10] POAU formed in 1947 to protest the Supreme Court's decision, in *Everson v. Board of Education,* that New Jersey could financially support busing expenses for parochial school children without violating the constitutional principle of church-state separation. Executive Director Glenn Archer, Associate Director C. Stanley Lowell, and legal counsel Paul B. Blanshard vigilantly pursued national support for complete separation between church and state.[11]

Accommodationist liberals, on the other hand, interpreted the First Amendment to support government assistance of religious goals, believing that the First Amendment's guarantee of religious liberty promoted institutional religion's favored status in American society. While they denied the state's right to favor any particular denomination, they also proscribed the government from suppressing or hindering religious organizations. In the nondenominational *Christianity and Crisis,* Union Theological Seminary officials John C. Bennett, Robert McAfee Brown, and Reinhold Niebuhr expressed great fear that insistence on complete church-state separation would undermine all religious faith and promote secularism. University of Chicago theologian Jaroslav Pelikan shared this opinion that government should accommodate religious belief, and he supported some Catholic requests for federal financial assistance.[12]

Most Catholics adopted an accommodationist viewpoint and perceived libertarian absolutism as anti-Catholic bias. Catholic priests and professional organizations advocated religious-governmental partnerships to assist the underprivileged, regulate movie content, and financially aid religious education. Catholics had largely supported the liberal President Franklin D. Roosevelt, who quoted papal encyclicals to justify government assistance for disadvantaged U.S. citizens.[13] Members of the Catholic Church hierarchy organized labor protests, boycotts of pornographic movies, and opposition to artificial birth control. Catholic organizations, such as the Knights of Columbus, and professional societies created subcultures within the broader U.S. political culture. Leading Catholics such as Archbishop Spellman perceived attempts to limit church participation in politics as prejudicial. Spellman's New York archdiocese frequently criticized POAU interpretations of absolute church-state separation and even depicted this organization as the modern equivalent of the Ku Klux Klan, which in earlier years had also led movements to restrict state support of Catholic institutions.[14] The conservative Catholic publication *Brooklyn Tablet* published a cartoon showing a POAU member replacing his Klan cloak with a business suit jacket. Jesuit theologian John Courtney Murray described POAU counsel Blanshard as a modern facsimile of traditional anti-Catholicism (Murray privately shortened POAU's acronym to "PU").[15] While the Catholic Church officially avoided an endorsement of either Kennedy or Nixon, Catholic publications did note criticisms of Catholicism and defended church policies.

Kennedy supporters perceived undeniable tension between liberalism and Catholicism. According to liberal historian and Kennedy advisor Arthur M. Schlesinger, Jr., "[Kennedy's] candidacy touched uglier strains in the liberal syndrome, especially the susceptibility to anti-Catholicism."[16] Another member of Kennedy's campaign staff, economist John Kenneth Galbraith, also recalled substantial anti-Catholic attitudes among U.S. liberals. During the campaign, Galbraith and other non-Catholics actively implored New York's Jewish American liberals to overcome traditional religious antagonisms and support Kennedy.[17] Noted journalist David Halberstam described "uneasiness" about a Catholic president within "the *New Republic* crowd, the intellectuals and the liberals," very much the same elite Michener encountered at Bennett Cerf's party.[18] According to these observers of the 1960 campaign, liberal anti-Catholicism presented a serious obstacle to Kennedy's candidacy.

Prior to 1960, Kennedy's attitude toward church-state separation appeared undefined, though increasingly independent from Catholic accommodationism. As a Massachusetts congressman, Kennedy rejected claims that Catholics were biased against non-Catholic schooling. Kennedy's own personal educational history, at a private nondenominational boarding school and Harvard University, demonstrated his own autonomy from Catholic Church instruction. During a congressional hearing, Kennedy once explained, "There is an old saying in Boston that we get our religion from Rome and our politics at home." While Congressman Kennedy sought to mediate compromise and ensure some federal aid to Catholic schools, as a presidential candidate he opposed the Roman Catholic Church's ambitions for both a U.S. ambassador to the Vatican and federal aid to parochial schools.[19]

In 1960, POAU lawyer and author Paul Blanshard was the most articulate and outspoken libertarian opponent of Catholic Church participation in U.S. politics. Since 1949, Blanshard's books had argued that Catholic power threatened American democracy and global religious liberty. With titles such as *American Freedom and Catholic Power; Communism, Democracy, and Catholic Power;* and *The Irish and Catholic Power: An American Interpretation,* Blanshard advocated a "resistance movement" against the Vatican's goals in the United States and the world.[20] Blanshard viewed the Catholic Kennedy's presidential ambitions as subversive to U.S. freedoms.

More than two years prior to the 1960 presidential campaign, Blanshard challenged all Catholic presidential candidates to answer specific questions about the Vatican's political authority. In the February 1958 issue of *Church and State,* POAU's monthly newsletter, Blanshard publicly demanded that Kennedy and other Catholic presidential candidates address three contentious church-state subjects: "the Catholic boycott of public schools, the drive of Catholic bishops for public funds, and the appointment of a Vatican ambassador." Though he denied any intent to organize a "blanket boycott" of Catholic presidential aspirants, Blanshard nonetheless issued no such requirements to non-Catholic candidates.[21]

Kennedy refused to respond specifically, claiming that Blanshard's inquiry violated the U.S. Constitution's guarantee of equality before the law: "The mere presentation of a list of questions such as you have suggested betrays a dangerous tendency which is not consistent with the spirit of our Constitutional principles." In particular, Kennedy invoked the Constitution's Article VI, which stipulated that "no religious Test shall ever be required as a qualification to any Office or public Trust under the United States." Libertarians mocked Kennedy's attempts to label Blanshard's questioning as discriminatory, countering that his response avoided legitimate questions about church-state relations. *Church and State* endorsed Catholics' right to pursue the executive office, but again demanded the Catholic candidates' opinions "concerning certain anti-democratic policies of the Catholic hierarchy."[22]

Debate within the ACLU revealed internal libertarian divisions about religious questioning of Catholic candidates. ACLU's leadership decried Kennedy's unwillingness to answer religious questions, denying that Article VI proscribed inquiry about political candidates' religion. Some Catholic supporters of absolute church-state separation, however, considered questioning only Catholic candidates a violation of civil liberties. In a letter to ACLU Associate Director Alan Reitman, Vincent Carrafiello, a Catholic ACLU member, asked the organization's leadership to defend Catholics from selective religious interrogation. He claimed that Article VI banned religious tests for public office and described such questioning of a Catholic candidate as "flagrant violation of our Constitutionally guaranteed civil liberties."[23] Reitman countered that the First Amendment's free speech clause protected individuals who questioned Catholic candidates' religious and political loyalties. Still, if anyone pursued legal restrictions on Catholic rights to enter public service, Reitman assured Carrafiello, "the American Civil Liberties Union would be the first to enter the fray."[24] POAU and ACLU leaders defended the questions to Catholic candidates as a legal and unbiased political challenge.

Kennedy spoke out on church-state issues in a March 1959 *Look* magazine article, denying any obligation to obey clerical political dictates. "Whatever one's religion in his private life," he said, "for the officeholder nothing takes precedence over his oath to uphold the Constitution and all its parts—including the First Amendment and its strict separation of church and state."[25] Kennedy also firmly opposed aid to parochial schools. Such statements supported the libertarians' demand for absolute boundaries between government and church actions, but accommodationist liberal Protestants and Catholics considered them too exclusive of religion. Believing rather that state policies should enhance religious institutions, accommodationists expressed shock and dismay over Kennedy's comments. Martin Marty, associate editor of the liberal *Christian Century,* called the Massachusetts senator "spiritually rootless and politically almost disturbingly secular."[26] Union Theological Seminary's Robert McAfee Brown characterized the Catholic candidate in *Christianity and Crisis* as "rather an irregular Christian."[27] In appearing to align with libertarians, Kennedy risked losing the support of accommodationist liberals.

Although Kennedy appeared to comply with libertarian requirements of a Catholic candidate, Blanshard remained unconvinced, and his 1960 book *God and Man in Washington* offered libertarians the most detailed argument yet against Catholic Church participation in U.S. politics and culture. In his private notes, Blanshard also revealed deeply entrenched beliefs that the Catholic Church's political goals threatened libertarianism and liberalism. "Belonging to the Cath. Ch. for a genuine liberal is like a Democrat belonging to the [anti-civil rights] Dixiecrat Party at the same time," he wrote. He characterized Catholics as deviant, ignorant, and illiberal, and stated in another note, "Blanshard's law of Catholics: the members of the Catholic hierarchy will be as reactionary as they dare to be and still retain favor."[28]

These confident criticisms of Catholic power veiled Blanshard's personal indecisiveness about Kennedy as he struggled to reconcile abstract arguments against Vatican laws and practices with Kennedy's support for absolute separation of church and state. Since Blanshard had obsessively dwelled in the theoretical realm of constitutional law and Roman Catholic canon law, concrete reality inserted emotions into his assessment of Catholic power. In his 1973 autobiography, Blanshard recalled, "As the 1960 presidential campaign approached I was intensely unhappy. . . . [W]ith the appearance of a Catholic presidential candidate who had a reasonable chance of election, discussion of the issues was personalized in a way I had tried to avoid."[29] But this discomfort failed to deter Blanshard from questioning Kennedy's susceptibility to religious pressures.

Blanshard justified inquiry into Kennedy's Catholicism by distinguishing criticism of church politics from opposition to private belief. In his 1949 book *American Freedom and Catholic Power,* Blanshard had depicted religious resistance to Catholic Democratic presidential nominee Alfred E. Smith's 1928 candidacy as largely motivated by "personal bigotry." Blanshard described criticism of Catholicism in 1960 as an ideological battle about public policy, not private religious faith: "The new opposition [to the Catholic Church] . . . is strongest among the liberals who have always stood most courageously for personal tolerance."[30] Liberal intellectuals could legitimately contradict Catholic political policy, Blanshard believed, without criticizing individual spiritual belief.

Based on this rationale for religious questions, *God and Man in Washington* detailed the specific issues any Catholic candidate should address. Seeking to expose Vatican interference in U.S. public policy, Blanshard defined six particular points of contention with Catholicism—state support of Catholic schools, censorship of movies and books, discrimination against Protestants and Jews in mixed marriages, segregation of Catholic children by schools, the prospect of a U.S. ambassador to the Vatican, and the banning of birth control in Catholic hospitals—and challenged voters to consider whether a Catholic presidential candidate would support the Vatican's stated positions on these issues.[31] By addressing such practical and personal issues as marriage and education, Blanshard sought a wider audience than lawyers and intellectuals, and his national tour to promote the book consistently raised criticisms and questions about Catholic presidential candidates. Blanshard's articles and books contained an explicit claim to defend liberalism from Catholic power, and inevitably they inspired liberal doubts about Kennedy's candidacy.

Kennedy's supporters quickly recognized that Blanshard's libertarian arguments presented serious challenges to any Catholic presidential candidate. Many anti-Kennedy pamphlets and letters—and even church bulletins—quoted and/or referenced Blanshard's works.[32] Liberal Protestant leaders consulted Blanshard before publicly discussing the issue in early 1960. Blanshard's occasional tennis partner and POAU's first president, Methodist Bishop G. Bromley Oxnam, and Episcopalian clergyman Eugene Carson Blake commissioned Blanshard to ghostwrite a *Look* magazine article on Catholics and the presidency.[33] Kennedy assistant Theodore C. Sorensen acknowledged Blanshard's authority on church-state issues and asked Blanshard to respond to a proposed statement by Boston archbishop, Richard Cardinal Cushing, who defended Catholic loyalty to the constitutional principle of church-state separation. When Blanshard declared in a three-page letter that Cushing's argument failed to support absolute separation of church and state, the Kennedy campaign decided not to distribute Cushing's document.[34] While Kennedy may have wanted merely to appease Blanshard's doubts through flattery, such deference to the libertarian leader's opinion reveals Blanshard's intellectual authority on church-state issues.

At the same time, prominent accommodationist liberals and Kennedy supporters confronted Blanshard's claim to profess the authoritative liberal view of Catholicism. In a late March edition of the *New Republic*, three non-Catholic liberal intellectuals defended Catholic perspectives on education, free speech, and diplomatic relations. While Blanshard chastised Catholics for "boycotting" state schools, Union Theological Seminary's John C. Bennett characterized the preference for parochial schooling as "a natural response to the secularization of public education." University of Chicago historical theology professor Jaroslav Pelikan directly confronted the libertarian position on church-state separation, asserting that this "militant minority" promoted "an authoritarian and totalitarian liberalism" that sought to suppress Vatican religious teaching. Such absolutism, Pelikan claimed, substituted "the Grand Inquisitor" with "the professional Pope-baiter." According to Pelikan, libertarians perceived a "democratic faith" and "the American way of life" as religious absolutes, revealing a "new idolatry" that subverted traditional religions.[35] In Pelikan's interpretation, Blanshard merely promoted one theological perspective over another by treating liberal democracy as a sacred institution.

Americans for Democratic Action (ADA) member and Kennedy advisor Arthur M. Schlesinger, Jr., applied this accommodationist liberal perspective to the presidential election, comparing anti-Catholicism to racial prejudice against African Americans: "It seems to me inconsistent with the whole theory of our democracy to deny nearly 40 million Americans the right to aspire to the highest office in the land. It is terrible to do this to the Negro, and it is no less terrible to do it to the Catholic (or, for that matter, to the agnostic or atheist)."[36] Schlesinger's words targeted liberals who supported civil rights for black Americans but who also questioned Catholic loyalty, while his parenthetical reference to nonbelievers appeared designed to attract anticlerical, secular humanists. Schlesinger rejected Blanshard's libertarian questions about a Catholic presidential candidate's commitment to religious liberty and portrayed the debate about Kennedy's Catholicism as a civil rights issue.

Although Pelikan had characterized libertarians as a "militant minority," *New Republic* editor and publisher Gilbert A. Harrison was surprised at the degree of reader resistance to these accommodationist opinions. In a letter to Schlesinger, Harrison admitted that "[E]ven though I had anticipated a rather fierce response from some readers, I was not prepared for the persistence and the emotional intensity and extent of the anti-Roman Catholic bias." No particular geographic or economic class predominated among the missives; rather, "They are clearly from the poorly educated and the well educated [and are] evenly distributed across the country." According to Harrison, 95 percent of the letters accused the magazine of disloyalty and "having 'sold out' to the Vatican."[37] Such significant anti-Catholicism among this liberal publication's readership dramatically confirmed the strength of libertarian resistance to a Catholic president.

In April, Kennedy again expressed support for absolute separation of church and state and conceded several specific policy issues to the libertarians. Before the American Society of Newspaper Editors in Washington, D.C., he distanced himself from the Catholic hierarchy, denying that he would "be responsive in any way to ecclesiastical pressures or obligations of any kind." Repudiating once again positions favored by many Catholics, Kennedy condemned federal aid to parochial schools as "clearly unconstitutional" and refused to support an ambassador to the Vatican. He avoided a clear stand regarding legislative proposals to provide U.S. funds for international birth control programs, but he clearly stated that religious values would not determine his political decisions about this procedure: "I would neither veto nor sign such a bill on any basis except what I considered to be the public interest."[38] Kennedy's statement impressed Blanshard, who quoted the speech in a column for the *Humanist*.[39]

Having struggled to distinguish criticism of the Catholic hierarchy from Kennedy's presidential candidacy, Blanshard urged POAU to avoid election politics. During the summer of 1960, however, Associate Director Lowell mobilized POAU efforts against Kennedy, characterizing religion as "the paramount issue in the campaign."[40] In a letter to Blanshard, Lowell outlined a plan to reprint past *Church and State* stories, including "much of the Kennedy material," and to distribute 750,000 copies of this publication "in newspaper form" only weeks before the Democratic convention. Lowell recognized potentially damaging ramifications: "I suppose the particular composite of stories will be suspect as to political intent," he said. "Of course we will throw in some innocuous ones to balance." Lowell claimed to act on behalf of POAU's constituency, particularly monetary contributors: "Bear in mind that we have been under terrific pressure from our members to do something, and that our financial appeal in the summer campaign also demands this."[41] In Lowell's view, political and economic ambitions justified POAU resistance to the Catholic presidential candidate. While Blanshard increasingly viewed Kennedy as sympathetic to libertarian absolutism, POAU's executives were determined to defeat the Catholic candidate.

When this publication—called *Church-State News*—appeared, Blanshard expressed stern opposition to POAU's strategy. "Horrible biased reprints looking like the worst kind of anti-Catholic denunciation," he wrote.[42] Next to a large cover photo of Roman Catholic Labor Secretary James P. Mitchell kneeling before a Catholic bishop, Blanshard inscribed, perhaps for posterity's sake, "I objected to this as too bigoted and one-sided."[43] Writing to Lowell and Archer, Blanshard reiterated that "it gives the impression of crude and unbalanced anti-Catholicism." Blanshard believed the paper required both presentation of issues "in a more rational manner" and a more balanced account of Kennedy's opinion on church-state relations. Further, antiliberal critics of Catholicism could use POAU's publication as "a tool in the Presidential Campaign directed against Kennedy." POAU members would subsequently feel "that we have broken faith," Blanshard feared, and acted irresponsibly with the leadership's mandate to defend church-state separation. Attempts to revoke POAU's tax-exempt status in the U.S. Congress also worried Blanshard, who specifically mentioned Catholic Majority Leader John W. McCormack's (MA) authority in the government's legislative branch, and he decried the directors' failure to obtain the POAU counsel's approval for this publication.[44] "I am . . . shocked by some of the things POAU puts out when I am not around to check them," he lamented in a letter to Edwin Lukas of the American Jewish Committee.[45] Lowell's actions undermined Blanshard's goal of focusing on the Catholic hierarchy rather than on Kennedy's presidential bid.

Throughout the Democratic Party primaries, no prominent Democrats had publicly supported libertarian challenges to Kennedy's candidacy. Kennedy had won several state primaries and secured endorsements from important party leaders. Leading Democratic officials could not publicly raise doubts about Kennedy's Catholicism without fatal political consequences. If liberal Democratic leaders rejected Kennedy on religious grounds, the party would alienate a critical voting base; in the 1958 Congressional elections, nearly 80 percent of Catholics voted Democratic.[46] In practical terms, libertarians threatened to alienate Catholic Democrats.

Evidence of latent anti-Catholic attitudes within the party nonetheless emerged in the primaries. In the April Wisconsin primary, Catholic voters overwhelmingly supported Kennedy, and Protestants largely endorsed Senator Hubert H. Humphrey (MN). After extensive interviews, reporter Samuel Lubell declared that "the question as to whether a Catholic should be President dominates the whole Wisconsin primary."[47] After national media focused attention on the Catholic issue in West Virginia's May primary, no prominent liberal Democrat publicly raised religious questions to block Kennedy's nomination, and some West Virginians even endorsed Kennedy merely to demonstrate the state's religious tolerance. In this 95 percent Protestant state, Kennedy's repeated pledges to support the absolute separation of church and state allayed libertarian doubts, and he won easily.[48]

As the Democratic National Convention approached, Kennedy's overwhelming success in the primaries and substantial support from various delegations appeared uncontestable. Privately, however, liberal resistance to a Catholic nominee persisted. In response to one anti-Catholic letter, ADA National Director Violet M. Gunther informed the organization's president, Samuel Beer, "I'm getting a flock of this kind of thing."[49] Just as *New Republic* editor Harrison acknowledged widespread religious skepticism about a Catholic president, the ADA leadership recognized that some liberals still perceived Kennedy's Catholicism as a critical flaw in his candidacy.

As Democratic divisions about Kennedy's religion persisted, Harry Truman pressured him to decline the party's presidential nomination. In a dramatic pre-convention press conference, Truman resigned as a Democratic convention delegate and criticized party leaders—including Catholic Democratic National Committee Chairman Paul Butler—for supporting Kennedy. Although Truman cited Kennedy's inexperience and not his religion, suspicion of a Catholic president undergirded his opposition. Less than a year earlier, Truman had privately argued that no Catholic could separate church and state issues as president, and in January he had warned that a Catholic nominee would inevitably attract substantial opposition on religious grounds.[50] Hundreds of anti-Catholic letters arrived daily in the former president's Independence, Missouri, office, encouraging Truman to continue to oppose any Catholic presidential candidate.[51] Deference to the Democratic Party's large Catholic constituency kept Truman from openly opposing Kennedy on religious grounds, but Kennedy's religion inspired the former president's private suspicions.

Although Kennedy secured the Democratic Party nomination on the first ballot, the libertarian ACLU continued to defend religious inquiries of the Catholic candidate. In mid-August, ACLU Executive Director Patrick Murphy Malin reiterated that the Constitution's Article VI prevented the government from excluding a candidate on religious grounds: "It would be unconstitutional," Malin declared, "formally to bar a Catholic or a Quaker—or a Baptist, a Jew, a Moslem, or an atheist—from becoming President, solely because of his religious, or non-religious, classification." Malin refused, however, to repudiate questions regarding the candidate's religious affiliation: "[I]t is not improper for voters to seek and consider information—including a particular candidate's own views—about the effect on governmental matters of organizational positions which his group may hold—for example, Quakers on the use of armed force, Catholics on the use of public funds for parochial schools."[52] While Democratic leaders discouraged further discussion of Kennedy's religion, Malin sought to guarantee that the ACLU could publicly discuss these policy differences without facing charges of religious bigotry.

After the convention, most liberal Democrats rallied in support of the party's nominee. Kennedy's repeated endorsements of absolute church-state separation allayed libertarian doubts, and liberal organizations and individuals rapidly provided Kennedy with the necessary cachet to distinguish the party's nominee from Republican standard-bearer Richard M. Nixon. The ADA's national board voted to support the Catholic Kennedy on August 27. Meeting minutes reveal only one reference to Catholicism, when Brandeis University Dean John Roche declared that Kennedy's religious affiliation created no barrier to ADA endorsement.[53]

In early September, liberals continued to characterize libertarian doubts about Kennedy's candidacy as partisan, gratuitous, and prejudicial. Despite his earlier reservations about a Catholic candidate, after hosting Kennedy in a visit to Independence, Harry Truman actively campaigned for the party nominee, even charging Nixon with tolerating anti-Catholic prejudice. "While [Nixon] stands at the front door proclaiming charity and tolerance," Truman stated publicly, "his supporters are herding the forces of racial, religious and anti-union bigotry in by way of the back door."[54] Party loyalty and Kennedy's personal assurances explain Truman's dramatic rejection of libertarian skepticism toward the Catholic presidential candidate.

POAU particularly attracted liberal ire for criticizing Kennedy's religious affiliation at the National Conference of Citizens for Religious Freedom (NCCRF) in early September. The National Association of Evangelicals (NAE) and popular author and Protestant minister Norman Vincent Peale adopted a leadership role in NCCRF, and most participants shared personal and political affinity for GOP nominee Nixon.[55] Prior to the conference, POAU's national advisory board recognized the risk of appearing anti-Kennedy and forfeiting the tax-exempt status available to nonpolitical organizations. As prominent Protestant liberals mistrusted the NAE, POAU also feared alienation from the liberal mainstream. Stanley Lowell vouched for NCCRF's freedom from political intentions, however, and the POAU board adopted a resolution to sponsor speakers who would address "the Roman Catholic problem in America." The POAU advisors also endorsed the organization's Executive Director Glenn Archer's participation in NCCRF.[56] Despite the stated nonpolitical intent of the conference, conservative Protestant evangelicals and some libertarians agreed that Kennedy's nomination risked the future status of church-state separation. The official conference statement concluded that Kennedy could not resist "the determined efforts of the hierarchy of his church . . . to breach the wall of separation between church and state."[57]

Many liberals perceived the NCCRF's assumptions about Kennedy as violations of liberal tolerance. Union Theological Seminary's Reinhold Niebuhr and John C. Bennett denounced both the NAE and POAU for having "loosed the floodgates of bigotry clothed in the respectability of apparently rational argument."[58] Bennett accused Kennedy's religious opponents of harboring Republican political goals, not legitimate fears about religious liberty: "Those who take the leadership in the Protestant attack on the Roman Church as a campaign issue are also persons who would not support a liberal Democrat no matter what his religion," he said.[59] But POAU members included Democrats as well as Republicans, and religious motives weighed as heavily as political goals.

The conference on religious liberty encouraged another liberal publication to abandon libertarian skepticism of Catholicism. *Christian Century* editors upbraided NCCRF's "myopic concentration on one issue" as intolerance and "a disservice to American Protestantism." While continuing to characterize the Roman Catholic Church as "politically monarchical and historically antidemocratic," this publication nonetheless criticized NCCRF for misrepresenting "the breadth of Protestant interests, the intelligence of Protestant concerns, [and] the charity of Protestant attitudes."[60]

Blanshard continued to worry that many liberals were naïvely ignorant about the Catholic threat to church-state separation, but realized that NCCRF had changed the political context of the campaign's religious issue. Frustrated with cries against "bigotry," he scribbled in the margins of a *New York Times* story, "complete avoidance of main issue, use of public support for sectarian institutions."[61] Public challenges to the Roman Catholic Church seemed politically unacceptable at this time, however. "Damn it, Peale is spoiling everything," Edward Darling, director of Boston's Beacon Press—the publisher of Blanshard's popular books—informed the author of Peale's negative financial impact on the industry of anti-Catholic literature. "Sales were great until *he* spilled over, but now people are reacting strongly against him—and against *us*, as a result. He's actually put up a roadblock."[62] By late September, Blanshard was discouraging POAU leaders from further comments on Kennedy's Catholicism, leaving only Protestant evangelical leaders to join POAU in promoting the campaign's religious issue. In a memorandum to Archer and Lowell, Blanshard warned against commitment to "the absolute position held by some affiliates of [the conservative evangelical publication] *Christianity Today*."[63] Further criticism of Kennedy on religious grounds, he believed, risked losing financial and political support for libertarian views of church-state separation.

Despite Blanshard's warning, POAU's Executive Director Archer traveled nationwide in late September through October to discuss Catholic power, portraying the Vatican as antithetical to modern democratic culture and American freedom. This "medieval church," he said, implemented "anti-democratic policies." Roman Catholic politicians dominated two-thirds of American cities. Such rhetoric revived antiurban impulses and liberal suspicions of Tammany Hall Catholic patronage politics that had plagued Al Smith's 1928 candidacy. The POAU director even described a "Vatican-inspired colossal political machine whose announced purpose is to control the world."[64] Though Archer refrained from specifically denouncing Kennedy, his virulent anti-Catholicism inspired Protestant hesitancy toward Kennedy's candidacy.

As Election Day approached, *Christian Century,* which frequently had criticized Vatican policy and supported absolute church-state separation, decried religious intolerance toward individual Catholics. Editors described Kennedy and most U.S. Catholics as more libertarian regarding church-state issues than the Vatican. Citing Kennedy's public opposition to parochial schools and a statement from 150 American Catholic laymen supporting church-state separation, they dispelled any reservations about a Catholic president: "In theology [American Catholics] allow the authoritarian principle to prevail; in politics they insist on using private judgment. Ecclesiastically they are Catholics; politically they are Protestants." Instead of dwelling on disagreements with Catholic Church leaders, *Christian Century* editors counseled tolerance in order to encourage the American Catholic majority's continued political independence from their church's clerical hierarchy. The magazine particularly cited NAE attempts to promote discussion of the Catholic issue on October 30, Reformation Sunday, which fell only a week prior to the general election: "[I]t would be deeply regrettable if Reformation Sunday were to be diverted this year into a gigantic anti-Catholic rally, as some fundamentalist groups urge should be done." Such Protestant "authoritarianism" would discourage Catholics from "using private judgment in widening fields of political and personal decision."[65] Intolerant anti-Catholicism would only deter Catholic liberalism, the editors argued. This publication spoke for absolutist libertarians who had joined establishment liberals behind Kennedy's candidacy much earlier.

In the 1960 election, the Democratic Party relied on a minority coalition of Catholic, Jewish, and African Americans who recognized a common purpose. Truman and the Democratic National Committee understood this political reality and, by portraying the Democrats as bigotry's eternal foes, appealed to racial and religious minorities. Seventy percent of African Americans supported the Democratic nominee,[66] and Jewish Americans voted for Kennedy in even larger percentages than American Catholics. Four of five Jews, and more than seven of ten Catholics, endorsed the Catholic candidate.[67] According to reporter Samuel Lubell, Kennedy's religion proved critical in recreating the Democratic New Deal coalition of minority groups.[68]

James Michener's reflections on this campaign underscore religion's profound significance for mid-century American liberalism. After working for Kennedy's campaign, Michener felt confident of one conclusion: "If, thirty years from now, all of this can be explained away in clever articles which prove that religion played no significant role in the 1960 election, it seems to me that the writers of that age will have to blind themselves to what actually happened."[69]

The struggle against totalitarian fascism and communism led many self-proclaimed liberal Americans to insist upon an absolute separation of church and state as necessary for complete individual liberty. Other liberals perceived tolerance of sectarian differences and avoidance of secularism as the best way to preserve religious freedom. While some doubts about Catholicism persisted, liberals and libertarians recognized that intolerance toward an individual Catholic would alienate an entire religious organization from political liberalism. In the twenty-first century, legal struggles about abortion, stem cell research, and same-sex unions again challenge liberals to choose between a total separation of religious morality from public life and compromise with orthodox Catholics and other sectarian groups.

Chapter Five

Defining Religious Bigotry

Pluralism and Political Strategy in the 1960 Presidential Election

The prominent Harlem congressman and Baptist minister, Adam Clayton Powell, highlighted the campaign's religious issue in several September 1960 speeches. Unlike many of his white Protestant counterparts, Powell did not express fears about the prospect of a Catholic president, but rather denounced those Americans who opposed John F. Kennedy on religious grounds. Speaking to an interfaith rally in New York City's Central Park, Powell charged "Republicans and Southerners" with propagating criticism of Kennedy's Catholicism. In clerical attire, Powell identified pastors of white-only churches as the primary purveyors of anti-Catholicism: "[T]he leaders are changing the white robes of the Klan for the black robes of the Protestant clergy."[1] According to Powell, the same elements that resisted Kennedy would also block Jewish Americans and African Americans from the presidency.

Powell again berated anti-Catholicism at a Harlem meeting entitled "Senator John F. Kennedy's National Conference of Constitutional Rights and American Freedom." Speaking to an audience that included Elijah Muhammad, Herbert Lehman, Averell Harriman, Eleanor Roosevelt, and Kennedy, Powell accused Republican vice president and presidential nominee Richard M. Nixon of representing "the worst forces of bigotry in America." Kennedy followed Powell to the microphone, a bit stunned, but nonetheless supportive: "After that speech, I am ready to put the question right now. Are we going to vote Democratic?" Surprised by Powell's passionate and strident remarks, Kennedy quipped, "Adam, I am going to sit down and turn it all over to you. Congressman Powell says he is my senior. I respect age. I admire his speech. It was very good."[2] Kennedy refused to temper or repudiate Powell's inflammatory charges of Republican complicity in spreading anti-Catholic prejudice. Although appearing overwhelmed by Powell's words, Kennedy understood how the specter of anti-Catholic bigotry served to unite African, Catholic, and Jewish Americans. Powell offered the most strident portrayal of American religious and racial minorities as common victims of the prejudices of the white, Protestant elite. Yet Kennedy's supporters frequently echoed the same theme.

This chapter examines how Kennedy managed the Catholic issue to attract Catholic, Jewish, and African American voters while his opponents struggled to avoid being labeled bigots. In the Democratic Party primaries, former President Harry S. Truman, Senator Hubert Humphrey (MN), and Senator Wayne Morse (OR) each expressed frustration about Kennedy's manipulation of the "Catholic issue." After Kennedy's nomination, however, these same Democrats strongly denounced religious prejudice, and some even accused Nixon of exploiting anti-Catholicism for political gain. Republican President Dwight D. Eisenhower and Vice President Nixon sought to marginalize discussion of Kennedy's Catholicism. In a time of heightened sensitivity to religious and racial differences, some Catholic Republicans encouraged Nixon to pursue Catholics as a political constituency. Rhode Island Governor Christopher Del Sesto actively promoted Catholic Labor Secretary James P. Mitchell for the vice presidency. But Nixon's unwillingness to engage in religious politics prevented Mitchell's nomination.

Although Kennedy pledged commitment to absolute separation of church and state, Democratic leaders recognized that voters would never completely ignore religion's role in this election. Harry Truman constantly denounced anti-Catholicism in addresses to Protestants and Jews, as well as Catholics. Kennedy's Civil Rights Division, led by law professor Harris Wofford and businessman and founding member of the National Catholic Interracial Council (and Kennedy brother-in-law) R. Sargent Shriver, lobbied Powell and Southern Christian Leadership Conference (SCLC) President Martin Luther King, Jr., to equate anti-Catholic prejudice with anti-black racism. While Democrats denounced bigotry, Nixon prevented Mitchell and other Catholics from any discussion of Kennedy's Catholicism.

Chairman of the Democratic Party Paul Butler demonstrated the potential to convert Kennedy's Catholicism from a liability to an advantage. As the Democratic National Convention approached, the Catholic Butler threatened Kennedy's opponents by invoking the candidate's religion. Since Kennedy had won several party primaries and secured numerous state delegations, Butler described Kennedy's nomination as a "cinch." In Butler's opinion, only religious bigotry could motivate an attempt to block the nomination of this Catholic candidate.

If the Democrats rejected Kennedy at the party convention, Butler warned, Catholics would vote as a bloc for the Republican presidential nominee.³

Both Catholic and Protestant Democrats protested Butler's statement. Catholic Representative Hale Boggs (LA) believed that Butler could inspire "a wave of hatred and misunderstanding" against Catholics by promising such religious retribution.⁴ The liberal Protestant publication *Christian Century* suggested that Butler's "thinly veiled threat" would "haunt" the Democratic Party in the fall election. Butler's statement, according to the article, would make "religion the test of Kennedy's acceptability to the Democratic convention."⁵ Such political extortion, these critics warned, could alienate non-Catholic Americans who perceived Kennedy's candidacy as the product of Catholic pressure tactics.

For many Democrats, Butler's comments echoed the argument of the 1956 "Bailey Memorandum" prepared by Kennedy aide Theodore Sorensen, and discussed in Chapter Two.⁶ In this memo, Sorensen surmised that concentrations of Catholic voters in fourteen states could help the Democratic Party secure sufficient electoral votes to win the presidency.⁷ By declaring an unwillingness to accept the vice presidency in 1960, however, Kennedy forced delegates to choose between two risky alternatives: Reviving anti-Catholicism by nominating a Catholic or alienating Catholics by rejecting Kennedy's candidacy.⁸

This question challenged Democratic unity in 1960. During the party primaries, Kennedy's opponents resented his special appeal to Catholics. Presidential hopeful Wayne Morse criticized Kennedy privately as exploiting religion for political gain. After receiving a letter that alleged an excessive number of Catholics occupied government offices, Morse blamed Catholic presidential aspirants for discussion of Catholicism: "[T]he sad part about this religious issue is the fact that some candidates of the Catholic faith have been heard to say that if they are denied the nomination of a Party [*sic*] or the election as President, it will be because of their religion." While refusing to mention any particular candidate, Morse certainly referred to Kennedy, the major Catholic contender. Morse equated such appeals to Catholics with anti-Catholicism: "In my book, that is an attempt to use religion on one's behalf and is just as bad as trying to use a man's religion against him."⁹

Hubert Humphrey, Kennedy's most significant challenger in the Wisconsin and West Virginia Democratic Party primaries, emphasized the potential for religion to assist, rather than harm, the Catholic candidate. An advertisement attributed to the "Square Deal for Humphrey Committee" accused Catholic Republicans of registering as

Democrats to vote for Kennedy in the state primary.[10] Amid charges of anti-Catholic bigotry, Humphrey repudiated this advertisement. After Kennedy secured a 60 to 40 percent victory, Humphrey warned that Kennedy would not receive the same religious advantage in the next primary battle in West Virginia, where only 4 percent of the population was Catholic. Writing to Kennedy aide Arthur Schlesinger, Jr., Humphrey noted, "the so-called religious issue [is] a two edged sword, working one way in [predominately Catholic districts in] Wisconsin and another in [majority Protestant] West Virginia."[11]

Democratic National Committee (DNC) Chairman Paul Butler's threat of a Catholic bloc vote against a non-Catholic Democratic nominee motivated former President Truman to challenge Kennedy's candidacy only days prior to the party's national convention. Truman's suspicion of Catholicism contributed to the former president's opposition to Kennedy. When Truman resigned as a Democratic delegate, the Rolla *Daily News* (Missouri) interpreted this decision as a silent protest against Kennedy's religion: "Truman doesn't want a Catholic to be President."[12] Truman denied any religious bias toward Catholics. Yet he had privately claimed, in two 1959 interviews for a political biography, that a Catholic could serve as chief of staff or chairman of the DNC, but never as commander-in-chief.[13] Speaking in a nationally televised press conference in 1960, Truman charged Butler with making the convention a "rigged, . . . pre-arranged affair" to anoint Kennedy. Despite repudiating religious bigotry and even offering Catholic Senator Eugene McCarthy (MN) as an alternative nominee, Truman's address inspired anti-Catholic hopes. Several self-identified Masons lobbied Truman, as a thirty-second degree member of this fraternity, to oppose a Catholic president.[14] One citizen agreed with Truman's assertion that Kennedy supporters dominated the convention, and added: "Butler is following his instructions from the Pope."[15] While these individuals applauded Truman's verbal protest, others asked the former president to attend the convention and actively resist Kennedy's nomination.[16] Truman neither encouraged nor denounced this anti-Catholic correspondence.

While several Democrats repudiated Kennedy's strategic attempts to attract Catholics, Republican politicians considered a conscious pursuit of Catholic voters. In 1959, some Republicans had promoted a Catholic as the Republican vice-presidential nominee. Ambassador to Brazil Clare Booth Luce, a convert to Catholicism, received brief consideration, and Eisenhower recommended his former chief of staff and allied commander in Europe, General Alfred M. Gruenther—also a Catholic—to Nixon in mid-1959.[17] GOP polling data also suggested

Nixon's chances would improve with a Catholic running-mate. In January 1960, Republican pollster Claude Robinson suggested that Nixon would receive a significant Catholic vote if opposed by a non-Catholic Democrat. According to Robinson's data, however, Nixon's Catholic support dropped precipitously when Kennedy's name appeared as an alternative. If California's Catholic Governor, Edmund G. Brown, occupied the Democratic vice-presidential position, furthermore, Catholics even favored Protestant Adlai E. Stevenson over Nixon. This evidence suggested that Catholic Democrats would receive a net gain from religious-based voting. In Robinson's opinion, "Kennedy's religion helps him."[18] The Wisconsin Democratic primary confirmed this theory for Nixon's campaign director, Robert Finch, who recalled dismay at Kennedy's ability to attract "crossover Catholic Republicans" who registered as Democrats to vote for Kennedy in that state's Democratic primary. In Finch's recollection, "our polls always showed us doing very well among Catholics." A non-Catholic Democratic nominee, such as Stevenson, failed to challenge Nixon as strongly among this religious constituency.[19]

Recognizing Nixon's weakness against a Catholic opponent, the incumbent Republican administration avoided substantial discussion that might further encourage Catholics to vote Democratic in November. In late April, Nixon publicly discouraged further discussion of Kennedy's Catholicism by characterizing all the presidential candidates as "men who cherish ... the religious and moral principles which are the very foundation of our American ideals."[20] In response to press conference questions, President Eisenhower dismissed religion's significance in the election. When asked to address religion in April, the president quoted the Constitution's prohibitions against religious tests for public office, and concluded that religion lacked any relevance to the campaign. After Kennedy won the May 10 West Virginia primary, a reporter asked the president whether this would end questions about religion in politics. Eisenhower responded: "I have made as strong a statement as I can, deploring the insertion of the religious issue in elections."[21] Nixon and Eisenhower believed that political leaders had very limited power to change prejudicial attitudes. These politicians demonstrated this distaste for radical cultural reform in pursuing a moderate civil rights policy during the 1950s. Confident that interfaith tolerance would evolve slowly, these Republicans sought to suppress discussion of Kennedy's religion.

Although Nixon and Eisenhower downplayed religion's role in the campaign, some Republican officials recommended a symbolic gesture to attract Catholic voters. As the Republican National Convention approached, Rhode Island Governor Christopher Del Sesto initiated a nationwide movement to nominate Labor Secretary James P. Mitchell as the party's vice-presidential candidate. After distributing this proposal to Republican leaders nationwide, Del Sesto claimed that favorable responses outnumbered negatives by a 326–10 margin. Del Sesto, a Catholic, denied that religion motivated this endorsement.[22] Other Republicans, however, perceived Mitchell's religion as a significant advantage. Wisconsin attorney Edward J. Zahn, Jr., claimed that Mitchell's religion would strengthen Catholic support for the GOP ticket. Having discussed the issue with Del Sesto and Mitchell's executive assistant Walter C. Wallace, Zahn wrote to Mitchell, "the Church hierarchy in Wisconsin is definitely opposed to Mr. Kennedy." Wisconsin's Republican Party Chairman, Zahn continued, knew leading Catholic prelates who compared Mitchell's "dedicated church work and affiliation" favorably against Kennedy's more modest support for Catholic political goals.[23] These Republicans believed that a Nixon-Mitchell ticket could frustrate Democratic hopes for Catholic bloc support in November.

The differences between Democratic and Republican strategy regarding the religious issue appear evident in two internal memoranda, distributed on two consecutive days in August, from top campaign officials of each respective camp. On August 15, Theodore Sorensen proposed initiatives to attract Jewish voters and to reduce anti-Catholic voting. "Senator Kennedy *will* win in November *unless* defeated by the religious issue." This interpretation contradicted Kennedy's opponents, who believed that his religion benefited him. Seeking "*neutralization*" of the religious issue, Sorensen suggested a "Community Relations" division within the campaign. This section would publicize arguments in favor of a Catholic president.[24]

The following day, Nixon's campaign chairman, Leonard W. Hall, and Campaign Director Finch issued a gag order that proscribed discussion of the religious issue. In a confidential memorandum to "all persons connected to [the Nixon] campaign," the chairmen quoted Nixon's statements on Kennedy's Catholicism: "[R]eligion will be in this campaign to the extent that the candidates of either side talk about it. I shall never talk about it and we'll start right now." The directors warned campaign staff against contact with any individual or group that offered support on religious grounds. No Republican volunteers, party organization, or campaign headquarters were to distribute literature addressing Catholicism. Even jokes or allusions to Kennedy's religion were off-limits; "staff and volunteer workers should avoid discussing the 'religious issue' either informally or casually since this might be construed as some kind of deliberate campaign."[25] Nixon exercised extreme caution to avoid any association with anti-Catholicism.

Nixon's strategy made the Republican Party appear apathetic toward anti-Catholicism when several conservative Protestant ministers challenged Kennedy's candidacy on religious grounds. Despite Nixon's refusal to permit official discussion of Kennedy's religion, Republican sympathizers among the Protestant clergy insisted on raising doubts about a Catholic president. At an August 24 press conference, a reporter asked for Eisenhower's reply to Baptist evangelical minister Billy Graham, who called Kennedy's Catholicism a legitimate campaign issue. Eisenhower refused to repudiate Graham's comment, and denied personal responsibility for anti-Catholic prejudice: "I certainly never encouraged it."[26] Eisenhower's comment neither attracted attention to anti-Catholic bigotry nor stigmatized the Republicans as prejudiced against Catholics. By scolding a popular religious figure and personal friend, Eisenhower would have risked alienating many voters. Eisenhower nonetheless bypassed an opportunity to demonstrate solidarity with Catholics against religious questions pertaining to public office.

When several Protestant ministers, including Nixon's friend and best-selling author Norman Vincent Peale, held a conference in Washington, D.C., to assert that a Catholic president could not resist Vatican pressures (as discussed in Chapter Three), both Democrats and Republicans reaffirmed their strategy regarding the religious issue. The Democratic leadership continued to associate anti-Catholicism with the GOP. Henry Jackson, recently selected as the first non-Catholic DNC chairman since 1928, demanded that Nixon repudiate Peale, the conference's spokesman and most prominent participant. Just as Eisenhower feared criticizing Graham, Nixon avoided a direct denunciation of Peale, a popular figure and personal friend of the vice president. Nixon's "gag order" further prevented any Republican official from denying Republican complicity in Peale's statement. On the national Sunday morning television program "Meet the Press," Nixon again claimed that Kennedy's religion lacked any relevance to the campaign: "I don't believe there is a religious issue as far as Senator Kennedy is concerned." Confident that general repudiation of religious prejudice should suffice, Nixon proposed a "cut-off date" when both candidates would cease discussing religion.[27] Democrats used Peale's comments, and Nixon's reluctance to repudiate them, as evidence to support the thesis that the Republicans countenanced and encouraged anti-Catholicism.

Nixon's appeal for an end to discussion of anti-Catholicism failed to deter Democrats. In mid-September, Kennedy devoted an entire speech, in response to an invitation by the Greater Houston Ministerial Association, to deny that religious obligations would impair his ability to serve as president. Truman accused Republicans of distributing anti-Catholic literature in his hometown of Independence, Missouri. Henry Jackson mocked Nixon's "cut-off date" as incompatible with "the reality of American politics," and characterized anti-Catholicism as a moral crisis that required more active resistance to anti-Catholicism; "It's not enough for the Vice President to say he's against religious bigotry."[28] Eugene McCarthy suggested that Nixon's current call for an end to discussion of the religious issue would change if anti-Catholic voters could help the Republican candidate win in November.[29] Republicans surmised that Americans wanted to avoid religious debates. But Kennedy supporters believed that public statements on religion would encourage many Americans to counter the anti-Catholic vote.

Democratic leaders specifically orchestrated Truman's speeches to accentuate the religious issue. Charles S. Murphy and David Lloyd, DNC officials who had served in the Truman administration, wrote the words and coordinated the former president's campaign efforts.[30] In a late September letter, Murphy stressed the importance of Truman's Texas speeches on religion. Sending Truman a speech draft, Murphy reiterated a phone conversation about Kennedy's Catholicism: "You will see that [the speech draft] includes some discussion of the religious question. . . . Dave Lloyd has been over this with me carefully, and we think [this discussion of the Catholic issue] would be very useful."[31] Truman demonstrated full comprehension of his role, writing to former Secretary of State Dean Acheson, "I am leaving tomorrow for Texas to talk principally to the Baptists at Waco."[32] Since the Southern Baptist Convention had publicly questioned Kennedy on religious grounds, Truman's appeal to this constituency held particular significance. Texas' Southern Baptists might help Kennedy in a state with substantial electoral votes.

Truman's speeches in Texas escalated the previous charges against Nixon of exploiting anti-Catholicism. A "widespread . . . un-American" group defamed Kennedy with Nixon's tacit approval, Truman claimed in Waco: "The Republican candidate pays lip service to tolerance, but he is quite willing to accept any votes that may come his way by reason of religious *intolerance*."[33] Repeating this address in other Texas cities, such as Dallas, Truman deviated from the script before a San Antonio audience: "If you vote for Nixon, you ought to go to hell."[34]

Fearing that African American voters might chose Nixon based on anti-Catholicism, Democrats sought to change this constituency's view of Catholics. African Americans expressed frustration with both parties' indifference and resistance to minority rights, but "black Americans, predominately Protestant, shared a prejudice with their white coreligionists," according to historian Carl Brauer.[35] In 1959, a survey by the popular African American magazine *Jet* reported, "many Negro ministers opposed [Kennedy] on the religious basis alone."[36] Kennedy's civil rights division director, Harris Wofford, recalled "an anti-Catholic mood" among "many deeply Protestant Negro clergymen."[37] According to the *New York Times,* Philadelphia's African American leaders recognized hostility toward Kennedy's religion within their communities.[38] Political scientist James Q. Wilson claimed that religious prejudice exacerbated blacks' discontent with Democrats' limited commitment to civil rights reform. Wilson's sources suggested that Baptist minister Martin Luther King, Jr., privately favored Nixon.[39] On October 18, the Atlanta Baptist Minister's Union—including Martin Luther King, Sr.—specified religious grounds for opposing Kennedy and publicly endorsed Nixon.[40] Fearing that religious opposition might alienate black voters from the Catholic candidate, Democrats sought to secure African American sympathy for Kennedy as a victim of religious prejudice.

In addressing this racial constituency, therefore, Democrats attempted to equate anti-Catholicism and white supremacy. Eleanor Roosevelt emphasized Kennedy's status as a religious minority while speaking to an African American audience in Baltimore. The former First Lady described resisting anti-Catholicism as important to the preservation of black Americans' civil rights: "[I]f we discriminate against Mr. Kennedy because he is a Catholic, other kinds of discrimination may soon follow."[41] Implying that Nixon's election would encourage anti-black racism, Roosevelt asked blacks to identify with Kennedy's struggle against bigotry.

Adam Clayton Powell repeated the analogy between racial and religious prejudice in strong terms. Since Powell had endorsed Eisenhower in 1956, Kennedy offered $50,000 to have this African American politician deliver ten campaign speeches for the Catholic candidate. Despite an initial demand for $300,000, Powell accepted the lower amount.[42] Powell's September and early October speeches for Kennedy echoed Democratic attempts to associate religious bias with racial prejudice. According to Powell, the same white supremacists that resisted Kennedy would prevent an African American from the presidency. Powell's speeches also endorsed Democratic appeals for a coalition of Jewish, Catholic, and African Americans for Kennedy. Describing the Klan as "riding again," Powell warned that "all bigots will vote for Nixon and all right-thinking Christians and Jews will vote for Kennedy rather than be found in the ranks of the Klan-minded."⁴³ When questioned about these charges in the first televised presidential debate, Kennedy refused to repudiate Powell.

A series of events in late October accelerated the attempt to link religious and racial prejudice in the minds of African Americans. Police arrested Martin Luther King, Jr. (who had not yet achieved recognition as one of the nation's most important African American political figures), for trespassing in white-only areas of an Atlanta department store. After several days in jail, King received a sentence, for an earlier misdemeanor, to serve four months of labor on a state road gang, which "meant cutthroat inmates and casually dismissed murders," according to historian Taylor Branch. King's six-months pregnant wife, Coretta Scott King, had broken down in tears after witnessing her husband led away in shackles and chains. As the King family feared for the life of the civil rights leader, Sargent Shriver encouraged Kennedy to telephone and offer support to Coretta King.⁴⁴

Although Kennedy's senior campaign staff, such as Campaign Manager Robert F. Kennedy, feared that overt support of King would rally white southerners against the Democratic nominee, this impulsive decision compelled King, Sr., to disavow religious opposition to Kennedy. "I'll vote for him, even though I don't want a Catholic," said the elder King, who felt indebted to transfer loyalty to Kennedy. "I'll take a Catholic or the Devil himself if he'll wipe the tears from my daughter-in-law's eyes." King, Sr., told Kennedy's Atlanta supporter Morris Abram, "I've got a suitcase full of votes—my whole church—for you to give to Senator Kennedy."⁴⁵ This gesture did not free King, Jr., from prison, but Kennedy had taken a bold step toward extinguishing anti-Catholicism in the African American community.

After Robert Kennedy's phone call to a Georgia judge secured bail for King, several African American ministers joined the Democratic Party's denunciations of anti-Catholic prejudice. Kennedy gained the younger King's assistance in linking opposition to anti-Catholicism with the civil rights movement's work against anti-black racial bias. The night of his release, King, Jr., delivered a sermon that denounced anti-Catholicism: "I never intend to be a religious bigot. I never intend to reject a man running for President of the United States just because he is a Catholic." While stopping short of a political endorsement of Kennedy, King passionately echoed the Democrats' campaign against religious prejudice, saying "Religious bigotry is as immoral, undemocratic, un-American, and un-Christian as racial bigotry."

Despite Robert Kennedy's demands that Wofford and Shriver avoid any further risk of alienating white southern voters, the campaign's civil rights division secretly sponsored a pamphlet to publicize Kennedy's phone call to Corretta King. Attributed to an organization of Philadelphia African American ministers, this document specifically included the younger King's sermon against anti-Catholic prejudice and the elder King's words, "I had expected to vote against Senator Kennedy because of his religion. But now he can be my President, Catholic or whatever he is."[46] The campaign's civil rights division targeted only African American communities when distributing this pamphlet, known as the "Blue Bomb" because of the paper's colorful background and controversial content.

In the campaign's final days, Kennedy's staff also raised the religious issue in order to attract support from Jewish Americans. Harvard economist John Kenneth Galbraith recalled being assigned, with former New York Governor Averell Harriman and Arthur Schlesinger, to pacify Jewish fears of a Catholic president.[47] While never admitting any intention to encourage bloc voting, Charles Murphy included religion even in speeches that Truman would deliver to a mostly Catholic and Jewish audience in Brooklyn, New York. In a letter attached to Truman's final speeches, Murphy pointedly addressed Kennedy's Catholicism: "You will note that the draft for Brooklyn is mainly about the religious question." While few Protestants lived in Brooklyn, Murphy "thought that Catholics and Jews need to be reminded of the extent to which religious freedom is involved in this situation."[48] Kennedy's party realized that a coalition of religious minorities could offset, and perhaps override, a substantial anti-Catholic vote.

America's highest-ranking Catholic official, Labor Secretary James Mitchell, perceived these accusations as an emotional appeal to Catholic resentment of anti-Catholicism. Early in September, Mitchell had called a press conference to charge Truman and Robert Kennedy with exploiting Catholic fears of prejudice. In Mitchell's interpretation, Democrats pursued Catholic votes by unfairly associating Nixon with anti-Catholicism.[49] Mitchell's comments, however, received much less attention than the statements by Peale and other Protestant ministers that a Catholic president would face Vatican pressures.

Mitchell prepared to respond publicly to Democratic charges again in early October when a Catholic correspondent criticized the labor secretary's refusal to sign a public endorsement of church-state separation by Catholic laymen.[50] Perceiving this process as a tool of the Kennedy campaign, Mitchell composed a six-page reply. Mitchell's letter quoted extensively from the 1956 "Bailey Memorandum," which Sorensen had written to demonstrate Kennedy's potential to attract Catholic voters for the Democratic Party. Mitchell even reproduced a table from this document to prove that Kennedy campaigned "almost exclusively" in states with large Catholic populations. Mitchell decried the Democratic strategy of targeting Catholic voters, writing, "we are witnessing a campaign based upon religious groupings, northern Catholics being the main target." Mitchell decried Kennedy's supporters—including Jackson and Truman—for seeking to "obfuscate this strategy" by portraying the Catholic candidate as a "religious underdog whom bigotry will deprive of a fair chance." The labor secretary characterized such tactics as "censurable," and even "reprehensible."

Mitchell's staff honored Nixon's restrictions on discussing religion, however, and prevented this response from reaching the public. Mitchell's executive assistant Walter Wallace proved particularly vigilant in keeping the labor secretary from publicly addressing the religious issue. A handwritten note attached to the letter addressed Wallace: "WCW—Are you interested that JPM signed this?" The original letter never left the labor secretary's office, and Mitchell sent a tempered, two-page reply on November 30, three weeks after Kennedy's victory.[51] Wallace also prevented Mitchell from sending a response to a Catholic priest who asked the labor secretary to denounce religious bigotry. On the copy of Mitchell's letter is written, "Do not reply. WCW."[52] Nixon's strategy frustrated Mitchell's attempts to counter Democratic tactics regarding religion.

Other Republican leaders shared Mitchell's views and sought to prove that Democrats were exploiting Kennedy's religion for political gain. An anonymous three-page GOP memorandum on the religious issue charged Democrats with raising Catholicism "in connection with the Kennedy candidacy" much more often than did Republicans. Citing Sorensen's 1956 thesis (presented in the "Bailey Memorandum") as the first detailed analysis of religion's strategic elements—such as Catholic bloc voting—the Republican memo counted 127 Democratic references to Kennedy's religion in comparison with 24 by Republicans.[53] This document suggested that Democrats, not Republicans, kept religious discussion alive. On October 18, the Republican National Committee's Research Division determined that Kennedy's comments on religion outnumbered Nixon's by 48–9.[54] Yet these studies remained unpublicized by Nixon's campaign, and Republicans received only a healthy conscience as reward for their magnanimous forbearance. To promote these studies publicly would violate Nixon's repeated calls for an end to discussion of Kennedy's religion and risk further Democratic accusations that the Republican Party defended anti-Catholic bigotry.

Although Republicans called upon the president to denounce Democratic discussion of Kennedy's religion for political gain, Eisenhower offered no dramatic condemnation of Democratic tactics. Only days before the election, a telegram implored Mitchell to repudiate Catholic bloc voting: "Get on radio and TV and urge [Catholics] to put their country first in the most critical time our country has ever known."[55] This individual assumed that Democrats had persuaded Catholics to support Kennedy and a Catholic could best communicate with co-religionists. In a November 1 phone message, businessman Dan Gainey accused Robert Kennedy of promoting pro-Catholic attitudes. Advising Eisenhower to schedule a national broadcast and explain the Democrats' misuse of Kennedy's religion, Gainey suggested, "It is just as much bigotry for Catholics to vote for Kennedy simply and only because he is a Catholic as it is for a Protestant to vote for Nixon simply and only because he is not a Catholic."[56] In Gainey's interpretation, many Americans believed that Catholics only related to bigotry as victims, not as perpetrators of bias.

Nixon also received pressure to criticize Kennedy's tactics regarding the religious issue. In the campaign's final days, aides encouraged the Republican nominee to challenge Democratic assertions about religion and politics. On November 3, Nixon's staff voted unanimously that the vice president should make a speech denouncing the Democrats' use of "reverse bigotry." Nixon responded that such a statement would "substantially set back" the cause of religious tolerance.[57]

In 1960, the Democrats successfully created an electoral coalition of Catholic, Jewish, and African Americans. Seventy percent of African Americans supported the Democratic nominee.[58] Jewish Americans voted for Kennedy in larger percentages than American Catholics. Four of five Jews, and more than seven of ten Catholics, endorsed the Catholic candidate.[59] Gallup surveys estimated that Jewish support for Kennedy increased from 69 percent in late October to 81 percent on Election Day. According to author and journalist Samuel Lubell, who conducted extensive interviews with voters to complement polling data, Kennedy's religion proved critical in recreating the Democratic coalition of minority groups.[60]

The Kennedy campaign managed the Catholic issue more effectively than Nixon by consciously pursuing a coalition of African, Catholic, and Jewish American voters in 1960. The historical precedent of New York Governor Alfred E. Smith offered Kennedy a strategy for responding to religion's unavoidable significance in the campaign. In the 1920s, Smith's image as a successful son of immigrants inspired widespread support among religious and racial minorities. Catholics, blacks, and Jews admired Smith as a fellow minority who rose to power in a Protestant nation. This spirit of interethnic and interfaith cooperation, or pluralism, was enhanced by the collective American experience of struggle against the Great Depression and Nazi Germany's Aryan racist regime. John Kennedy' 1958 book *A Nation of Immigrants* invoked this pluralist ideal. His father, Joseph P. Kennedy, adopted the concept as a political mantra prior to the 1960 campaign: "There's a whole new generation out there and it's filled with the sons and daughters of immigrants from all over the world and those people are going to be mighty proud that one of their own is running for President."[61]

Pluralism signified assimilation, rather than respect for group identities, to Republicans in 1960. As a Quaker, Richard Nixon might have similarly claimed status as a religious minority. Republican presidential nominee Herbert Hoover, also a Quaker, had made this case in the 1928 campaign against Al Smith. Nixon and President Eisenhower refused to recognize denominational or ethnic differences as important. In a message to Nationalities for Nixon, the president had warned against religious balkanization: "I don't know how to speak to a Jewish group or a Catholic group or a Presbyterian group, or any other. I like to talk to Americans."[62] Echoing former President Woodrow Wilson's disdain for hyphenated Americans, Eisenhower refused to appeal to group loyalties, but emphasized common traits and beliefs. In Eisenhower's account of the campaign for a 1965 memoir, *Waging Peace,* he made no mention of Kennedy's religion.[63] Eisenhower viewed foreign policy experience as most critical in presidential candidates. As Americans fought a Cold War against communist nations, Nixon and the president would only discuss religion in relation to the Judeo-Christian anticommunist consensus against atheistic regimes, such as the Soviet Union and People's Republic of China.

The Kennedy and Nixon campaigns revealed two competing views of pluralist philosophy. Kennedy's supporters promoted the idea that pluralism required aggressive repudiation of religious and racial bigotry. Republican Party leaders portrayed ignoring and ostracizing anti-Catholic critics as the best means of defending pluralist ideals. After conservative Protestant ministers and anti-Catholic bigots continued to challenge Kennedy on religious grounds, however, Nixon's silence appeared as disinterest rather than magnanimity. Kennedy's success in the primaries persuaded Democrats to promote solidarity, among religious and racial minorities, against the Protestant establishment—symbolized by the Republican Party. Nixon suppressed attempts by Catholic Republicans to indict Kennedy's loyalists for employing "reverse bigotry."

Campaign strategy regarding the 1960 campaign's "Catholic issue" had significant consequences for subsequent U.S. politics. Nixon felt abused by Kennedy's exploitation of religion and "savage" tactics, which he felt justified later tolerance for "dirty tricks" within his own campaign team. Republicans nominated a Catholic vice presidential candidate in 1964. Today American Catholics are divided evenly as Republicans and Democrats, and the two parties continue to battle for the votes of religious and racial minorities. Republican candidates have tended to align themselves with the Catholic bishops on issues of federal aid to parochial schools and abortion, while Democrats continue to present themselves as struggling against an establishment that limits equal opportunity for African and immigrant Americans. In continued debates about preferential treatment for African and Latino Americans, bigotry and prejudice remain powerful terms in political discourse. One can view the 1960 campaign as a rehearsal for the politics of group identity characteristic of the late twentieth century.

"THE PROMISED LAND," AS SEEN FROM THE DOME OF SAINT PETER'S, ROME.—[See Page 926.]

New York illustrator Thomas Nast graphically depicted the Roman Catholic Church as a medieval institution bent on colonizing North America. This image, entitled "'The Promised Land,' as seen from the Dome of Saint Peter's, Rome," evoked the conspiracy theories of early-nineteenth-century ministers and writers, such as Reverend Lyman Beecher and inventor of the telegraph Samuel F. B. Morse, who portrayed the pope and his faithful minions as plotting conquest of the United States through Irish immigration, Jesuit missionaries, and Catholic schools. Originally published in *Harper's Weekly* (1870). Provided courtesy HarpWeek LLC.

When European leaders suppressed Catholic Church authority in Europe, Thomas Nast depicted the pope as desperate to create a religious establishment in the United States. This cartoon contrasts the European ideal of church-state separation, supported by British Queen Victoria and German Chancellor Otto von Bismarck on the above right, with a clerical assault on religious freedom below, symbolized by ape-like Irish immigrant thugs, corrupt politicians, and a regal pope. Originally published in *Harper's Weekly* (1870). Provided courtesy HarpWeek LLC.

In pursuing the presidency during the 1920s, New York Governor Alfred E. Smith confronted anti-Catholic critics, as well as nativists who disparaged the Catholic candidate as alien to U.S. traditions. This 1921 cartoon caricatured Smith's "immigrant" characteristics, such as the ubiquitous cigar, brown derby, and opposition to Prohibition. Smith's unabashed urban, New York City style attracted many religious and racial minorities, who viewed the Catholic politician as a champion of the underdog. Yet these same mannerisms appeared un-statesmanlike to rural Americans. Other Catholic presidential candidates—such as Senator Thomas J. Walsh (MT), Postmaster General James Farley, and John F. Kennedy—consciously avoided association with such stereotypes. Originally published in the *New York World-Telegram and Sun* (January 3, 1921). From the Cartoon Drawings collection of the Library of Congress Prints and Photographs Division.

Boston Archbishop Richard Cushing proved John F. Kennedy's most fervent supporter in the Roman Catholic hierarchy. Since serving as a U.S. congressman and senator from Massachusetts, Kennedy cultivated good relations with Cushing, who lobbied Catholic politicians, such as Pennsylvania Governor David Lawrence, on his behalf as the 1960 campaign approached. (Photo No. PC542 in the John F. Kennedy Library.)

During the campaign, Cushing submitted to Kennedy an article that explained Catholic policy regarding the separation of church and state. Kennedy's aide Theodore C. Sorensen consulted the author and critic of Catholicism Paul B. Blanshard, who wrote a lengthy criticism of Cushing's arguments. The Kennedy campaign respectfully asked Cushing not to publish the piece, which might attract greater attention to the religious issue. (Photo No. PC2208 in the John F. Kennedy Library.)

As part of a strategy to show independence from the Roman Catholic Church's staunch anticommunism, Massachusetts Senator John F. Kennedy repudiated "red scare" tactics at the 1959 Alfred E. Smith Memorial Dinner. Hosted annually by Catholic Archbishop of New York Cardinal Francis Spellman in honor of the 1928 Catholic presidential candidate, this event attracted nationally recognized U.S. politicians. Kennedy's speech appealed particularly to liberals, who viewed his family's connection to Spellman and former U.S. Senator Joseph R. McCarthy (WI) with great suspicion. (Photo No. Px 88–7:2 in the John F. Kennedy Library. Photo by Jack Schildkraut.)

Protestant evangelical minister Billy Graham, seen here with President Kennedy, eagerly encouraged Vice President Richard M. Nixon and President Dwight D. Eisenhower to exploit anti-Catholicism among Protestant voters, especially in the South. After Kennedy's victory, the nation's first Catholic president-elect skillfully maneuvered Graham into a public endorsement of religious toleration. (Photo No. PC805 in the John F. Kennedy Library.)

Protestants and Other Americans United for Separation of Church and State (POAU) aggressively challenged Kennedy and other Catholic presidential candidates to answer specific questions about religion's role in politics. Many Catholics viewed such skepticism of Kennedy's religion—shared by several self-proclaimed liberals—as thinly disguised nativist bigotry. This *Brooklyn Tablet* cartoon echoed Roman Catholic Archbishop of New York Francis Spellman's characterization of POAU as "unhooded Klansmen." Originally published in *The Tablet* (November 7, 1959). Reprinted with permission of *The Tablet*.

Former President Harry S. Truman's unpublished comments in 1959 revealed his firm resistance to the prospect of a Catholic president. Asserting that Catholics would not respect the principle of separation of church and state, Truman nonetheless changed his mind after a personal visit from John Kennedy in August 1960. In the following months, Truman denounced Nixon and the Republicans for anti-Catholic bigotry. Even in speeches to Catholic and Jewish audiences, as well as to southern Baptists, Truman accused Kennedy's enemies of religious prejudice. (Photo No. 79-AR-6284-D in the John F. Kennedy Library. Photo by Abbie Rowe, White House.)

At the 1960 Alfred E. Smith Memorial Dinner, Nixon pointedly and soberly praised the nation's Judeo-Christian, interfaith consensus, while Kennedy joked irreverently about the campaign's "Catholic issue." Ironically thanking New York Archbishop Spellman for showing "the proper spirit" by inviting the Quaker Nixon, Kennedy quipped, "I assume that shortly I will be invited to a Quaker dinner honoring [Smith's opponent in the 1928 presidential election and Quaker] Herbert Hoover." Noting that the *Wall Street Journal* had recently chastised Nixon's campaign tactics, Kennedy joked, "That is like [Vatican publication] *Osservatore Romano* criticizing the Pope." (Photo No. Px88–7:4 in the John F. Kennedy Library. Photo by Jack Schildkraut.)

Michigan Governor G. Mennen Williams, a Protestant, endorsed Kennedy early in the primary season, which helped the Catholic candidate overcome religious prejudice. Michigan's Democratic political machine—a coalition of Catholic labor unions, such as the United Auto Workers, and liberals—provided Kennedy with a slim victory in November. Williams' repudiation of anti-Catholic opponents in Michigan proved critical to Kennedy's success in that state. (Photo No. AR 6347-A in the John F. Kennedy Library. Photo by Abbie Rowe, White House.)

California Governor Eugene "Pat" Brown, a Roman Catholic, balanced his own presidential ambitions with modest support for John Kennedy's candidacy in 1960. Protestant Adlai Stevenson's nomination would make Brown's selection as a running mate more likely, since the Democrats would not select two Catholics for the national ticket. Brown also feared that Kennedy's campaign would revive California's anti-Catholic voters. Yet Brown's advisors counseled support for the Catholic candidate, since Kennedy's defeat on religious grounds would discourage both parties from nominating Catholics for higher office. Brown's son Jerry and John Kennedy's brother Edward both challenged President Jimmy Carter for the Democratic Party presidential nomination in 1980. (Photo No. AR-6528-A in the John F. Kennedy Library. Photo by Abbie Rowe, White House.)

Democratic Presidential nominee John F. Kennedy addressed the Al Smith Memorial Dinner in 1960. In the presence of Roman Catholic Cardinal Francis Spellman, Archbishop of New York, Republican candidate Richard M. Nixon spoke somberly and seriously about religion's positive role in public life. Kennedy's speech lightheartedly mocked the campaign's religious controversy. Nixon later chastised Kennedy for wearing a black tie, which was less formal than Nixon's white tie. (Photo No. Px88–7:3 in the John F. Kennedy Library. Photo by Jack Schildkraut.)

Chapter Six

The Cold War and the Domestic Response to Kennedy's Catholicism

Conventional wisdom in the 1960 campaign suggested that John F. Kennedy's Catholicism would insulate the Democratic Party from charges of softness on communism that had been leveled at its prominent liberals like two-time presidential nominee Adlai Stevenson. Several political observers, even conservative Catholics, initially portrayed Kennedy's religious affiliation as such a political advantage. Conservative *Wall Street Journal* columnist Robert D. Novak suggested that Kennedy's Catholicism "is his best weapon" against those who charged the Massachusetts senator with appeasing communism.[1] In the liberal *New Republic,* former Stevenson speech-writer Gerald W. Johnson characterized Catholicism as "the one triple-plated guarantee of a candidate's anti-Communism."[2] In a publication that featured many conservative Catholics, William F. Buckley, Jr.'s *National Review,* veteran journalist John Chamberlain admitted that religion assured Kennedy's anticommunism, saying, "As a Catholic he could hardly capitulate to Communism. That *would* be letting his coreligionists down!"[3] The Roman Catholic Church's dogmatic approach to anticommunism appeared to protect the Catholic candidate from conservative opponents who might challenge Kennedy's national security strategy.

Many non-Catholic liberals, however, argued that the American Catholic Church's moralistic, inflexible opposition to communism would undermine attempts to engage the Soviet Union and People's Republic of China with pragmatic diplomacy. Memories of Catholic Senator Joseph R. McCarthy's (WI) militant pursuit of communist subversives within the U.S. government heightened these suspicions. To secure the Democratic nomination, Kennedy needed support from liberals, a fundamental wing of the party. While Kennedy's advocacy of peaceful coexistence with communist nations pleased liberals, conservative Catholics and non-Catholics portrayed this strategic toleration of communism as contrary to Catholic doctrine. Republican Party nominee Richard M. Nixon nonetheless rejected the effort of some

Catholic Republicans to portray Kennedy's weakness against communism as a legitimate religious issue. Kennedy betrayed Catholic principles, conservatives insisted, by failing to treat communist nations as incompatible with religious belief. In the 1960 campaign, therefore, Kennedy sought to articulate a Cold War policy acceptable both to liberals and Catholics.

This chapter examines the impact of Cold War politics on responses to Kennedy's Catholicism in the presidential campaign. In the months prior to the Democratic National Convention, Kennedy seized several opportunities to repudiate Joseph McCarthy's tactics of militant anticommunism. Kennedy defended the National Council of Churches (NCC) when, in early 1960, an Air Force manual published charges that this organization harbored communists. When the Soviet Union shot down a U.S. spy plane in May, Kennedy joined Adlai Stevenson in denouncing President Dwight D. Eisenhower's refusal to apologize to the Soviet leader. The conservative Catholic *Brooklyn Tablet* and Protestant fundamentalists, such as Gerald L. K. Smith, portrayed Kennedy's tolerance of communism as directly violating the Roman Catholic Church's clear teachings against a system that seeks the destruction of all religion. Although liberal endorsements helped Kennedy gain the Democratic nomination, conservative Catholic James L. Buckley, brother of *National Review* founder William F. Buckley, Jr., encouraged Nixon to present anticommunism as the campaign's only significant religious issue. Nixon's refusal to challenge the Catholic candidate's adherence to church dogma regarding communism enabled Kennedy to secure overwhelming support from Catholic voters.

As a Massachusetts congressman in the late 1940s, Kennedy embraced the American Catholic Church's militant anticommunism. Kennedy joined conservative Republicans in denouncing the administration of fellow Democrat President Harry S. Truman for insufficiently strong anticommunist policies. Under Truman's leadership, these critics noted, the communist party successfully captured power in China in 1949, and communist North Korea nearly conquered the entire Korean peninsula. Kennedy also outraged liberals by supporting the McCarran Act—named after Catholic Senator Patrick A. McCarran (NV)—that legally demanded communist registration with the government. Kennedy's endorsement of Republican congressman Richard M. Nixon (CA), who characterized his liberal Democratic opponent Helen Gahagan Douglas as the "Pink Lady" in a 1950 campaign for a California Senate seat, established Kennedy as a conservative Cold Warrior.[4]

Such political positions created a real liability for Kennedy's attempt at attracting liberal support in 1960. Liberal suspicion of Catholic anticommunism intensified in the 1950s as McCarthy—the nation's most recognizable Catholic—accused liberal Democrats, such as Adlai Stevenson, of betraying U.S. institutions because of ideological sympathy with communism. By openly supporting McCarthy's crusade against communist subversives, New York Archbishop Francis Cardinal Spellman gave credibility to fears of Catholicism's incompatibility with liberal anticommunism. Catholics increasingly voted for Republican presidential candidates in the 1950s, and former First Lady Eleanor Roosevelt chastised Kennedy, as a Catholic Democrat, for failing to lead resistance to McCarthy.

Kennedy's refusal to repudiate Joseph McCarthy prompted the greatest suspicion from liberal Protestants. Kennedy's father, Joseph P. Kennedy, maintained close friendships with Spellman and McCarthy, who employed John's younger brother Robert. McCarthy even dated John's sisters Patricia and Jean.[5] In February 1952, John Kennedy publicly showed sympathy for McCarthy's vigilant anticommunism. After a speaker criticized in the same breath both McCarthy and former State Department official Alger Hiss, who stood accused of spying for the Soviet Union, Kennedy responded with outrage, "How dare you couple the name of a great American patriot with that of a traitor!"[6] Eleanor Roosevelt never forgave Kennedy for failing to discourage Catholic support of McCarthy, by his not endorsing the U.S. Senate's 1954 censure of the Wisconsin Senator. Mocking the title of Kennedy's book *Profiles in Courage,* Roosevelt chastised the Massachusetts senator for not having shown "less profile, and more courage." This issue prompted Roosevelt to oppose Kennedy's nomination for the vice-presidency in 1956 and the presidency in early 1960.[7]

Months prior to the election year, however, Kennedy demonstrated a desire to adopt liberal positions regarding communism. In 1959, Kennedy's public statements included repudiation of the domestic anticommunism associated with McCarthy. Kennedy used an address at the October 1959 Alfred E. Smith Memorial Dinner to challenge the American Catholic hierarchy's militant anticommunist stance. New York City's Archbishop Spellman hosted national politicians annually at this event to honor former New York Governor Al Smith, the first American Catholic nominated by a major party to run for president. On this occasion, Kennedy appealed for liberal sympathy by portraying Smith as a politician who repudiated extreme anticommunism. Warning against exaggerating the communist menace, Kennedy praised Smith's refusal to foster excessive anticommunism in the years following World War I. As governor, Smith had vetoed state bills "which rode a crest of popular anti-socialist hysteria after the First World War,"

Kennedy noted. Smith's courage to denounce "those who had built this 'red scare' up out of all proportions" earned Kennedy's praise.[8] Choosing to highlight Smith's earlier denunciation of red-baiting, Kennedy significantly ignored this Catholic politician's portrayal of President Franklin D. Roosevelt's New Deal as "socialistic" in 1936, as discussed in Chapter Two.

Recognizing success among liberal Democrats as essential to securing the party nomination, Kennedy seized another opportunity to defend liberals from accusations of harboring communist sympathies. In the early months of 1960, an Air Force training manual published fundamentalist Protestant Reverend Billy James Hargis' charges that communists infiltrated the NCC. Kennedy rejected the Air Force manual's accusations as "shocking and distasteful." In criticizing the manual, Kennedy specifically denounced the use of government publications to attack a church organization. Such action amounted to infringement upon the principle of church-state separation, Kennedy alleged.[9] "Under the First Amendment our Government cannot—directly or indirectly—select any religious body for either favorable or unfavorable treatment."[10] Kennedy asserted that this manual transgressed public institutions' obligation to maintain official neutrality toward religious bodies.[11] Sensing an opportunity to secure liberal allies in the Democratic primaries, Kennedy enthusiastically and unreservedly defended the NCC against these allegations of disloyalty.

Kennedy's open support for a liberal Protestant institution under siege also distinguished the Catholic candidate from Archbishop Spellman's uncompromising anticommunism. Spellman initially defended the NCC against the Air Force manual's indictment.[12] When Congressman Donald Jackson (CA), a Republican member of the militantly anticommunist House Un-American Activities Committee (HUAC), vaguely claimed that reporters distorted Spellman's intent, however, the Catholic bishop expressed admiration for Jackson and HUAC.[13] Spellman failed to reaffirm his opposition to the Air Force manual's aspersions against the NCC.

Kennedy also asserted independence from the American Catholic bishops' dogmatic anticommunism by advocating greater diplomacy in the Cold War. Criticizing Eisenhower's handling of an American U-2 spy plane in May 1960, Kennedy called for the president to make strategic concessions to the Soviet Union. Conservative Democrats, such as Senate Majority Leader Lyndon B. Johnson (TX), supported Eisenhower's refusal to concede Soviet Premier Nikita Khrushchev's demand for an apology. Kennedy, however, advocated a sign of contrition. In Kennedy's opinion, Eisenhower had allowed "the risk of war [to] hang on the possibility of an engine failure" by approving the U-2 missions. When Kruschchev walked out of a Paris summit because of Eisenhower's unwillingness to apologize for spying on the Soviets, Kennedy argued that the president should have "expressed regret" in order to salvage the summit's goals. Such a position aligned Kennedy squarely with the opinion of liberal Democrat Adlai Stevenson.[14] Appealing to the party's liberal wing, Kennedy called for compromise with communist governments.

While Kennedy's repudiation of militant anticommunism pleased non-Catholic liberals, Catholic and non-Catholic conservatives portrayed these policies toward communism as incompatible with Catholicism. In the conservative Catholic diocese of Brooklyn, New York, the *Brooklyn Tablet* published the views of political science professor Anthony Bouscaren, a conservative foreign policy scholar who taught at Jesuit institutions Marquette University in Milwaukee and LeMoyne College in Syracuse, New York.[15] In Bouscaren's opinion, Kennedy failed to demonstrate sufficient vigilance against communism. Characterizing Kennedy's unwillingness to defend two Chinese Nationalist offshore islands, Quemoy and Matsu, as "appeasement" of communist China, Bouscaren also expressed "grave doubts" about the Catholic candidate's suggestion of a U.S. apology for U-2 espionage flights. "If these two stands of Senator Kennedy are any indication of his general approach to Communism, I believe many Catholics are going to cast their votes for the anti-Communist candidate," Bouscaren concluded.[16] By portraying American Catholics as convinced that anticommunism required an uncompromising stance, Bouscaren perpetuated the notion that loyal adherence to Catholicism required subservience to doctrine.

Other Catholic conservatives argued that Catholics would reject Kennedy's willingness to coexist with communist governments. The right-wing publication *Human Events* promoted this idea in an article entitled "Kennedy for President? A Catholic Priest Says 'No.'" In this article, Reverend Juniper Carol publicly criticized Kennedy's "liberal attitude toward communism," and urged opposition to the Democratic nominee.[17] The *Brooklyn Tablet* also encouraged Catholic opposition to Kennedy by publishing letters that challenged Kennedy's anticommunist credentials. Brooklyn resident Joseph F. Murray denounced the Massachusetts senator's endorsement of aid to Communist Poland and Yugoslavia. Chastising Kennedy for considering Adlai Stevenson as secretary of state, Murray also questioned Kennedy's tacit approval of Soviet Premier Khrushchev's 1959 visit to the United States. Finally, Murray's letter criticized Kennedy for rejecting a bill that would require a loyalty oath from students who sought federal loans.[18] These Catholics required a rigid, uncompromising anticommunism from a president of any denomination. Even Republican President Eisenhower failed to support most of the policies these writers advocated. According to these Catholic conservatives, Catholicism was incompatible with moderate or liberal anticommunism.

Conservative Protestants shared the liberal assumption about Catholicism's stringent anticommunism, but several members of the "radical Right" rejected the anti-Catholicism common to traditional Protestant fundamentalism. Approving the Catholic Church's militancy against communism, these fundamentalist Protestants instead criticized Kennedy for showing insufficient attention to his church's anticommunist teachings. Leading radical right antisemites like Elizabeth Dilling, Conde McGinley, and Gerald L. K. Smith each opposed Kennedy without repudiating Catholicism. "Catholics are being led into a horrible trap," warned McGinley's *Common Sense: The Nation's Anticommunist Newspaper* in June 1960. "If elected, Kennedy will not be able to reject the liberals, socialists, communists, Marxist Jews, etc. who have put him in office."[19] Seeking to mobilize Catholics against Kennedy, two articles in Smith's magazine, *The Cross and The Flag*, cited several public positions where the Democratic candidate contradicted "Catholic policy." An unattributed editorial entitled "Is Kennedy a Catholic?" rebuked Kennedy's legislation to prohibit loyalty oath requirements for students receiving federal loans. This action violated Catholic beliefs, the writer argued. In this interpretation, Kennedy's support for United Auto Workers President Walter Reuther—"who was trained in Moscow for his socialist, pro-Marxist, and revolutionary activities"—also opposed the Catholic Church's teachings.[20] Depicting "Catholic policy" as equivalent to the *Brooklyn Tablet*'s conservative anticommunism, *The Cross and The Flag* argued that Kennedy betrayed Catholicism. Reversing the nativist argument that a Catholic president would honor religious loyalties before political duties, Smith's publication accused Kennedy of insufficient allegiance to the Catholic Church's religious teaching regarding communism.

Smith's personal editorial, "Suicide in Los Angeles," cited these same issues to portray Kennedy's view of communism as heretical toward "Catholic policy." Referring in the title to the location of the Democratic National Convention, Smith claimed that the party's nomination of Kennedy was a self-inflicted, fatal wound. Denying any anti-Catholic sentiment, Smith claimed a personal friendship with both the late Joseph McCarthy—"the great patriotic martyr from Wisconsin"—and former Notre Dame University Law School Dean Clarence E. Manion.[21]

These two Catholics charged liberals with appeasement of communism. In Smith's interpretation, Kennedy served as agent for the Democratic Party's liberals, communists, and "Muscovite platform." Smith endorsed Nixon despite some reservations about the GOP nominee. Nixon's repudiation of Smith's antisemitism frustrated the fundamentalist minister, but Kennedy bothered Smith far more than Nixon.[22] Kennedy's liberal policy toward communism perhaps alienated the Protestant Right more than his Catholicism. The Roman Catholic Church's intolerance of communism provided some basis for Smith's arguments. If Catholics recognized Kennedy's liberal approach to communist countries, Smith believed they would oppose him at the polls.

While the Holy See never addressed Kennedy's policies toward communism, official statements from Vatican City encouraged speculation that the Roman Catholic Church's anticommunist stance required strict obedience from faithful members, even public officials. The Vatican's official newspaper, *L'Osservatore Romano*, publicly defended the church's right to assert binding doctrine on certain public issues. Expressing opposition to communist candidates for Italian electoral offices, *Osservatore* contended that some political issues—such as America's racial segregation, South African apartheid, and Algerian terrorism—carried religious implications. Although some Americans argued that church direction of political decisions exceeded religious authority, *Osservatore* declared that communism propagated morally incorrect activity, and thus undermined basic human dignity.[23] The Catholic hierarchy's insistence on obedience regarding the immorality of communism perpetuated the image that American Catholics lacked freedom of thought in this critical area of public policy. If this impression of unquestioning Catholic anticommunism had gained popular acceptance, Kennedy would likely have faced opposition from liberals who viewed such militancy as a threat to diplomacy and peaceful coexistence. These statements also appeared to justify conservative Protestants who claimed that membership in the Catholic Church required adherence to militant anticommunism.

Catholic Republicans interpreted these Vatican pronouncements to signify that Nixon could attract Catholics by portraying Kennedy's liberal anticommunism as incompatible with Catholicism. If Nixon's campaign team would publicize the disparity between the Catholic Church's positions regarding communism and Kennedy's, these Catholics believed, many Catholics would repudiate the Democratic nominee. By advocating toughness against domestic and foreign communism in earlier political contests, Nixon previously had demonstrated an ability to attract Catholic support. The Republican presidential ticket of

Eisenhower and Nixon had attracted traditionally Democratic Catholic voters, and Nixon's record of uncompromising anticommunism as vice president fortified his appeal in this regard.

Nixon's staunch anticommunism previously had brought him to the attention of the American Catholic hierarchy, benefiting his political career. Father John Cronin, a Catholic priest who taught at a Baltimore seminary, propelled Nixon's advance to national recognition by revealing evidence that encouraged him to pursue the investigation of Alger Hiss' communist past in 1948. Cronin's confidential sources confirmed that Hiss lied when denying prior membership in the Communist Party. In following years, Nixon employed Cronin as a speechwriter.[24] California Catholics helped Nixon defeat Helen Gahagan Douglas in the 1950 senate campaign. Blaming northern California Catholics for her defeat, Douglas quoted northern California campaign manager Harold Tipton, in her 1982 autobiography, as saying, "The campaigning of the Catholic church, especially in the building trades unions in the north, was very important."[25] Conservative Catholic leaders, such as Los Angeles Archbishop J. Francis McIntyre, campaigned for Nixon's election.[26]

The Eisenhower-Nixon presidential ticket also proved attractive to Catholic voters in 1952 and 1956. Although Catholics had overwhelmingly voted Democratic for more than one hundred years, the Republicans appeared favorable in comparison to the Democrats' 1952 and 1956 presidential nominee Adlai Stevenson, whom some Catholics perceived as "soft on communism." In 1956, Kennedy's supporters argued that a Catholic vice-presidential nominee would quell these suspicions and "win back Catholics."[27] Eisenhower and Nixon received the support of 53 percent of Catholic voters in 1952.[28] In the award-winning book *The Future of American Politics,* reporter Samuel Lubell portrayed anticommunism as the primary explanation of the Catholic trend toward supporting Eisenhower and Nixon, writing, "The Church hierarchy has clearly interpreted the present world crisis as a challenge to reaffirm the all-pervasive character of the moral doctrines of the Church and to establish Catholicism as the irreconcilable 'we or they' antagonist of 'atheistic communism'."[29] Nixon particularly embodied the uncompromising anticommunism that satisfied many Catholic voters.

Nixon's confrontations with communism just prior to the 1960 campaign earned particular praise from many Catholic organizations. In 1959, Nixon traveled to overwhelmingly Catholic South America. Crowds attacked Nixon's car in Venezuela and students refused to allow the vice president to speak at one Peruvian college. Nixon presented these incidents as evidence of communism's violent repression and censorship of open intellectual exchange.[30] In a model kitchen at the American trade exhibition in Moscow that same year, television cameras captured an impromptu verbal exchange in which Nixon wagged his finger derisively at Soviet Premier Nikita Khrushchev for closing the Soviet economy to innovative, practical U.S. consumer products. The national Jesuit weekly *America* praised the vice president for openly and firmly challenging communist ideology, writing, "It was our good fortune that when Premier Khrushchev decided to turn the [American Exhibition in Moscow] into a propaganda circus, we had on hand for a change a man who can give as good as he takes."[31] This publication implied that Nixon's critique of communism greatly exceeded the record of President Eisenhower, who had established a reputation for characteristically uninspiring press conferences. Catholic bishops Spellman and Cushing publicly opposed Eisenhower's invitation to Khrushchev, who came to the United States in 1959.[32] After the vice president's repeated, firm stands against communism, the senior class at America's most famous Catholic university, Notre Dame, awarded Nixon the honor of "Patriot of the Year" in February 1960.[33] Nixon enjoyed the recognition and respect of many Catholics.

Ironically, Protestant minister and best-selling author Norman Vincent Peale's anti-Catholic statements harmed Nixon and aroused sympathy for Kennedy from certain staunch anticommunists. In early September, Catholics and non-Catholics alike expressed resentment of Peale's infamous statements that a Catholic president would succumb to Vatican pressure. Writing to Eisenhower's Catholic Labor Secretary James Mitchell, an Indiana resident insisted that Peale aided the Soviet Union by promoting internal U.S. "discord."[34] The editor of *National Defense,* an American Legion publication, denounced Peale as "impregnated with Sovietism."[35] These writers invoked the anticommunist consensus to defend Kennedy from critics of Catholicism.

Peale's public doubts about a Catholic president also complicated Nixon's appeal to conservative anticommunists. In a letter to Peale, a supporter of conservative Senator Barry Goldwater (AZ) for president rallied to defend the Roman Catholic Church's reputation as an equal, if not leading, partner in the anticommunist consensus. Praising Catholics as devoted allies against communism, this writer asserted, "there would be a good deal less tolerance of Communism in this country if the Vatican had any influence on our national affairs." The Catholic hierarchy's consistent anticommunism compared favorably, the writer continued, with the Protestant establishment's liberalism.

While Catholic Cardinals Spellman and Cushing "loudly" protested America's "red carpet" response to Khrushchev's 1959 visit, the Protestant National Council of Churches approved. America's interfaith alliance against communism superseded religious differences for this individual, who would vote for Goldwater "even if he were a brother of the Pope."[36] Although right-wing anticommunists such as Gerald Smith had tried to portray Kennedy as appeasing communist governments, Peale's anti-Catholic statements alienated both Catholics and conservatives who valued interfaith cooperation against communism.

In several campaign speeches following Peale's public doubts about Kennedy's Catholicism, Nixon pursued Catholic support by stressing an interfaith consensus against atheistic communism. Nixon's advisors began to suggest that the Republican nominee directly connect the campaign's "Catholic issue" and the candidates' policies toward communism. GOP convention platform chairman and future Illinois Senator Charles Percy, a member of the Church of Christ, Scientist, drafted a speech that echoed Nixon's earlier emphasis on atheistic communism's threat to Judeo-Christian tradition.[37] "There is only one religious issue in the campaign," Percy wrote, "It exists because the power of world Communism today menaces the freedom of any and every religion."[38] Percy's words sought to redirect resentment about Kennedy's encounter with anti-Catholicism toward vigilance against communism.

In mid-October, evidence suggested that Nixon's anticommunist reputation had failed to attract Catholics. If even a small percentage of Catholics who had voted Republican previously switched their loyalties to Kennedy on religious grounds, this shift could determine the results of a very close election. On October 18, journalist and pollster Samuel Lubell announced that 36 percent of "Eisenhower Catholics"—Catholic Americans who supported Eisenhower's 1956 presidential bid—favored Kennedy.[39]

Lubell's earlier book, *The Future of American Politics,* had identified Republican anticommunism as attractive to Catholic voters, but his 1960 door-to-door interviews in key precincts uncovered Catholics' greater loyalty to Kennedy as a co-religionist. While "Eisenhower Catholics" tended to respect Republican foreign policy, this group felt religious affinity for Kennedy. Lubell quoted one representative interviewee, who said, "Nixon would handle the Russians better but I want to show the world this country is broad-minded enough to elect a Catholic."[40] "If only Nixon were a Catholic!" exclaimed one 55-year-old engineer in East Meadow, Long Island. "He's the better man on foreign policy. But I'm Catholic and it's not right that all men shouldn't have an equal chance to be President."[41] Whether due to resentment of anti-Catholicism or pride in a Catholic candidate, Catholics demonstrated an unwillingness to perceive Nixon's vigilance against communism as the campaign's decisive issue.

Lubell's analysis did not preclude Nixon from persuading Catholics to make their Election Day decisions on the basis of the communist issue. Nixon's anticommunism continued to impress Catholic Americans, Lubell argued. "So strong is the pull of Nixon and [GOP vice-presidential candidate] Henry Cabot Lodge on foreign policy that many of these Catholic suburbanites may still switch back to Nixon."[42] On October 20, Lubell reported that 10 percent of "Eisenhower Catholics" opposed Kennedy's positions regarding communism.[43] Lubell's assertion that Nixon might still entice Catholic voters, however, required Republican strategists to discover quickly a means of securing this constituency.

Republican Catholics called on Nixon to challenge Kennedy's Cold War policies as an authentic religious issue. Since many Catholic Americans believed in a firm anticommunist stance, Nixon's Catholic supporters argued, Kennedy did not best represent Catholicism's attitude toward communist states. In an October 20 press conference, Catholic Congressman William E. Miller (NY) accused Kennedy's supporters of exploiting Catholic resentment against religious prejudice to obscure Nixon's stronger reputation for resisting communism. Democratic leaders appealed to Catholic Americans on religious grounds, Miller claimed, "rather than because of his qualifications to lead our country and the West against atheistic Communism which would wipe out all religions." The Republican National Committee released Miller's statement to the press. By promoting Judeo-Christian unity against communism, an antireligious political, economic, and social system, Nixon's allies believed that voters would question Kennedy's experience as a defender of U.S. values.[44]

Behind the headlines, Republicans considered a direct appeal to Catholic voters by portraying the Democratic Party and Kennedy as "soft" on communism. Nixon's supporters prepared detailed arguments to attract Catholics who favored right-wing anticommunism. Two proposed pamphlets in Nixon's manuscript collections revealed the GOP strategy. According to one argument, entitled "YES, THERE IS A 'CATHOLIC BLOC' VOTE—UNITED AGAINST COMMUNISM," the "Eisenhower-Nixon-Lodge administration" prevented communist expansion "without apology, appeasement, or war." To aid such internal reflection, the author quoted Al Smith's characteristic suggestion to "look at the record." By employing words from the Democrats' 1928 Catholic presidential nominee, the pamphlet's author implied that Smith, who denounced President Roosevelt's New Deal federal programs as "socialistic" in 1936, would have endorsed Nixon. This document's definition of firm anticommunism relied on a right-wing perspective. In this interpretation, Republicans ended the Korean War and prevented communist China's entry in the Untied Nations. The "Truman-Kennedy-Johnson Team," by contrast, forfeited America's atomic monopoly and surrendered China to communism.[45] This Republican interpretation of Cold War politics would not convince partisan Catholic Democrats, but might persuade undecided, independent, and GOP Catholics.

The second document, entitled "WHY CATHOLICS SHOULD VOTE FOR NIXON: *The Real Issue is Atheistic Communism*," presented a more strident appeal to Catholics. While recognizing some Americans' anti-Catholicism, the author discouraged Catholics from taking their resentment out against the Republican Party. This author criticized Kennedy for advocating a U.S. apology for U-2 espionage flights, conceding Chinese Nationalist islands to Communist China, and voting for federal aid to communist governments in Poland and Yugoslavia. In conclusion, the author celebrated Nixon's struggle against Alger Hiss "and his fellow travelers . . . [who] were selling out your country to Godless Communism."[46] These documents overtly linked religion and anticommunism. But no widespread distribution of either pamphlet occurred. Nixon continued to avoid even indirect public references to Kennedy's Catholicism.

Although the GOP offered no direct appeal to Catholic voters, an ad hoc, conservative Catholic organization publicly promoted Nixon's candidacy as the best choice for American Catholics. This group deemphasized anti-Catholicism and highlighted anticommunism. In a full-page *New York Times* advertisement, the "Communism Is The Issue" Committee conveyed an "Open Letter" to "Catholics hurt by hostility toward the Vatican in recent months." The committee's chairman, future New York Senator James L. Buckley, portrayed Catholicism and communism as irreconcilable opponents. Communists perceived the Roman Catholic Church as "the prime enemy," Buckley claimed, but the Catholic Kennedy nonetheless retained close associates who regarded communism as merely "a childish bugaboo." In Buckley's interpretation, this attitude demonstrated naiveté, and disqualified a candidate, of any religion, from leading America. Kennedy's positions on the U-2 incident, the Chinese Nationalist Islands, and the loyalty oath for students seeking federal loans also demonstrated weak resolve against communism, Buckley believed.[47] These charges echoed Gerald L. K. Smith and other right-wing critics of Kennedy. In Buckley's interpretation, the communist threat superseded resentment about anti-Catholicism.

Buckley reversed the traditional anti-Catholic argument that Catholics harbored dual, divided loyalties to religious and political authorities. In Buckley's interpretation, Catholic Americans had complimentary dual allegiance to the world's leading secular and spiritual anticommunist institutions—the U.S. government and the Roman Catholic Church. Buckley viewed this unique status, however, as carrying "a special obligation to consider chiefly which candidate has the will to fight the most determined enemy Christian society has known."[48] Beyond an appeal to a Judeo-Christian alliance, or even a right-wing anticommunist consensus, this argument charged Catholics specifically with a profound political and religious duty to resist communism. In 1960, Buckley argued, American Catholics' secular and religious loyalties both required a vote for Nixon.

Nixon resolutely refused to endorse any discussion of Kennedy's Catholicism. James Buckley asked Catholic investment banker and Nixon aide Peter Flanigan to propose that the Republican Party sponsor some advertisements with this theme.[49] Nixon immediately rejected Buckley's message that anticommunism was the campaign's true "Catholic issue." Nixon "chewed me out," Flanigan recalled. "Don't you play the religious card under any circumstances whatever," Nixon responded to Flanigan's suggestion. "I absolutely forbid you to do anything which suggests that my campaign has a religious bias to it."[50] Whether Nixon's unwillingness to risk accusations of religious bigotry was motivated by principles or pragmatism, he refused to deviate from his policy of withholding comments about religious differences in the campaign.

Kennedy did not appeal specifically to Catholics on the anticommunist issue but sought to portray himself as a more hard-nosed Cold Warrior than the Republicans. Kennedy's polling data revealed that Nixon gained public support by portraying his foreign policy stance as "tough" and opponents as "soft."[51] Years prior to the presidential campaign, Kennedy had begun to redefine the foreign policy debate. In August 1958, Kennedy initially challenged the Republican administration to account for a "missile gap" with the Soviet Union. Quoting an air force general, Kennedy warned that U.S. weapons stockpiles could no longer deter a Soviet attack. Two years later, Kennedy marshaled evidence from H. Rowan Gaither, Jr., of the Ford Foundation, to support this critique of the Eisenhower-Nixon defense policy.[52] While conservatives had blasted the Truman administration for failure to prevent communism from expanding into China and South Korea, liberals attacked the Republicans for losing ground to the Soviet military.

Kennedy furthered his hardliner anticommunist reputation with his aggressive, militant approach to communist Cuba. Since Cuba's 1959 revolution and President Fidel Castro's alliance with the Soviet Union occurred during the administration of Eisenhower and Nixon, Kennedy could hold the Republican Party responsible for communism's expansion to this island merely ninety miles from Florida. On October 19, Kennedy decided to pursue the "toughness against communism" label by calling for U.S. aid to anti-Castro "fighters for freedom [who] have had virtually no support from our government." After the *New York Times* published Kennedy's statement as a front-page headline, the two candidates clashed publicly on this topic in the fourth and final televised debate. Although Nixon had advocated an invasion of Cuba since mid-1959, Kennedy portrayed the Republican administration as delinquent by not acting more promptly and decisively against Cuban communism. Several liberal Protestants, such as pundit Walter Lippmann, protested Kennedy's intensified anticommunist rhetoric.[53] This assertion of aggressive resistance to communism, especially regarding an overwhelmingly Catholic nation, nonetheless challenged the charge that Kennedy abandoned the Catholic Church's uncompromising opposition to communism.

On Election Day, reporter Samuel Lubell suggested that religion indeed conditioned Catholic voters. In Lubell's interpretation, Catholics weighed anti-Catholicism greater than anticommunism: "Much of the Kennedy vote will be cast, not for the specific proposals he has voiced but for his personality and 'to break the barrier against a Catholic president.'"[54] Catholicism's strong resistance to anticommunism represented a spiritual imperative. But this group perceived the anti-Catholic attitudes expressed by right-wing Protestants as more immoral and more immediate than the global communist threat. Neither did this group choose to respond to the charges of Kennedy's shallowness of religious belief. Kennedy received more than 70 percent of the Catholic vote.[55]

The 1960 campaign's "Catholic issue" threatened to fracture America's anticommunist consensus, but Kennedy maintained support from both liberal and conservative Cold Warriors. Kennedy's attacks on right-wing anticommunists, who portrayed Protestant liberals as sympathetic to communism, relieved fears that a Catholic president would prompt a third world war by militancy toward the Soviet Union and People's Republic of China. Republican Catholics and non-Catholics sought to arouse Catholic outrage at Kennedy's apparent willingness to compromise with communism. Nixon refused to encourage these doubts about Kennedy's loyalty to his church's anticommunism. Confident that Kennedy's Catholicism guaranteed his freedom from communist wiles, many Catholics voted to overturn the unwritten law that no Catholics could occupy the White House.

Chapter Seven

Testing the "Bailey Thesis"

State-level Reactions to a Catholic Presidential Candidate in California, Georgia, Michigan, and New York

"The Catholic vote is far more important than its numbers—about one out of every four voters who turn out—because of its concentration in the key states and cities of the North," contended Theodore C. Sorensen, Massachusetts Senator John F. Kennedy's chief advisor, who catalyzed a controversial debate about American Catholics in his 1956 "Bailey Memorandum." In Sorensen's interpretation, fourteen states contained substantial Catholic populations that would vote overwhelmingly for a Catholic vice-presidential nominee. Sorensen included Michigan, New York, and California among these key "Catholic states" that would determine the presidential election. Although substantial anti-Catholic attitudes existed in the South, Georgia and the other southern states lacked sufficient electoral votes, Sorensen argued, to undermine a candidate's success. Sorensen concluded that the Catholic vote essentially could determine the election's results.[1]

At this time, some scholars resolutely rejected this theory about Catholicism's electoral role. Political analyst Louis H. Bean denied that religion represented an isolated factor in voter decisions. According to Bean's studies, a combination of elements determined electoral choices, and social scientists Dr. Ralph M. Goldman and Dr. John H. Romani discovered "no significant difference" in Catholic districts' support for Catholic and non-Catholic congressional candidates.[2] Since Kennedy failed to receive the vice-presidential nomination in 1956, however, these researchers could not generate data to test Sorensen's theory about religion's role in presidential campaigns. Would Kennedy's Catholicism determine the election results in critical states in 1960, proving Sorensen correct? Could certain states be defined as Catholic? Would non-Catholic states demonstrate anti-Catholic attitudes?

This chapter assesses religion's role in responses to Kennedy's candidacy within four states—California, Georgia, Michigan, and New York. Each indeed proved critical in the 1960 presidential campaign. Kennedy's political analyst, Louis Harris, described Catholicism as a crucial factor in all of these states. He viewed religion as the primary obstacle to Kennedy in California, noting that Catholicism "is easily the most frequent and most serious negative expressed about Senator Kennedy." Ten percent of California's Democrats vocalized hesitancy regarding Kennedy's religion.[3] In a state with eighty-one Democratic delegates and thirty-two electoral votes, California's voters would have a significant impact on Kennedy's attempts to secure the party nomination and presidency. Although California elected a Catholic governor, Edmund G. "Pat" Brown, in 1958, Harris viewed the state's potential for anti-Catholicism as a serious challenge for Kennedy. While some non-Catholics assumed Brown's 1960 loyalties would reside with Kennedy as a co-religionist, the governor's personal ambitions actually clashed with the Massachusetts senator's goals.

In Michigan, New York, and Georgia—states that Harris also noted as important for strategic reasons—religion played an indeterminate role. Harris described Michigan as "an integral part of the Northern chain of big electoral vote states swinging westward from Massachusetts to Missouri." Sorensen had identified Michigan and several midwestern states, such as Illinois and Ohio, among America's fourteen "Catholic states." Capturing Michigan's fifty-one-member Democratic delegation might prove "key" to the party's nomination, Harris argued, and the state's twenty electoral votes constituted a "significant" general election prize.[4] Although many Catholics lived and worked in Michigan, Protestant Democratic Governor G. Mennen Williams had remained in office since 1948. In the words of one Kennedy advisor, Williams consciously used religion to justify public policy, saying "He is a devout Episcopalian . . . [who] apparently sees himself as having been tapped to put the Sermon on the Mount into governmental practice."[5] Williams and State Party Chairman Neil Staebler initially withheld endorsement of any particular Democrat. These Michigan leaders wanted to sponsor a candidate they viewed as electable and who would reward their support with national recognition.

Harris described New York, another of Sorensen's "Catholic states," as "the most important prize of any Presidential Campaign." Since 1900, Harris noted, only two candidates won New York State and still lost the general election. In Harris' interpretation, this made New York's voters "pivotal and barometric."[6] New York liberals, such as former First Lady Eleanor Roosevelt, initially resisted the efforts of local Catholic officials, such as New York City Mayor Robert F. Wagner and state Democratic Party Chairman Carmine DeSapio, to nominate Kennedy for the presidency.

In Harris' interpretation, Georgia would present a challenge for Kennedy because of its small Catholic population and a predominant anti-Catholic sentiment. For much of the nation's history, southern states demonstrated firm loyalty to Democratic candidates, and Harris viewed Georgia's vote as "a portent of victory for the Democratic Party in such other states of the Solid South as Alabama, Mississippi, and Arkansas."[7] The Democratic Party worked as a virtual one-party system in these southern states, but anti-Catholicism threatened to undermine Kennedy's expected popularity in Georgia.

Unique local political circumstances conditioned reactions to a Catholic presidential candidate in the critical states California, Michigan, New York, and Georgia. These received substantial study by Kennedy's research team, and deserve exacting attention from historians.

California—Brown's Dilemma

Should Sorensen have included California among the nation's fourteen "Catholic states"? In 1960, several political and religious characteristics appeared to favor a Catholic presidential candidate in California. The state's registered Democrats outnumbered Republicans by one million voters, a three-to-two margin. Exceptional religious diversity characterized California's population, as well as the state's congressional delegation, which derived from nine separate denominations, including the Sikh religion.[8] Political anti-Catholicism received a major blow in the 1958 elections. A three-to-one Californian majority rejected a referendum to repeal tax exemptions for Catholic schools. In that same year, Catholic candidate Pat Brown received a one-million-vote majority for governor.[9] Brown's leadership of a majority Democratic state augured positively for Kennedy's prospects in the state.

Yet California's election of Brown obscured the significant challenges that a Catholic presidential candidate faced in that state. Catholics comprised a smaller ratio of California's voters than the national average.[10] This state's Protestant representatives to the U.S. Congress outnumbered Catholics by twenty-six to three. Political trends revealed increasing anti-Catholicism in the late 1950s. A successful legal battle to repeal the tax-exempt status of the Catholic Church's Christian Brothers Vineyard encouraged Californians who sought to restrict government partnership with Catholic institutions.[11] Although Californians elected a Catholic governor in 1958, the nonpartisan Fair Campaign Practices Committee specifically cited the state as emblematic of a "sharp and disquieting increase in anti-Catholicism" in that year's congressional elections. In the campaign to tax private and parochial schools, some pamphlets blamed Catholic schools for producing Mafia gangsters. If this motion had passed, California would have stood alone among the fifty states in taxing Catholic schooling.[12] In a state characterized by such intense religious debate, it would seem that a united front with Governor Brown would be essential to Kennedy's efforts in California, and thus his chances to obtain the Democratic Party presidential nomination and the presidency in November.

Kennedy needed to overcome liberal suspicion of Catholics within California based on his own, and his church's, attitude toward communism. Several California liberals blamed Catholics for supporting Republican Richard M. Nixon in the 1950 race for the U.S. Senate. Nixon portrayed his opponent, Hollywood actress Helen Gahagan Douglas, as "the pink lady" sympathetic to communism. Los Angeles Archbishop J. Francis McIntyre abetted Nixon's campaign that year by ordering all parish priests to address, in October sermons to parishioners, the dangers of communism in the U.S. government. Kennedy's father donated money to Nixon's campaign, and both father and son privately supported Nixon. Appealing to Californians for the vice-presidential nomination in 1956, Kennedy apologized to California party official and Beverly Hills tax lawyer Paul Ziffren, who had led fund-raising for Douglas' campaign. Calling his secret endorsement of Nixon "the biggest damnfool mistake I ever made," Kennedy still failed to attract California's liberals in that year.[13] Governor Brown's executive secretary, Frederick G. Dutton, recalled that at the Democratic National Convention, "[U.S. Senator from Minnesota Hubert] Humphrey's group was made up of liberals who especially could not take Kennedy—i.e., the Catholic aspect." Anti-Catholicism contributed to Kennedy's inability to secure the state delegates, Brown believed: "[The Masons] were affirmatively against [Kennedy]."[14]

While Brown proved important to Kennedy's presidential ambitions in California, the governor's own political goals discouraged an early endorsement of Kennedy. Brown's national aspirations fostered this initial reluctance to support Kennedy's campaign, which threatened to mobilize anti-Catholic attitudes in his state. Controversy about Catholicism might prevent all Catholic candidates from reaching the nation's highest office. About a year before the party convention, Pennsylvania's

Richard Graves and Brown's Executive Secretary Frederick Dutton discussed the California governor's own presidential prospects. Graves noted that Brown's ambitions would suffer if Democratic leaders characterized Catholics as unelectable: "[T]his is a real problem and one with which you must reckon."[15] Brown's political future on the national level was tied inextricably to Kennedy's.

Since the Democratic National Convention would never nominate Catholics to both positions on the national ticket, Graves portrayed Kennedy's presidential ambitions as a direct threat to Brown's pursuit of higher office. If Kennedy obtained the party nomination for either president or vice president, neither Brown nor another Catholic would receive consideration on the national ticket. Because Democratic leaders feared alienating non-Catholic voters by nominating two Catholics, Graves suggested that Brown should defend a Catholic's right to serve in the White House without actively promoting Kennedy's candidacy. In Graves' words, Brown needed "to overcome the carefully cultivated opposition to a Catholic nominee without handing Kennedy the nomination." Brown's personal ambition for the vice presidency rested on the rise of a non-Catholic, such as two-time presidential nominee Adlai Stevenson, as the party's standard bearer. Graves concluded, nonetheless, that Brown needed to defend Kennedy against anti-Catholicism, which could undermine Brown. Graves' recommendation amounted to cautious encouragement of Kennedy's campaign. According to Graves, "In a very peculiar sense, Pat has to sell Kennedy to sell Brown."[16] Kennedy's early success might convince Democrats to accept a Catholic presidential or vice-presidential candidate. The party's leadership might prefer Brown as a more mature Catholic than the precocious Massachusetts senator.

Events in February 1960 provided Brown with the opportunity to implement Graves' complex strategy. Meeting secretly with several Catholic Democrats to discuss the presidential campaign, Brown recalled standing alone in support of Kennedy despite the skepticism of New York City Mayor Robert Wagner, Pennsylvania Governor David L. Lawrence, Chicago Mayor Richard J. Daley, and Congressman William J. Green from Philadelphia. According to oral history interviews with Brown, the California governor backed Kennedy's candidacy without reservation despite the fears of these other Catholic politicians. "I was all-out for Kennedy. I thought he could win," Brown asserted. On the following day, Brown and Kennedy negotiated a deal. If the Massachusetts senator would bypass the California primary, Brown agreed not to pursue the vice-presidential nomination. In Brown's recollection, Kennedy perceived this agreement as pragmatic and sensible "because they're not going to put two Catholics on the ticket, that's a cinch."[17] The Democrats might risk an anti-Catholic backlash by nominating a popular Catholic presidential candidate. But a Kennedy-Brown campaign would instantly alarm those Americans who suspected a Catholic conspiracy to subvert U.S. democracy.

Brown's commitment therefore struck the delicate balance that Graves advised. Without Kennedy's competition in the state primary, Brown would likely receive state Democratic endorsement. This would elevate Brown's name among other potential presidential nominees. Brown's private, verbal commitment to Kennedy, furthermore, depended upon Kennedy's uncertain success in the party primaries. If Kennedy swept these Democratic contests, Brown would have earned potential leverage with the party's nominee. Kennedy's defeat by voters or party bosses, alternatively, could place Brown's name on a short-list of candidates for the vice presidency—the party's consolation prize to American Catholics.

Although this arrangement allowed Brown to win the state's Democratic primary, Kennedy's pursuit of the party's presidential nomination propagated suspicions of Catholics in California. Some observers accused Brown of political favoritism toward other Catholics, and of orchestrating a "secret pact" with Kennedy to guarantee Kennedy's endorsement by the California delegation.[18] Brown's legislative secretary, Alexander H. Pope, defended the governor from charges of special assistance to Catholic politicians and institutions. But Pope remained significantly silent about Brown's meeting with Kennedy.[19] Brown's surreptitious negotiations with Kennedy in February threatened to damage the governor's political popularity by giving credence to those who perceived a Catholic conspiracy.

Despite these allegations of religious pressures, Brown favored the Protestant Adlai Stevenson's nomination. In May and June, Brown denied any commitment to Kennedy's candidacy. Brown's substantial constituent correspondence contained both favor and disapproval of a Catholic presidential candidate. Brown answered all these letters with the ambivalent response that the California delegation's decision should embody "the wishes of the people of our State."[20] Media reports suggested that Brown refused to promote Kennedy's cause in the state delegation. Although Michigan's political leaders expected Brown to endorse Kennedy in early June, Brown's personal "man-in-the-street-poll" revealed that Stevenson enjoyed the majority of California Democrats' loyalty.[21] Sensitivity to California constituents may have discouraged Brown's open support for Kennedy's candidacy at this time. But

Brown also recognized that Stevenson's nomination would strengthen the California governor's chances to obtain the vice presidential nomination.

A state party rift in late June revealed Brown's political self-interest. The California governor's prospects for the vice presidential position on a Stevenson ticket threatened to breach the February agreement with Kennedy. Brown removed Paul Ziffren as California's national committeeman without explanation. Ziffren's 1958 efforts in liberal southern California significantly contributed to Brown's gubernatorial victory. But in 1960, Ziffren encouraged Kennedy to challenge Governor Brown's "favorite-son" candidacy. Brown appointed Attorney General Stanley Mosk to replace Ziffren. By offering no reason for this decision, Brown inspired suspicions about his true intentions.[22] Kennedy's ability to secure the support of Ziffren, Helen Gahagan Douglas' primary fund-raiser in the 1950 senate campaign, suggested that he had reconciled with liberals, who resented his support of Nixon in that race. Brown's attempt to block Kennedy's entry into the state's primary suggested that the Catholic governor would help Kennedy only when it would benefit his own political goals. By dismissing an early advocate of Kennedy's nomination, Brown betrayed his wavering commitment to Kennedy.

At the Democratic National Convention in Los Angeles, Brown's refusal to secure a monolithic voice from California's delegation angered both Kennedy's supporters and detractors. In early 1960, polling data suggested that Kennedy would beat Brown in the California primary. In exchange for Kennedy's promise not to challenge Brown in his home state, the California governor pledged support for the Catholic candidate under specific conditions. By the convention, Kennedy had met each of Brown's requirements: finish first in the three Democratic primaries—New Hampshire, Wisconsin, and West Virginia; place at least second in Oregon's primary (Kennedy won); and lead all other Democrats in the July Gallup poll.[23] Convention rallies for Stevenson, however, aroused Brown's personal and political ambitions. By July 12, the state delegation split, with Stevenson's supporters slightly outnumbering Kennedy's.[24] While the California governor endorsed Kennedy, Brown encouraged independent judgment from individual delegates.[25] Kennedy's brother and campaign manager Robert F. Kennedy recalled a sense of panic, as if "California was falling apart."[26] As a result, Kennedy only received thirty-three of California's eighty-one delegates. This delegation's opposition failed to prevent Kennedy's nomination on the first ballot, but this victory did not dispel his family's bitterness about Brown's failure to persuade California delegates to show greater support for Kennedy. According to California delegate Thomas Lynch, "I think the Kennedys always held that against Pat [Brown]. I know that [Kennedy Campaign Director Lawrence F.] O'Brien did."[27] If Kennedy and Brown had reached an agreement earlier in the campaign, each apparently conceived of the terms in a different manner.

California Attorney General Mosk assessed Brown's motives as personal and political. In Mosk's recollection, Brown privately hoped the convention would select a non-Catholic presidential candidate. According to Mosk, Brown's earlier negotiations with the Massachusetts senator did not bring the California governor into Kennedy's camp: "Pat was not enthusiastic for Kennedy." Brown maintained vice-presidential ambitions: "I think Pat secretly hoped that the nominee would be a typical, white Protestant. Then to balance the ticket they might well look for a Catholic governor, and that would be Pat."[28] Mosk's theory reflected the reasoning that Brown's supporter Richard Graves expressed in 1959. Brown hoped to dispel suspicions of a Catholic on the national ticket, but Kennedy's presidential nomination completely undermined Brown's prospects for the vice presidency.

Brown never admitted this ulterior motive, and blamed anti-Catholic attitudes for California's split delegation. In an oral history interview, the California governor recalled "a tremendous anti-Catholic feeling" among the state's delegates. Brown perceived these attitudes as based in pragmatic politics rather than theological disagreements or social prejudice characteristic of old, "right-wing Protestant sects." Nonetheless many "very active [Masons] just wouldn't go for Kennedy," Brown recalled. The Masonic Order and the Roman Catholic Church traditionally clashed over spiritual and temporal issues. In Brown's account, delegates from many religious perspectives questioned whether Kennedy could win a general election in a predominately Protestant nation: "[T]his feeling was shared by a lot of Catholics."[29] If Brown accurately described the delegation's multiple bitter divisions regarding Kennedy's religion, one could not expect unanimous support for Kennedy. But this explanation conveniently excused Brown from responsibility for Kennedy's failure to secure a majority of California's delegates.

After the convention, anti-Catholic attitudes encouraged some California Democrats to abandon the party in favor of Republican New York Governor Nelson Rockefeller. In July, a San Joaquin Valley group, Democrats for Rockefeller, lobbied California Republicans to nominate Rockefeller rather than Vice President Richard Nixon. According to the organization's secretary, C. P. Stevens, a San Joaquin County poll showed that "more than three times as many Democrats would leave Kennedy to support Rockefeller as would leave to support Nixon." Since California voter registration, as in many other states, favored the Democratic Party by a three to two margin, the GOP needed Democratic votes. Stevens openly appealed to anti-Catholicism in this campaign for Rockefeller's nomination, writing, "For those who may say that they would rather lose with Nixon we ask: 'Are you sure, considering the history of England before they outlawed Catholic kings, and other countries, that it is wise to set a precedent for Catholic presidents in the U.S.A.?'" If Republicans chose Rockefeller instead, Stevens argued, more than three times as many Democrats would eschew party loyalty in the general election.[30] In Stevens' interpretation, Nixon's praise of Catholic prelates in South America, "and elsewhere," discredited the vice president. Such compromise with Catholicism would also attract opposition, Stevens believed, "particularly in the South."[31] For those liberal Democrats who opposed Kennedy on religious grounds and Nixon as too conservative, Rockefeller seemed the most reasonable choice. If the more liberal Rockefeller captured the Republican nomination, author James A. Michener surmised, this would encourage anti-Catholic liberals to bolt the Democratic party. Michener's wife endorsed this theory by claiming that she would support Rockefeller before Kennedy.[32]

Despite the California governor's half-hearted support for Kennedy, the left-liberal *Nation* magazine editor Carey McWilliams credited prominent Catholic politicians, especially Brown, with securing Kennedy's nomination. In McWilliams' interpretation, Kennedy won without the support of the Democratic Party's traditional voter bases—labor unions, African Americans, farmers, Jews, intellectuals, or oil companies. Kennedy's victory depended upon the Irish Catholic political machines "in the big cities of the big states." Although Brown proved unable to secure the majority of California delegates, McWilliams particularly chastised Brown for supporting Kennedy "at zero hour" and refusing to release California's delegation. Using the term commonly applied to Adolf Hitler's seizure of power in 1930s Germany, McWilliams argued that California delegates should have blocked Kennedy's nomination: "Brown alone could have stopped the Kennedy *putsch*." Brown's support for Kennedy defied the California governor's personal polling data that revealed Stevenson's "remarkable strength" in that state. Citing a rumored meeting between Brown and Joseph P. Kennedy in Lake Tahoe, McWilliams explained Brown's convention behavior as motivated by service to the Kennedys: "[I]t is hard to escape the conclusion that Brown had a working agreement with Senator

Kennedy from the outset."[33] McWilliams' accusations confirmed conspiracy theories that religious loyalty motivated Brown's convention behavior.

Protestant minister and pamphleteer Dan Gilbert specifically attributed Brown's endorsement of Kennedy to clerical pressure. In Gilbert's view, Brown submitted to a papal conspiracy for Kennedy's election: "Rome ordered Brown to cut his own throat, and that is what he obediently did." According to Gilbert, Brown's sudden endorsement of Kennedy, after supporting Stevenson since 1952, demonstrated the Catholic hierarchy's power over individual Catholics. Brown and Pennsylvania Governor David Lawrence, Gilbert argued, acted with political independence before the 1960 Convention. At this point, however, the Vatican seized "the Papal ring in their noses."[34] Gilbert's publications encouraged readers to view Catholic politicians, such as Brown, as motivated by religious rather than patriotic loyalties. While few respected political observers would give credence to this theory of a Catholic cabal, the distribution of this idea in the *Nation* and other venues threatened Kennedy's attempt to dispel fears of papal power in the United States.

Perhaps fueled by this notion of a Catholic conspiracy, Kennedy's religion prompted substantial discussion during the Catholic candidate's early September visit to California. In a letter to Kennedy, a San Jose lawyer expressed fear that "Stevensonites" refused to support a Catholic presidential candidate: "If these people had had their choice certainly you would not be the nominee."[35] Democrats exceeded Republicans in the 500-mile Central Valley's official voter registration, and Stevenson secured many of this region's voters in 1956. But leaders of both parties admitted that religious attitudes conditioned the Valley's response to Kennedy. As the *New York Times* reported, "During a two-day survey of the valley, by automobile and telephone, almost every political leader and rank-and-file voter who was interviewed for more than thirty seconds voluntarily broached the subject of religion."[36] Californians' preoccupation with Kennedy's Catholicism alarmed Democrats.

Anti-Catholicism declined in political importance for Californians after major California newspapers rallied behind the cause of religious tolerance in response to the two pivotal September events: Protestant minister Norman Vincent Peale's assertion that a Catholic president would succumb to Vatican pressures, and Kennedy's defense of religious liberty before the Greater Houston Ministerial Association. An editorial in the Democratic *San Francisco Chronicle* strongly and animatedly criticized Peale's comments. A nearby political cartoon depicted Peale as a first-century Roman emperor releasing a hungry lion, labeled "Religious Bias," to an arena where the helpless Kennedy awaits. Comparing Peale's attacks on Kennedy to imperial Rome's persecution of Christians in gladiator spectacles, the caption asked, "Didn't this go out of style 1900 years ago?"[37] Kennedy's address to Protestant ministers in Houston prompted editors at the Republican *San Diego Union* to repudiate religion's role in the campaign. These writers advocated religious faith without specifying adherence to one particular denomination: "His belief in God is important, his form of expressing it is not."[38] Adjacent to this editorial, a drawing of the Statue of Liberty bore the words from the Constitution's Article VI, which opposed religious tests for public office.[39]

Peale's offensive and Kennedy's subsequent defense generally silenced anti-Catholic critics while inspiring Catholic support for Kennedy. Michigan Governor G. Mennen Williams toured California in September, and noted little discussion of the religious issue—"in fact hardly [any] at all." Williams instead chronicled growing Catholic resentment of anti-Catholicism. Peale's well-publicized warnings of papal pressures particularly bothered and mobilized Catholics: "Loyola (Catholic) College was apathetic until Peale, then real political interest."[40] These attacks on Catholicism encouraged an already defensive Catholic population to rally behind Kennedy. In early October, Democratic National Chairman Henry M. Jackson received reports from chairpersons in Richmond, Riverside, Onondaga, and San Joaquin counties, but none made reference to the religious issue. If the Democratic nominee faced significant religious opposition, this would have surely appeared in these letters. Only Orange County's chairman requested printed material that explained Kennedy's position on church-state relations.[41]

Samuel Lubell also recognized California Catholics' increasing resentment of religious prejudice. In Lubell's analysis, public expressions of suspicion about a Catholic president fostered a "surge of anger" that might translate into a "Religious Spite Vote." Even before Peale's comments, 70 percent of Catholics favored Kennedy. Of those Catholics who supported Eisenhower in 1956, only about 33 percent, Lubell estimated, would vote for Nixon in 1960.[42] Catholic voters had shown strong affinity for Nixon in earlier campaigns, such as his victory over actress Helen Gahagan Douglas in the 1950 California Senate race.[43] Nixon's appeal to Catholic voters, therefore, should have equaled Eisenhower's. After encountering reports of anti-Catholic prejudice, however, many Catholic Americans now wanted to see a Catholic in the

White House. A Los Angeles housewife, for example, opposed Kennedy's union associates, such as United Auto Workers President Walter Reuther, but concluded, "it would be wonderful to show that a Catholic can be elected president."[44] Unregulated discussion of religion resulted in Catholic defensiveness. Responding to social ostracism and alienation, Catholics felt increasing solidarity toward Kennedy as a co-religionist.

However, anti-Catholicism contributed to Kennedy's failure to win California. Despite superior Democratic registration in California, Kennedy failed to carry this important western state. Earlier in election night, Governor Brown predicted an 800,000-vote majority for Kennedy.[45] But California, Nixon's home state, provided the Republican nominee with a 40,000-vote plurality.[46] Nixon received substantial pluralities in San Francisco, Alameda County, and San Diego County. In Los Angeles County, a liberal Protestant stronghold, Nixon's total exceeded Republican registration by 140,000 votes.[47] Anti-Catholic attitudes may also explain Kennedy's poor performance in California's agrarian Central Valley, especially Fresno and Bakersfield, where Nixon surpassed Eisenhower's 1956 returns.[48]

Despite this evidence, several election observers deny that religion played the decisive role in Kennedy's failure to win California. Political analyst Kevin P. Phillips, who later advised Nixon in the 1968 presidential campaign, has argued that anti-Catholicism was only one of several factors that explained this movement away from the Democratic candidate. Rural white voters in this "Pacific Interior" expressed increasing resentment at government programs that benefited urban areas and minority groups. In this region, Phillips even found socially conservative Irish, German, and Italian Americans who similarly perceived Democrats as excessively liberal.[49] In Phillips' interpretation, religion alone could not explain Nixon's victory.

A *Los Angeles Times* editorial blamed California's governor, not anti-Catholicism, for Kennedy's defeat. Responding to Governor Brown's claim that anti-Catholic attitudes undermined Kennedy in California, the editorialist credited Nixon's victory to the vice president's popularity and the state Republican Party's superior organization. As evidence of Californians' freedom from religious prejudice, the author noted that the Catholic Brown received substantial non-Catholic support in two 1950s races for attorney general and governor. Entitled "Pat Brown's Phony Alibi," the editorial suggested that the governor advanced religious bias as an excuse for his personal failure to secure the state for Kennedy.[50] Indeed, Brown had also cited anti-Catholic attitudes to justify his inability to persuade the entire Democratic state delegation to endorse Kennedy at the 1960 Democratic National Convention.

Governor Brown's ambiguous response to Kennedy's Catholicism closely reflected the behavior of many Californians. Pat Brown's perception of this ambitious Catholic candidate as a political adversary discouraged him from pressing for the California delegation's unanimous support of Kennedy at the convention. Governor Brown also feared that Kennedy's candidacy would inspire anti-Catholicism. Heightened religious bigotry would undermine the governor's later political ambitions, Brown feared. Brown's lukewarm response to Kennedy contributed to the Catholic candidate's failure to secure this predominately Democratic state in the general election. Catholicism had a complex, contradictory impact on California, which did not resemble Sorensen's description of a "Catholic State."

Michigan—Driving Over Bigotry with the Democratic Machine

While California demonstrated indistinct responses to Kennedy's Catholicism, Michigan showed more promising signs for a Catholic presidential candidate. If Sorensen's theory about a Catholic bloc vote proved correct, Kennedy could expect to garner Michigan's electoral votes. Catholics represented 22 percent of the state's population and 33 percent of Michigan's U.S. congressmen.[51] Detroit's Wayne County elected Catholics to four of six congressional seats.[52] By 1960, both U.S. senators from Michigan were Catholic. The state's Democratic coalition in the 1950s depended significantly on Catholic political participation. In the 1958 congressional elections, midwestern Catholics voted for Democratic candidates by 23 percentage points more than did Protestants. Three of four Catholic voters endorsed Democrats. Gallup Poll managing editor John M. Fenton estimated that Catholic voters cost Republicans twenty-four to forty congressional seats.[53]

Kennedy's presidential ambitions in Michigan largely depended on the support of a Democratic "triumvirate"—National Committeeman Neil C. Staebler, United Auto Workers President Walter P. Reuther, and Governor G. Mennen Williams. Kennedy would need active support from these Democrats to overcome several challenges to a Catholic Democrat in that state. Many Michigan residents had welcomed the anti-Catholic American Protective Association in the 1890s and the Ku

Klux Klan in the 1920s.[54] Michigan's Republicans, who dominated state politics prior to 1948, still contested Democrats for state power. In 1960, the Republican Party also enjoyed an eleven to seven advantage in Michigan's delegation to the U.S. Congress. A powerful GOP, pro-business constituency resisted the Democratic public works programs. Since 1948, however, a liberal-labor political machine constructed an alliance that elected Williams to six consecutive, two-year gubernatorial terms.[55]

Would Governor Williams campaign actively for a Catholic presidential candidate? Several Michigan residents sought the leadership of Williams, as a Christian liberal, against a Catholic presidential candidate.[56] Despite not having endorsed Kennedy in early 1960, Williams refused to accept the suggestion that religion should disqualify the Catholic candidate. "I am not participating in this debate because I feel that a man's qualifications for the Presidency have nothing to do with his race, his color, or his religious beliefs," Williams responded to one anti-Catholic letter.[57] Williams' unqualified intolerance of anti-Catholicism demonstrated magnanimity and courage. In contrast to Governor Brown, however, Williams experienced no immediate political threat from a Kennedy candidacy. Kennedy's potential presidential nomination might even allow consideration of the Michigan governor—who had declined the opportunity to pursue a seventh term—for appointment to a cabinet position or even the vice presidency.

Williams' defense of Kennedy did not initially translate into an endorsement by Michigan's Democratic leadership. Williams and Neil Staebler pledged delegate support for Minnesota Senator Hubert H. Humphrey if he won the April Wisconsin primary.[58] Humphrey's liberal credentials and geographical proximity as a fellow midwesterner cultivated favor with Michigan politicians. In March, nonetheless, the Michigan governor negotiated terms upon which he could endorse Kennedy. Williams received Kennedy's commitment of a cabinet position in exchange for the Michigan governor's support at the party's national convention.[59]

This agreement solidified Williams' support despite continued criticism of Kennedy's religious affiliation in Michigan. Fifty Michigan residents signed a letter that accused the National Catholic Welfare Council of dominating America's legislative agenda.[60] More than two hundred individuals endorsed a petition, sent to the governor, that opposed the presidential nomination of a Roman Catholic.[61] Despite these constituent pressures, Williams continued to repudiate skepticism about the prospect of a Catholic president. At this point, this state's powerful liberal-labor leadership withheld an endorsement, but refused to tolerate criticism of Kennedy's religion.

After Kennedy's April Wisconsin primary victory against Humphrey, Michigan's Democratic leaders viewed the Catholic candidate as the most likely liberal to gain the party's nomination. Democratic National Committeeman Neil Staebler even began to orchestrate general election strategy regarding the religious issue. The Michigan Council of Christian Churches (MCCC) director of general operations, Harold C. McKinney, volunteered to act as liaison between Democrats and the state's Protestant ministers. Staebler encouraged McKinley's plans for a September MCCC conference on the 1960 election. In Staebler's opinion, this might serve as "a dramatic means of responding to the misgivings of many people on the intrusion of the religious issue in the campaign."[62] Such foresight demonstrated Staebler's confidence in Kennedy's ability to secure the party nomination.

By winning the West Virginia and Oregon primaries with little competition, Kennedy convinced the Michigan triumvirate to wager on the Catholic candidate. According to journalist Theodore White, "the Massachusetts Senator had proved himself a clean, hard, organizational fighter in Staebler's terms; had given his commitments and friendship to labor clearly enough to satisfy Reuther; and had passed all of Williams' tests of liberalism and humanitarianism." Kennedy's offer of a cabinet post to Williams surely helped secure the endorsement of Michigan's Democratic leadership. Kennedy traveled to Michigan on June 2 to receive formal approval from Williams, who claimed to represent the "majority" opinion of Michigan's fifty-one delegates. According to Theodore White, Williams' authority over the state delegation resembled Soviet Premier Nikita Khrushchev's command of the one-party Supreme Soviet.[63] *Presidential Preview*, a Michigan-based newsletter that covered the presidential primaries and party conventions, reported that Williams had questioned the Catholic candidate on both McCarthyism and "technical" issues regarding religion and church-state separation. After this session, the Michigan governor "repeatedly" denied that religion would hamper Kennedy's general election campaign.[64] Although Williams had declared religion's irrelevance to the campaign several times, he likely issued this statement to allay any lingering, liberal fears about a Catholic presidential candidate. Kennedy may have even requested this statement from Williams. While Governor Brown remained suspiciously silent about the Catholic issue, Michigan Democrats lobbied aggressively against anti-Catholic attitudes.

After Kennedy's presidential nomination at the national convention, Staebler mobilized the state's party officials to confront the "Catholic issue." In a memorandum to Michigan county chairmen, Staebler provided standardized, specific "procedure for handling scurrilous literature." Each county was instructed to appoint a "Committee on Honest Elections," which would accumulate anti-Catholic literature or "any suspect pieces of material." These committees would forward anti-Catholic pamphlets and letters to the local Fair Campaign Practices Committee or the Michigan Fair Election Practices Commission. County headquarters should also create a "Crackpot Corner," which would display the most outrageous, bigoted publications.[65] In a broader mailing, Staebler enclosed excerpts of Kennedy's September speech to Houston's ministers as well as facts about Catholicism to use as replies to "meet these vicious, un-American attacks." Asking Democrats to forward published hate material—"so that we can determine the size of this movement"—Staebler also requested that recipients of anti-Catholic bigotry send this material to the Michigan Fair Election Practices Commission.[66] By publicizing the most outrageous examples of extreme anti-Catholicism, the state's Democratic Party machine served the Catholic candidate's goal of portraying such sentiments as those of a lunatic fringe.

Michigan's Protestant ministers, mainstream media, and public opinion proved favorable toward the Catholic candidate. Norman Vincent Peale's suggestion that a Catholic president would encounter Vatican pressures encouraged some debate within the MCCC. Methodist Bishop and MCCC President Marshall R. Reed defended Peale from criticism.[67] MCCC's director of general operations Harold McKinney, however, repudiated Peale's comments as divisive: "If it is not kept within bounds, the religious question can tear us apart."[68] While Michigan Protestants demonstrated diverse reaction to Kennedy's Catholicism, no prominent ministers publicly opposed Kennedy on religious grounds. The opinion pages of Detroit newspapers supported McKinney's view. In September, a *Detroit Free Press* illustration depicted "Religious, Racial Bigotry" as a hurricane that threatened a frightened Uncle Sam, the symbol of American patriotism.[69] The *Detroit News* published two editorial cartoons that respectively portrayed the religious issue as a snake and a skunk.[70] Public opinion reflected a general rejection of anti-Catholicism in Michigan. In mid-October, a *Detroit News* poll reported a substantial 53 to 46 percent advantage for Kennedy. Catholic resentment of attacks on Kennedy's religion may have contributed to the Democratic nominee's favorable numbers. Eighty percent of Michigan Catholics endorsed Kennedy, suggesting his ability to secure a comfortable victory in that state.[71]

Despite the success of Staebler's party organization, Kennedy's Michigan supporters also prompted a backlash against one pamphlet that took the religion issue a bit too far. A United Auto Workers (UAW) enclosure in the union's magazine *Solidarity* generated outrage by portraying the election as a contest between freedom and prejudice. In bold, threatening letters, the cover stated "Liberty or Bigotry? Which Do You Choose?" The accompanying graphic depicted an image of intolerance, a torch-bearing Ku Klux Klansmen, opposite the Statue of Liberty, America's symbol of acceptance and freedom to immigrants. Republicans interpreted this pamphlet as an intentional smear of Kennedy's opponents. This overly simplistic analysis portrayed Nixon's supporters as racists and bigots, in order to promote sympathy for Kennedy. Only a vote for the Catholic candidate, the image implied, would prove America's commitment to openness and tolerance of diversity. Even President Dwight D. Eisenhower, who had campaigned infrequently for Nixon, entered this debate, calling this publication "evil propaganda."[72] Such blatant attempts to exploit guilt about anti-Catholic prejudice did inspire a minor Protestant backlash, but one that did not have serious repercussions.

Michigan's Democratic leadership effectively managed the religious issue in 1960, but religion's role remains ambiguous in that state. Kennedy won a mere 67,000-vote majority in Michigan despite several favorable conditions for a Catholic candidate in that state.[73] Kennedy enjoyed strong support from Catholic cities, such as Detroit, as well as areas around Lake Huron, Lake Michigan, and Lake Superior that harbored many Catholics.[74] The leadership of Michigan's Democratic triumvirate proved critical to Kennedy's success. Governor Williams persuaded many non-Catholic liberals that Kennedy would defend liberalism. Unlike Governor Brown, Williams viewed Kennedy less as a rival than as an ally. (While he expected at least an appointment to a cabinet position, such as secretary of Health, Education, and Welfare for these efforts, Williams accepted appointment as assistant secretary of state for African Affairs.)[75] Staebler's party organization mobilized effectively against anti-Catholic literature. At some point, the state's Democratic Party organization may have been too effective. President Eisenhower chose to make a late entry into the campaign by denouncing Reuther's UAW pamphlet that portrayed the election as a choice between "Liberty or Bigotry." This incident likely inspired an anti-Kennedy backlash, certainly among those non-Catholics who had petitioned Governor Williams to oppose Kennedy on religious grounds.

New York—A Legitimate "Catholic State"

Among the fourteen states that Sorensen's memo labeled as "Catholic states," New York offered several characteristics that appeared to favor Kennedy's candidacy. New York City Catholics traditionally dominated Tammany Hall, the urban Democratic political machine. Through political patronage and recruitment of immigrant voters, Tammany Hall bosses nurtured strong loyalty among the city's Democrats. This organization had elevated a poor, Catholic youth from Brooklyn, Alfred E. Smith, to the state legislature, the governor's office, and even the Democratic nomination for president in 1928. John Kennedy's father, Joseph P. Kennedy, maintained close political connections with Democratic National Committeeman and Tammany Hall boss Carmine DeSapio, Bronx Congressman Charles A. Buckley, and New York Democratic Party Chairman Michael H. Prendergast. In 1960, Catholics constituted 30 to 35 percent of the state's population, while Protestants represented less than 40 percent. Catholics occupied more than a third of New York's U.S. congressional seats, and 50 percent of those representing New York City.[76] This city's five boroughs contained about one million Irish Catholic voters, and 3.2 million total registered voters. Since the rest of the state's registration equaled only 3.9 million, an overwhelmingly pro-Kennedy urban vote could counter rural returns, which typically favored the GOP. Even outside the city, Catholics represented an important electoral constituency. Suburban Catholic voter registration increased 33 percent from 1956 to 1960. The predominately Protestant, rural regions in the north also contained largely Catholic cities, such as Buffalo and Rochester.[77] New York's 114 delegates to the Democratic National Convention represented one seventh of the total required for nomination, and the state held forty-five electoral votes that would significantly affect the national results.[78]

Despite these advantages, Kennedy encountered several potential forces of opposition in New York. Al Smith failed to win his home state in the 1928 presidential campaign. As 1960 approached, nationally known liberal reformers—former First Lady Eleanor Roosevelt, onetime U.S. Senator Herbert H. Lehman, and past Secretary of the Air Force Thomas K. Finletter—challenged the state's largely Catholic

Democratic leadership. According to author Theodore H. White, a "vast . . . gulf" existed between New York's intellectuals and the state's Democratic Party machine.[79] Kennedy pollster Louis Harris predicted "internecine warfare" between these two Democratic factions. Kennedy lacked strong support from New York liberals, who promoted two-time party presidential nominee Adlai Stevenson for a third attempt at the presidency. Despite denying anti-Catholic motives, liberal Protestants and Jews threatened Kennedy's bid to control New York's delegation to the party's national convention.[80]

Kennedy also faced a Republican-dominated state leadership. New York Republicans occupied the governorship and both U.S. Senate seats. While the two parties remained virtually even in U.S. congressional seats, the GOP also outnumbered Democrats in the state legislature. Two Catholic Democrats had recently failed to win election to the U.S. Senate from New York. A Jewish candidate, Jacob K. Javits, defeated Catholic Robert F. Wagner in 1956, and Presbyterian Kenneth B. Keating won a slim 1958 plurality over Catholic Frank S. Hogan. Republican Governor Nelson A. Rockefeller even received consideration as the Republican's 1960 presidential nominee. Republican President Dwight D. Eisenhower carried this state in 1952 and 1956.[81]

Eleanor Roosevelt lobbied for the presidential nomination of Adlai Stevenson, but the state's Catholic political leaders limited liberal power in the New York delegation. When Michigan's Democratic leadership prepared to endorse Kennedy in May, Eleanor Roosevelt confidentially lobbied Governor Williams against the Catholic candidate. Committed to Adlai Stevenson and unconvinced of Kennedy's experience and maturity, Mrs. Roosevelt claimed to have received several letters expressing a growing national desire for Stevenson.[82] Some anti-Kennedy letters appealed to Roosevelt for leadership against a Catholic president.[83] Yet Roosevelt's political weakness was revealed in liberals' inability to break the Catholic machine politicians' hold on the state's delegation to the Democratic National Convention. A challenge from Stevenson's supporters failed to remove New York Party Chairman Michael Prendergast, and liberal former Governor Lehman could not even secure a seat on the New York delegation.[84]

Did anti-Catholicism motivate Roosevelt's opposition to Kennedy? Manhattan architect and Kennedy supporter Peter Blake asserted that this was indeed the case.[85] In 1928, Roosevelt actively supported Catholic presidential candidate and New York Governor Alfred E. Smith. According to close friend Joseph Lash, however, an anti-Catholic "part of her Protestant heritage" existed "deep in her subconscious." Historian Allida Black suggested that Roosevelt feared the

Catholic Church "as a temporal institution." Roosevelt's public and acrid disagreements with Catholic New York Archbishop Francis Spellman had left "scars" and inspired mistrust. As previously noted, Roosevelt strongly opposed the American Catholic hierarchy's pursuit of government assistance to Catholic schools. In 1949, Spellman publicly characterized Roosevelt's denial of federal aid to parochial school children as anti-Catholicism "unfit for an American mother."[86] Historian David Burner associated Mrs. Roosevelt's mistrust of Catholics with antipathy toward Wisconsin Senator Joseph R. McCarthy.[87] Kennedy's family connections to both Spellman and McCarthy certainly contributed to her misgivings. According to authors Peter Collier and David Horowitz, Roosevelt believed that Kennedy "had never satisfactorily dealt with questions posed by his Catholicism."[88] Despite expressing confidence that a Catholic could become president by showing an ability to maintain church-state separation, Roosevelt in May 1958 was "not sure Kennedy could do this."[89] In a 1960 statement to the Associated Press, she repeated this same doubt about Kennedy.[90]

Just as California Governor Pat Brown felt ambivalent about the prospect of an anti-Catholic response to Kennedy, New York's Catholic leaders viewed the Catholic presidential candidate as problematic. Kennedy's candidacy threatened the ambitions of New York's Catholic politicians Carmine DeSapio and New York City Mayor Robert Wagner. Having pursued the Democratic nomination for vice president in 1956, Wagner could not hope that the convention would select a Catholic as a running mate for Kennedy. If Democrats nominated a Catholic for president, furthermore, the party would need to select a non-Catholic National Chairman despite DeSapio's pursuit of this post.[91] But Connecticut National Committeeman and Kennedy loyalist John Bailey had lobbied upstate New York politicians, such as Erie (Buffalo) County Chairman Peter Crotty and New York Democratic State Secretary Ben Wetzler, since 1959. Joseph Kennedy brokered deals with Congressman Charles Buckley of the Bronx and Eugene J. Keogh of Brooklyn.[92] In Michael Prendergast's recollection, the elder Kennedy "sent a lot of people in to donate money to the state organization, which we used for Jack's election."[93] In the words of journalist Theodore White, New York's Democratic politicians could only "scramble aboard the rolling bandwagon with what little grace and dignity they could muster."[94] The Kennedy's financial power proved sufficient to hold these politicians' personal ambitions in check, at least for the duration of the 1960 campaign.

As the senior Kennedy lobbied Catholic politicians in New York, candidate Kennedy actively appealed to this state's liberals. In an address to New York's Liberal Party, Kennedy implied that liberals and Catholics might form a powerful alliance against the conservative South. As liberals pressured for African American integration in white-dominated southern states, Kennedy announced the goal of winning the Democratic Party's nomination without a single southern ballot. Such strategy appeared to challenge Democrats' traditional reliance on "the Solid South." In one interpretation, Kennedy had jettisoned southern voters to pursue the unanimous support of American Catholics. This theory bothered those who hoped to unify Democrats around liberal issues, "not regional, traditional, or religious emotions." A few even perceived Catholic conspirators lurking behind this plan: "[The] proposed realignment *requires* that Kennedy [as a Catholic] head the ticket." Therefore, the party would "be committed *indefinitely* to nominating Catholic candidates for President simply to hold the new coalition together, and with little or no regard to issues."[95] Such hysterical views relegated both southerners and Catholics as unfit for leadership and potentially threatening to liberal authority.

Other New York liberals, however, rejected such extreme fears of Catholicism and endorsed Kennedy's liberalism. U.S. Congressman Chester Bowles (CT), Kennedy's choice for platform committee chairman, created a Democratic plank that advocated expanded civil rights legislation. This liberal victory encouraged several non-Catholics, such as former Governor Averell Harriman, to support Kennedy in New York's delegate caucus.[96] Another New York delegate, Franklin D. Roosevelt, Jr., had endorsed Kennedy's candidacy. Despite his mother's objections, FDR, Jr., had helped Kennedy overcome anti-Catholic opposition by campaigning with the Catholic candidate prior to the West Virginia primary.[97] At a New York Liberal Party dinner, Kennedy's wife Jacqueline secured the support of Protestant theologian Reinhold Niebuhr, who happily confirmed after several hours of conversation, "She's read every book I ever wrote."[98] New York's Liberal Party Chairman Paul Hays listed Kennedy, along with Stevenson and Missouri Senator Stuart Symington, as a legitimate liberal. These particular New York liberals perceived Kennedy as ideologically acceptable, and electable. By month's end, eighty-seven of the state's one hundred and fourteen Democratic delegates endorsed the Catholic candidate.[99] Left-wing mistrust of Kennedy's Catholicism failed to disrupt the formation of a liberal-Catholic coalition behind his candidacy.

Economic factors combined with the "Catholic issue" to frustrate Nixon's pursuit of voters in New York's staunchly Republican, and predominately Protestant, upstate counties. Recession in this region's heavily Catholic cities fostered deep discontent with Republican leadership. Unemployment exceeded 6 percent in Buffalo, Albany, Schenectady, Utica, Troy, and Amsterdam. In this context, financial motives reinforced Catholics' religious sympathies toward Kennedy. Democrats encouraged Catholics in these cities to identify with Kennedy by rebroadcasting the Catholic candidate's televised September speech to Houston's ministers. The image of Kennedy "in the lion's den of Houston Protestant preachers"—according to *Time* magazine—made the Democratic nominee appear as a courageous opponent of religious bigotry. Republicans disliked this apparent exploitation of Catholics' emotional resentment of anti-Catholic prejudice. Persistent anti-Catholicism nonetheless frustrated Republican attempts to change the topic. A Rome, New York, GOP leader lamented; "Every time one of those blankety-blank Southerners opens his mouth about the Catholic Church, we lose 20 votes for Nixon up here." Any Catholic inroads into the upstate vote would impair Republican attempts "to offset downstate Democratic pluralities."[100] As Catholics increasingly identified with Kennedy for economic and religious reasons, Nixon's prospects for New York appeared bleak.

Kennedy's Catholicism also proved significant in New York City's typically Republican suburbs. Reporter Samuel Lubell's mid-October study of fifty precincts surrounding the city revealed that Kennedy procured at least 20 percent of those voters who supported Eisenhower in 1956. Nassau and Westchester counties had provided the incumbent president with critical votes in that year. Thirty-five percent of Eisenhower's support in New York had come from these two counties.[101] Catholics represented 60 percent of newcomers in these "traditionally rich and two-thirds Republican" regions. Nixon still appeared likely to win New York's suburbs, but these recent Catholic arrivals could reduce the Republican margin of victory in the suburbs.[102] Lubell discovered that only 6 percent of suburban non-Catholics endorsed Kennedy. Yet Nixon needed to reverse this Catholic trend toward a co-religionist in order to win the state.[103]

New York did demonstrate many characteristics of a "Catholic state" in 1960. Manhattan's elite liberal, "Silk Stocking" district demonstrated resistance to Kennedy's candidacy, but Catholics in New York's cities, suburbs, and rural counties provided Kennedy with more than enough votes to carry this state.[104] Despite the Democratic Party's internal divisions, Kennedy's father proved able to unite Democrats around the Catholic candidate. Liberals agreed that Catholics could serve as useful allies in securing a nominee that rejected the conservative politics of the Democratic Party in the South. Democrats also attracted

Catholic resentment against anti-Catholicism, especially after Kennedy's Houston speech to Protestant ministers. Machine politics and resentment about anti-Catholicism allowed the state's Catholics to give Kennedy New York's substantial electoral votes—which voters had denied Al Smith in 1928.

Georgia—Party Loyalty in the "Solid South"

In the 1956 "Bailey Memorandum," Sorensen deemphasized southern states, such as Georgia, which comparatively lacked large populations and controlled substantially fewer electoral votes. But Georgia's consistent support of Democratic presidential nominees provided this party's candidates with a consistent southern base of support. The Democrats' essentially one-party rule in these states also allowed Democrats to pursue the electoral votes of more closely contested states. Although polling research revealed that 30 percent of Southerners would not support a Catholic Democratic presidential nominee in any circumstance, survey data also suggested that anti-Catholicism primarily existed among poorly educated individuals who rarely voted.[105] Kennedy's choice of U.S. Senate Majority Leader Lyndon B. Johnson (TX), a political apprentice of longtime Senator Richard B. Russell (GA), seemed likely to reassure many Georgia Democrats.[106]

Despite Democratic Party domination of Georgia politics, Catholicism remained alien to most Georgians. This state's less than 1 percent Catholic minority generally proved unwilling or unable to challenge anti-Catholic assumptions and attitudes. Georgia's heavily Baptist and Methodist citizenry harbored deep-seated structural and theological disagreements with the Roman Catholic Church. Conservative evangelicals resented Catholic resistance to Protestant missionaries in Latin America. Southern Baptists, who democratically elected local pastors, mistrusted the Roman Catholic hierarchy that ruled a global church from a distant, European, and sovereign state.[107] To secure Georgians' endorsement, Kennedy needed to persuade Baptists and Methodists to overlook these fundamental religious disagreements.

Early analysis suggested that Kennedy's religious affiliation could prove fatal to the Catholic candidate in southern states. In Georgia, journalist Samuel Lubell discovered evidence that Kennedy's nomination might undermine Democratic strength in the predominately Protestant, "Solid South." Lubell's lengthy, detailed interviews with local residents revealed latent anti-Catholicism among many Georgians. For example, a retired Atlanta railroad engineer weakly disguised his mistrust of Catholics: "I'm against Kennedy. But I'm not going to explain why. You might be a Catholic." If many others shared this reluctance to express openly anti-Catholic attitudes, resistance to Kennedy might exceed the substantial percentage exposed by survey research. According to Lubell, religious opposition to Kennedy's candidacy might allow Richard Nixon to sweep Georgia, and perhaps the South: "If Sen. Kennedy were nominated, anti-Catholic defections could provide the extra margin that might swing some Southern states to Mr. Nixon."[108]

Kennedy also encountered open, even combative, anti-Catholicism in Georgia. Prior to 1960, Georgians mobilized against the prospect of a Catholic president. In the city of Albany in the state's southwest, a Catholic sent advertisements for public lectures to the Kennedy campaign to give them an idea of what they were up against—these were entitled "Immorality of the Catholic System" and "Roman Catholicism Un-American."[109] In a letter to Kennedy, Decatur resident Mary F. McCay accused him of dual loyalties, asserting that "your FIRST allegiance is to a foreign political power, which . . . hides behind a cloak of Religion."[110] In April 1960, McCay urged former President Harry S. Truman to lead resistance to the Catholic candidate: "[T]his is not bigotry, but necessary action to keep our country free from oppressive rule."[111] An Atlanta minister published and distributed a sermon entitled, "Can A Loyal Catholic Be A Good President of the United States?" This pamphlet's cover depicted a closely cropped, well-dressed white man, labeled "Rest of Us," obsequiously kissing the foot of a regal, crowned, and Italian-featured pope.[112] This image of humble obedience to a kingly figure implied that Kennedy's election would dramatically alter America's character and liberty. Such stern suspicion of a Catholic president graphically authenticated polling data that exposed Georgia's widespread anti-Catholicism.

Democratic Party strength and economic class consciousness offered a potential counterbalance to anti-Catholicism in Georgia. Samuel Lubell's analysis of religion's role in the West Virginia primary showed that the "overwhelming majority" expressed willingness to support a Catholic Democrat in November. "Intense party loyalty," Lubell argued, superseded any religious skepticism toward Kennedy in West Virginia. Confidence in the Democratic Party's financial policies specifically discouraged most West Virginians from endorsing a Republican candidate, even for religious reasons. In southern states generally, however, Lubell's interviews corroborated Gallup Poll reports that 20 to 25 percent of southerners would oppose any Catholic presidential nominee.[113] If Kennedy obtained the Democratic presidential nomination, Georgia's Democrats would need strong economic or other motives to compensate for this significant anti-Catholicism.

Kennedy's liberal party platform, especially regarding civil rights, provided another strong motive for southern resistance to the Catholic candidate. In response to the platform's denunciation of segregation, Georgians and other southerners endorsed Lyndon Johnson. Assuming that religious opposition, along with Kennedy's youth and inexperience, would prevent the Catholic candidate from receiving the nomination, Johnson entered no presidential primaries but felt confident that convention delegates would rally behind him as an experienced, nationally known, and Protestant senator. To enflame fears of a Catholic president, Johnson's advocates secretly spread doubts of Catholic willingness to support non-Catholic candidates.[114] In a nationally televised interview, Johnson wistfully expressed hope that states with large Catholic populations would emulate predominately Protestant West Virginia's religious tolerance. *Presidential Preview* reported Johnson's comments, and elaborated on this position: "Catholics who are supporting someone other than Kennedy are conspicuous in their absence." In covering this story, the publication noted that 50 percent of Kennedy's delegate base derived from five states—California, Illinois, New York, Ohio, and Pennsylvania. A Catholic led each of these state delegations—respectively, Governor Brown, Chicago Mayor Richard Daley, New York City Mayor Robert Wagner, Governor Michael J. DiSalle, and Governor David Lawrence.[115] Such theories exacerbated southern suspicion of a Catholic cabal.

Kennedy's selection of Johnson as vice-presidential nominee dampened fears of a Catholic conspiracy. Delegates from the South had publicly protested Kennedy's nomination on the convention floor.[116] Johnson's position as running-mate, however, pleased voters in Georgia. This active pursuit of the "Solid South" also dismissed suspicions that Kennedy sought to replace southern voters with Catholics. According to *Presidential Preview,* Kennedy successfully allayed fears that Catholics would perpetually determine Democratic presidential nominees: "[This religious ticket-balancing] reduced the objections of some to the possibility that [Kennedy] sought to reorganize the Party along liberal lines, but dependent upon a Catholic bloc vote to replace the Democrats' dependence on the South."[117] Georgians, therefore, gained reassurance that Kennedy's campaign did not intend to replace the South with a Catholic bloc within the Democratic coalition.

Despite evidence of strong anti-Catholicism in Georgia, Kennedy's religion did not fragment the state's Democratic Party. Georgia's secretary of state accused Republicans of promoting anti-Catholic pamphlets: "It is the same sort of smut that was traced back to the Republican organization in 1928, and, in my opinion, it will be so traced back to them this time."[118] A Fulton County Republican denied this charge, and claimed to have Catholics among Nixon's statewide campaigners: "From the moment of his nomination for the presidency, Richard Nixon has made it clear that he will not stoop to the use of the religious issue in his campaign."[119] Rather than encouraging anti-Catholicism, Democratic leaders accused the Republicans of religious bigotry.

Reporting on the religious issue in Georgia peaked in September. Five southern Democratic political leaders agreed, in an Atlanta meeting, that religion posed Kennedy's greatest challenge in this region.[120] The *Atlanta Journal* candidly described Catholicism as "important . . . particularly in this area."[121] Racial and religious tensions coincided when a burning cross appeared outside a Catholic church in Tilton, mere hours following an African American couple's wedding.[122] Georgia Democrats voted against pledging the state's electors to Kennedy. Although columnist William S. White credited Kennedy's liberal politics, especially regarding civil rights, as much as Catholicism for this potential defection, he wrote, "It is a heavy blow, at the very least."[123] According to National Media Analysis—a study provided for the Republican National Committee—references to Kennedy's religion in the *Atlanta Constitution* increased dramatically in September. While only twenty-one appeared in August's final week, this topic accounted for nearly two hundred stories in mid-September.[124] The "Catholic issue" complicated Democratic pursuit of Georgia's voters in a year when debates about racial segregation became widespread.

The mainstream Atlanta media's response to anti-Catholic attitudes showed a trend toward tolerance, especially after Norman Vincent Peale and other Protestant ministers questioned Kennedy's ability to resist church pressures. The *Atlanta Constitution*'s editors wrote several pieces that boasted of Georgia's respect for Catholicism. One editorial praised Georgians for refusing to engage in "the vicious anti-Catholic position seen in some other places."[125] Challenging the assumption that Baptists generally opposed a Catholic president, the editors cited Baptist Governor Ernest Vandiver's recent affinity for Kennedy as evidence of this religious body's tolerance. Even Senator Herman E. Talmadge's refusal to endorse the Democrat's standard-bearer derived from dissatisfaction with the party platform, not anti-Catholicism, since "he seems to have no reservations about the candidate's religion or loyalty."[126] This paper both promoted tolerance toward Kennedy's Catholicism and disassociated Baptists from religious prejudice.

By October, Kennedy's Catholicism appeared less significant as a campaign issue. Reports in Georgia revealed little organized anti-Catholicism while ministerial groups openly orchestrated efforts to defeat Kennedy on religious grounds in Texas and North Carolina. Some of Georgia's pastors absolutely rejected Kennedy on religious grounds, but others withheld judgment.[127] By mid-October, Kennedy pollster Louis Harris still discovered a "high degree of religious bigotry" among Georgians. Forty percent of Georgians believed that religion "makes a difference," and 23 percent admitted opposition to Kennedy "because he is a Catholic." Despite these alarming numbers, Harris believed that this state would maintain party loyalty: "Barring some unexpected event, Georgia will vote solidly for the Democratic ticket." Baptists and Methodists endorsed Kennedy "even more solidly than the total electorate." Kennedy enjoyed greater than 72 percent support from these two religious groups, while polls revealed 66 percent of Georgians favored the Democratic nominee.[128]

In the campaign's final stages, Kennedy received significant endorsements from Georgians, who promoted the Catholic candidate throughout the South. Writing to a constituent, Senator Russell opposed the party's "socialistic" platform, but asserted that religion played no role in his lack of enthusiasm toward the party ticket. Russell's letter even noted that he had supported the 1928 presidential bid of Catholic New York Governor Alfred E. Smith, who won the state. Despite this reluctant endorsement, Russell actively campaigned with Johnson in Texas in late October. Atlanta newspapers reported this fact, which suggested that the Democrats needed little help in Russell's home state.[129] Kennedy received greater assistance in Georgia, however, from the state's African American ministers, such as Martin Luther King, Sr., who had initially opposed the election of a Catholic president. After Kennedy's overt and covert efforts to obtain Martin Luther King, Jr.'s release from prison, both father and son King led several black Protestants to view anti-Catholicism as equally repugnant as racism. As discussed in Chapter Five, Kennedy received a vast majority of African American votes in the election.

Anti-Catholicism proved unable to dissuade Georgia's voters from supporting the Democratic Party's economic policies in the 1960 campaign. Harris felt confident enough to suggest that the Democratic ticket could bypass this state in the campaign's final weeks.[130] *Time* magazine, in a state-by-state October analysis of the campaign, described Georgia as "Loyally Democratic."[131] Only heavily Catholic

Rhode Island provided a greater margin of victory than Kennedy's 63 to 37 percent landslide in Georgia.[132]

Although a substantial minority voted against a Catholic candidate, the majority of Georgians displayed party loyalty and economic class consciousness. Kennedy managed religious and racial issues with great skill and good fortune. Georgia's newspapers and politicians avoided association with anti-Catholic and anti-black attitudes, and no native, white Protestant movement emerged. Even African American ministers, who initially opposed Kennedy on religious grounds, rallied behind the Catholic candidate. Kennedy's private assistance to Martin Luther King, Jr., earned black support without reviving nativism, anti-Catholicism, or racism.

Conclusions—Confirmation of the Bailey Thesis

While Sorensen's theory of "Catholic states" may have some flaws, the concentration of Catholics in particular northeastern and midwestern states helped Kennedy win in 1960. On the one hand, Kennedy's religion cost more votes than it bought. This net loss may explain Nixon's close victory in California as well as Kennedy's failure to win Michigan by a wider margin. On the other hand, the overpopulation of Protestants in southern states such as Georgia may have diluted the effect of this anti-Catholic vote. Since most Georgians remained loyal to the Democratic candidate, Kennedy won that state despite the substantial minority that voted based on anti-Catholicism. When Catholics in states such as Michigan and New York chose Kennedy on the basis of religion, furthermore, Kennedy secured significant Electoral College votes. In short, Catholic voters who endorsed one of their own in New York City, Detroit, and Chicago helped Kennedy win critical states New York, Michigan, and Illinois, respectively.

Although political scientists found religion to be a major factor in determining voter behavior, Kennedy benefited from voters' heightened religious consciousness in 1960. University of Michigan researchers concluded that Kennedy's Catholicism proved the most significant explanation for voter shifts in party loyalty from 1956 to 1960. Of the 6 percent of Americans who voted for both the Democrat Stevenson (in 1956) and the Republican Nixon (in 1960), 90 percent were Protestant. By contrast, 60 percent of voters who switched from Eisenhower in 1956 to Kennedy in 1960 were Catholic.

Kennedy's religion lost the Catholic candidate more votes than he gained, especially in the Midwest and South. The University of Michigan study suggested that a Democratic nominee should have received more votes in 1960, since Democrats running in congressional races outperformed Kennedy by about 5 percent.[133] A computer model, created by Massachusetts Institute of Technology (MIT) researchers, determined that Kennedy suffered a net loss of 1.5 million votes, or 2.3 percent of the total. These analysts estimated that 20 percent of Protestant Democrats and Independents voted against Kennedy for religious reasons.[134] These figures suggest that Kennedy's Catholicism made the election, determined by less than 150,000 votes, closer than necessary.

Catholics in Sorensen's fourteen "Catholic states" proved pivotal to this shift toward Kennedy, analysts have argued. Kennedy's vote exceeded the Democratic proportion of the vote in 97 percent of Michigan counties. In all three California counties with less than 5 percent Catholics, Democrats made substantial gains. "The most marked accretions to Democratic strength from 1956 to 1960 occurred in the states with extremely high proportions of Roman Catholics," concluded political scientist V. O. Key, Jr.[135] This impact proved most important in the Electoral College. The MIT study estimated that the religious issue cost Kennedy the electoral votes of several states, such as California, Kentucky, Oklahoma, and Tennessee. Yet Catholicism enabled Kennedy's victories in other "Catholic" states, including New York, Connecticut, Illinois, and Pennsylvania. Kennedy received a net gain of twenty-two electoral votes, the computer analysis reported.[136]

Individual states and local politicians greatly affected the 1960 presidential campaign's "Catholic issue." Kennedy's Catholicism played differently in each state. In California and New York, Catholic politicians Pat Brown and Robert Wager reluctantly sacrificed personal ambition to support Kennedy. Nixon narrowly won California's electoral votes amid suspicions about a Catholic conspiracy between Brown and Kennedy. Michigan and Georgia Democratic leaders mobilized loyal Democrats to overcome the inevitable anti-Catholicism. Catholics helped Kennedy win New York and Michigan, where non-Catholic liberals—such as Eleanor Roosevelt and Governor Williams—eventually rallied behind the Democratic nominee. Major newspapers in each of these states, including Georgia, publicly repudiated anti-Catholic attitudes, and Kennedy's impressive televised appearances in Houston and the presidential debates eased non-Catholic fears. If all politics is local, Kennedy effectively managed regional politicians, the public, and the media in each of these states. Kennedy's 1956 strategy, recorded in the Bailey Memorandum, proved prophetic.

Epilogue

Catholics and Presidential Elections since 1960

Mere months into John F. Kennedy's presidency, a contentious dispute arose about federal aid to Catholic schools. America's Catholic bishops advocated the inclusion of parochial institutions in a federal aid to education bill. The nation's first Catholic president opposed his church's hierarchy by interpreting the First Amendment to require absolute church-state separation.[1] Non-Catholic libertarians and liberals expressed pleasant surprise at Kennedy's defiance of Catholic clerics. In early March 1961, Paul B. Blanshard—the long-time critic of the Roman Catholic Church—gleefully recorded pleasure at the attention he received from Kennedy. "I feel kinda important," Blanshard wrote to a friend, "because I have been called to the White House twice during this month to talk to [White House Aide Theodore C.] Sorensen and the President on the education bills."[2] In a letter to family members, Blanshard admitted profound surprise about the treatment that Kennedy provided to "a public critic of Catholicism."[3] After Kennedy's first year in office, the liberal Protestant *Christian Century* lauded Kennedy for a "better record on the issue of separation of Church and State than any other President we have had in the past 30 years."[4] The Catholic president's uncompromising resistance to federally aiding parochial schools alleviated the liberal fear of Kennedy's supposed fealty to the Vatican.

This epilogue discusses the complex, and often counterintuitive, ways in which Catholicism has affected presidential politics since Kennedy's breach of the Protestant monopoly on the White House in 1960. Kennedy and Pope John XXIII dispelled fears of clerical pressure on American Catholic politicians by defying the stereotype of Catholicism's hostility toward the modern, secular world. In 1968, two liberal Catholic presidential candidates, Eugene McCarthy and Robert F. Kennedy, reinforced a new image of Catholicism by challenging the church's uncompromising anticommunism and opposing U.S. intervention in Vietnam. Although Democrats considered several Catholics—Edward Kennedy, Edmund Muskie, Thomas Eagleton, and ultimately Sargent Shriver—for a place on the national ticket in 1972, President Richard M. Nixon secured the largest Catholic vote of any Republican presidential candidate in history. After Shriver failed to recapture Catholic voters for the Democratic Party, no Catholic appeared on a major party presidential ticket until 1984. In that year, Catholic bishops criticized the Democrats' vice-presidential nominee Geraldine Ferraro for supporting abortion rights.

Senator John F. Kerry's nomination in 2004 ends a period of marginalization of Catholic politicians from presidential tickets of both parties. Nearly twenty years since Ferraro's nomination, only a conservative anti-abortion Catholic, Patrick J. Buchanan, had received a presidential nomination, by the marginal Reform Party in 2000. As a pro-choice Catholic, New York Governor Mario Cuomo may have feared religious opposition from his church's leadership in refusing to pursue the presidency in 1988 and 1992. Even prior to the 2004 Democratic National Convention, Kerry confronted questions about the Catholic teaching on abortion, stem cell research, and same-sex marriage. While Kennedy's election proved that anti-Catholicism could be overcome, Catholic presidential aspirants encounter challenges from the church's clerical hierarchy to uphold doctrinal principles in political decisions. The shifting significance of Catholicism in presidential politics further demonstrates the unique circumstances that Kennedy managed to his benefit in 1960.

In the early 1960s, John Kennedy and Pope John XXIII prompted national and global reevaluation of Catholicism. The nation's first Catholic president opposed federal aid to parochial schools, the appointment of a U.S. ambassador to the Vatican, and other public policies traditionally supported by Catholic bishops. Kennedy also avoided foreign policy decisions that might suggest favorable bias toward Catholic politicians abroad. In October 1963, for example, Kennedy refused to authorize protection for South Vietnam's Catholic President Ngo Dinh Diem, who subsequently died during a coup d'état.[5]

Unprecedented Vatican innovations also persuaded Americans to refashion perceptions of Catholicism. In 1962, Pope John XXIII convened an ecumenical council—or global conference—known as Vatican II. Over three years, church leaders reconsidered fundamental Catholic teachings and practices. The council advocated a greater role for laypersons, and endorsed the authority of individual conscience.

Catholic leaders also opposed civil coercion in religious affairs, and officially recognized Protestants as true Christians.[6] The Vatican invited several non-Catholic observers, including Paul Blanshard, who expressed limited approval of church reforms.[7] President Kennedy's support for church-state separation and Pope John's liberalizing of Catholic traditions encouraged some observers to credit the "two Johns" with reconciling Catholicism and the modern world.[8]

In 1964, several Catholics—including Attorney General Robert F. Kennedy and Kennedy's brother-in-law Sargent Shriver—received consideration for the vice-presidential nomination. A Catholic vice president appeared logical for the Texan Protestant, President Lyndon B. Johnson, whom Kennedy had selected for religious ticket-balancing in 1960. Now, four years later, Johnson's list of potential Catholic running-mates also included California Governor Edmund G. "Pat" Brown, New York City Mayor Robert F. Wagner, Maine Governor Edmund Muskie, and Senator Eugene McCarthy (MN). Choosing a Catholic on religious grounds alone, however, would appear too contrived. Some feared religious ticket-balancing would oblige the party to select a lower caliber candidate.[9]

Certain Catholics rejected the idea of choosing a Catholic vice president on religious grounds alone. The Jesuit publication *America* opposed any preferential treatment for Catholic candidates. In December 1963, *America* repudiated those who advised the political parties to select Catholics for religiously balanced presidential tickets: "A candidate's Catholic faith should not become a qualification for office. . . . If the old 'religious issue' was shameful, its new version is 'ridiculous.'"[10]

Republican presidential nominee Barry M. Goldwater's choice of a Catholic vice-presidential candidate, however, did appear to follow this model. Republicans privately attributed Kennedy's 1960 victory to Catholic bloc voting. In an April 1961 memo, GOP researchers interpreted Catholic voters' motivation in supporting Kennedy as "to end a custom which seemed to bar one of their faith from the highest office in the United States."[11] Goldwater may have chosen Catholic Congressman William E. Miller of New York for this purpose. Miller lacked widespread name recognition, a fact that served as a premise for his renowned post-election American Express commercials, in which he asked, "Do you know me?"[12] Miller's political career offered a religious counterpoint to the Protestant Arizona senator.

Although Johnson did not nominate a Catholic vice president in 1964, Catholic support for the Democratic president approached Kennedy's astonishing 75 percent in 1960. The president also returned predominately Protestant border states—such as Kentucky, Missouri,

Oklahoma, Tennessee, and West Virginia—to the party. Many of these states' voters opposed Kennedy on religious grounds in 1960. The Republican ticket won only five southern states and Arizona, Goldwater's home state. Miller's presence as the vice-presidential candidate mobilized no substantial Catholic support for the GOP.[13] Johnson's victory demonstrated the power of a coalition of both Catholic and non-Catholic voters. Would Catholics continue to support Democratic candidates in such high numbers after the Kennedy legacy faded?

Catholic support for the Democratic Party weakened in 1968 as the Vietnam War divided all Americans. In that year, two Catholic presidential candidates merged a political and religious critique of Johnson's foreign policy. Eugene McCarthy and Robert Kennedy actively confronted the escalating U.S. intervention in Vietnam. McCarthy overtly challenged the United States to follow Vatican leadership by repudiating militant anticommunism. In a late 1967 interview with *America,* McCarthy called on the Johnson administration to recognize the Catholic Church's moderation of its earlier refusal to compromise with communism: "[E]verything the Church seems to have given up at Vatican II has now been picked up by the Pentagon and the Administration. The Church has more or less said holy wars are out." Although this Jesuit magazine supported the U.S. government's efforts against communist North Vietnam, McCarthy cited papal reforms to challenge the traditional Catholic, and American, view of anticommunism as a moral and religious imperative. A one-time Benedictine monk, McCarthy frequently employed religious language, even quoting papal encyclicals to justify legislation that aided poorer Americans. Such public references to the Holy See's spiritual authority contrasted dramatically with John Kennedy's secular declarations of complete independence from Vatican dictates.[14] McCarthy asserted religious values to counter American images of militant Catholic anticommunism.

New York Senator Robert Kennedy, who also entered the 1968 presidential primaries, avoided any overt connections with Catholicism but echoed McCarthy's opposition to militaristic anticommunism. Kennedy similarly used moral arguments against America's military participation in Vietnam's civil war. According to the liberal Catholic lay publication *Commonweal,* which supported the Vietnam policies of both McCarthy and Kennedy, these two Catholic candidates articulated a Christian message of justice. After McCarthy's campaign faltered and Robert Kennedy fell to an assassin's bullet, *Commonweal* editors repudiated Vice President Hubert H. Humphrey, the Democrats' inevitable presidential nominee, for not responding to these passionate calls for reform. Criticizing national security arguments with appeals to religious ethics, this publication characterized Humphrey as "the pleader of platitudes and the defender of policies that have split the country and left it morally bankrupt before the world."[15] Humphrey's defense of Johnson's Vietnam policy lacked credibility with these liberal Catholics, who bitterly regretted America's lost opportunity for a religious and moral reevaluation of U.S. foreign policy. No Catholic candidate could translate this constituency's support into the Democratic Party nomination. But these Catholic candidates had publicly challenged American Catholicism's reputation for monolithic and unquestioning anticommunism.

Although communism dominated much of presidential politics in 1968, Catholic candidates also encountered religious questions about a domestic church-state issue—birth control. Reporters asked McCarthy whether the Roman Catholic Church's proscription of artificial contraception would affect a Catholic layman's public policy regarding population control. In response to this question, McCarthy offered flippant responses, such as, "That's a question for vice presidential candidates." This quotation served as "my standard answer, implying that the issue of religion was out of the question." On one occasion, McCarthy dismissed such an inquiry with the retort, "I would favor putting intrauterine devices into all sacred cows."[16] After Pope Paul VI reaffirmed the church proscription in a July papal encyclical, *Humanae Vitae* ("On Human Life"), Humphrey's Catholic vice-presidential nominee Edmund Muskie deflected questions about birth control with an evasive response: "I don't intend to issue an encyclical."[17] No organized campaign against Catholic clerical pressures emerged, however, and these noncommittal answers proved sufficient.

In the 1968 election, the Democratic ticket's success with Catholic voters encouraged the Democrats to nominate another Catholic for vice president in 1972. In that year, political analyst Louis H. Bean revised an earlier criticism of Kennedy advisor Theodore Sorensen, who had characterized fourteen "Catholic states" as pivotal to the Democratic Party in 1956. Sorensen's advocacy of a Catholic vice president, namely Kennedy, in that year's "Bailey Memorandum," attracted Bean's criticism. To counter Sorensen, Bean produced research to demonstrate that Catholics evaluated political candidates without regard to religion.[18] With a Catholic on the Democrats' 1960 and 1968 tickets, however, Bean recognized that Catholics in large northeastern states, such as New York, Pennsylvania, and Ohio, voted for Democratic presidential nominees. Bean also discovered that Catholics in San Francisco, California, and Baton Rogue, Louisiana, supported the Humphrey-Muskie ticket in 1968.[19] Less than twenty years after challenging Sorensen's analysis, Bean perceived the existence of a Catholic bloc in presidential campaigns. "This does not mean that every Catholic votes according to his religion; it does mean that a Catholic candidate can bank on a certain measure of Catholic backing." Northeastern Catholics could provide a Democratic candidate with a strong base of electoral support. For these reasons, Bean advocated a Catholic for the Democratic nomination.[20]

Democrats seemed committed to having a Catholic on the Democratic ticket in 1972, even when several nonreligious issues intervened. Senator Edward Kennedy's (MA) religion, name recognition, and a filial relationship with two slain national heroes all appeared favorable qualifications for the presidency. In 1969, however, Kennedy's abandonment of a fatal automobile accident scene badly tarnished his public image. Encountering questions about character and personal judgment, Kennedy chose not to seek higher office. The Democrat's 1968 vice-presidential nominee Edmund Muskie emerged as an early front-runner again after a January 1972 Harris Poll revealed that his national support equaled President Nixon's. Not much later, however, Muskie cried on television after a New Hampshire newspaper criticized his wife. When this image attracted national attention, some Americans interpreted this public emotional display as personal weakness. The Democratic presidential nominee, Protestant Senator George McGovern (SD) nonetheless selected another Catholic, Senator Thomas Eagleton (MO), as the vice-presidential nominee. Eagleton's medical history revealed electric shock therapy for nervous exhaustion. Eagleton withdrew at the request of McGovern, who believed that Americans would perceive this running-mate as unstable. Another Catholic, John Kennedy's brother-in-law Sargent Shriver, obtained the nomination after guaranteeing a scandal-free background.[21] Democrats' aggressive pursuit of a Catholic presidential or vice-presidential nominee likely contributed to hasty selection of candidates with liabilities other than religious affiliation.

Despite Shriver's presence on the Democratic ticket, President Nixon actively pursued Catholic voters. Nixon's 1972 northern strategy, in fact, included an aggressive appeal to traditionally Catholic ethnic groups. The president particularly aligned himself with official Catholic positions on two church-state issues—aid to parochial schools and abortion. In 1961, John Kennedy provoked some Catholic resentment by publicly opposing federal assistance to Catholic schools. Nixon had endorsed such aid in 1960. As president in late 1971 and early 1972, Nixon pledged to prevent Catholic school closings and advocated federal assistance for these institutions. Nixon addressed this topic during campaign speeches to Catholics in New York City and Philadelphia.[22]

President Nixon also addressed the increasingly controversial topic of abortion in the 1972 campaign. Abortion received national significance only in the late 1960s and early 1970s when citizen groups first lobbied for federal guarantees of the right to terminate pregnancies. The National Organization for Women and the National Women's Political Caucus exemplified this political movement, which George McGovern inelegantly described as "the Nylon Revolution."[23] Catholic teaching consistently depicted this practice as immoral.[24] Nixon, against the advice of many staff members, emphasized this issue in order to attract Catholic voters. Although most of Nixon's campaign team discouraged the president from issuing a public statement on abortion, the president followed the counsel of two aides, Protestant Charles Colson and Catholic Patrick J. Buchanan. In a letter to New York's Catholic archbishop, Terence Cardinal Cooke, Nixon repudiated that state's legalization of abortion. Cooke's decision to publish Nixon's letter clearly distinguished the Republican candidate from Democratic nominee McGovern. Several traditional Democrats perceived McGovern's abortion rights advocacy as unacceptable.[25] On these issues of particular concern to Catholic leaders, Nixon created a clear division between the two presidential candidates.

Nixon's remarkable success among Catholic voters in the 1972 presidential election rewarded the president's strategic maneuvers. Nixon received 53 percent of the Catholic vote. Socioeconomic issues partially affected how Catholics voted in 1972. Largely blue-collar Catholics sympathized with the Republican president's attempts to crack down on upper-class protesters of the Vietnam War. Yet Nixon's support for the American Catholic hierarchy's policies on federal aid to parochial schools and abortion also made a significant impact on the election results. No Republican presidential candidate had ever received a Catholic majority.[26] Despite Shriver's nomination and Catholics' 60 percent Democratic registration, only 26 percent of Catholics endorsed McGovern.[27] These results seriously challenged the theory of a Catholic voting bloc. In 1972, Catholics clearly made the distinction between Catholic issues and Catholic candidates at the polls.

The 1976 election revealed the limitations of attempts to attract Catholic voters through endorsement of "Catholic" issues. No Catholic received nomination to a national ticket in 1976, but the volatile "Catholic" issue of abortion played a large role in the campaign. After the Supreme Court's *Roe v. Wade* decision defined the procedure as a constitutional right in 1973, conservative Catholics, Protestants, and orthodox Jews sought to have this decision overturned. Both parties' presidential nominees expressed personal opposition to abortion. Catholic Archbishop of Chicago Joseph Bernardin, however, publicly rebuked Democratic standard-bearer James E. Carter—a self-proclaimed evangelical Christian—for tolerating the party's platform declaration of support for abortion's legality. The GOP endorsed a constitutional amendment that would restore individual state sovereignty over abortion's legality.[28] Despite Bernardin's comments, 57 percent of Catholics favored the victorious Carter and vice-presidential nominee Walter Mondale. After failing twice with a Catholic on the ticket, the Democrats succeeded with non-Catholic presidential and vice-presidential candidates. One cannot ignore the significance of Watergate in this campaign. Republican President Gerald Ford's pardon of Nixon following the president's resignation created suspicion and resentment. Carter's victory, however, revealed potential political divisions between Catholic clergy and laity.

The Catholic vote became even more difficult to anticipate in the 1980s. Two Catholics challenged President Carter for the party's nomination in 1980. In three Democratic primaries—New Hampshire, Illinois, and Wisconsin—Carter attracted more Catholic votes than either California Governor Jerry Brown or Senator Edward Kennedy. Although Kennedy secured a majority of Catholics in Massachusetts, New York, New Jersey, and California, Carter's substantial success among this group elsewhere ensured the president's renomination.[29] These results further undermined the theory that Catholics instinctively favored a Catholic presidential candidate.

A non-American event, however, initiated a more profound shift in the American Catholic hierarchy's role in U.S. politics. Pope John Paul II, elected in 1978, gave countenance to some liberal fears of Catholic dogma, especially with regard to abortion and communism. During the 1980 campaign, the Catholic hierarchy conveyed covert and overt opposition to abortion. The new pope proscribed Congressman Robert Drinan (MA)—a Jesuit priest and liberal Democrat—from seeking reelection. Some speculated that Drinan's endorsement of legalized abortion prompted this papal dictate. Boston's Humberto Cardinal Medeiros also distributed a pastoral letter that encouraged Catholics to support candidates who opposed legalized abortion.[30] This issue increasingly polarized the two parties. The Republican platform promoted a constitutional amendment to outlaw abortion, while some Democrats advocated federal funding of abortions for poorer Americans. Abortion's opponents in the American Catholic hierarchy perceived the Democratic policy as beyond just tolerating, but rather encouraging, an immoral procedure.[31]

This Polish-born "bishop of Rome" also revived Catholicism's active opposition to global communism. The new pope's praise for Poland's Solidarity, an anticommunist labor organization, excited more active anticommunism among Polish Americans.[32] Although U.S. Catholic bishops strongly criticized the nuclear arms race and President Ronald Reagan's military spending in the early 1980s, Pope John Paul II reaffirmed Catholicism's image as irrevocably opposed to communism. Americans perceived Catholicism as increasingly intransigent about abortion and anticommunism. Whether the Catholic laity fully shared the church hierarchy's views remained unclear.

The Republican presidential victory in 1980 encouraged political analyst Wilson Carey McWilliams to advocate a Catholic presidential nominee for the Democratic Party. Former California Governor Ronald W. Reagan won a slim majority of Catholics, 51 percent, by stressing the communist threat and appealing to traditional morality. Carter's Catholic percentage represented a nearly 20 point drop from his 1976 result.[33] According to McWilliams, a Catholic standard-bearer would revive the Democratic Party in 1984. In 1980, Reagan secured the "Catholic ethnic communities" that had dominated President Franklin D. Roosevelt's New Deal coalition prior to World War II. This group's rising socioeconomic status weakened loyalties to Democratic social programs. In McWilliams' interpretation, Kennedy's 1960 campaign promoted religious and ethnic consciousness among Irish, Italian, and Polish Catholics. By 1984, McWilliams predicted, this religious group would again rally behind a co-religionist: "Kennedy will increasingly be the symbol whose memory excites Democratic partisans." A Catholic Democratic presidential nominee would attract the Irish, Italians, and Poles who abandoned the party in 1980.[34] Viewing Catholicism as a completely favorable characteristic for a presidential candidate, McWilliams perceived no potential for anti-Catholicism in 1984.

The Democratic Party's nomination of a Catholic vice-presidential candidate in 1984 prompted no anti-Catholic revival, but McWilliams failed to predict the American Catholic hierarchy's response to the nomination of a liberal Catholic. By nominating Catholic Congresswoman Geraldine Ferraro (NY), the Democrats aroused bitter divisions within the American Catholic community, particularly about abortion. While John Kennedy encountered Protestant and secular skepticism about Catholic perspectives on church-state separation in 1960, Ferraro's co-religionists emerged as her loudest religious critics. Some Catholics berated Ferraro for ignoring the church's uncompromising opposition to abortion. One sign, which appeared in heavily Catholic Scranton, Pennsylvania, symbolized this discontent: "FERRARO—A CATHOLIC JUDAS." Scranton's Bishop James Timlin and New York Archbishop John O'Connor both publicly rebuked Ferraro's advocacy of legal abortion.[35]

Despite the appearance of intra-Catholic disputes in response to Ferraro's nomination, Democratic strategy regarding religion resembled John Kennedy's 1960 response to the Catholic issue. Campaigning for the Democratic ticket in 1984, Edward Kennedy defined abortion, school prayer, and homosexuality within the authority of individual conscience, not "the coercive rule of secular law."[36] Kennedy also warned against partisanship among religious leaders: "[W]e cannot be a tolerant country if churches bless some candidates as God's candidates—and brand others as ungodly and immoral." These statements rearticulated the elder Kennedy's support for absolute church-state boundaries. Ferraro's references to religion similarly relied on firm distinctions between sacred and secular matters. Ferraro treated O'Connor's criticism as incompatible with America's hallowed principle of church-state separation: "For the first time in over twenty years, religion has been injected into a presidential campaign." In Ferraro's interpretation, her "personal" faith did not diminish her political obligation to tolerate diverse moral and ethical worldviews: "I cannot, and I will not, seek to impose my religious views on others."[37] While such appeals to religious liberty may have pleased Protestant and nonreligious Americans, conservative Catholics remained unsatisfied.

Cardinal O'Connor's criticism of Ferraro revealed fundamental differences between American Catholics and the national Democratic Party. Campaigning in a 70 percent Catholic congressional district, Ferraro had supported tuition tax credits for parochial schools. Since the national platform opposed this government aid to religious institutions, the Catholic vice-presidential candidate could offer little compromise with her church's political goals.[38] Ferraro nonetheless portrayed O'Connor's criticism as motivated by partisanship rather than religious principle. Ferraro's 1985 autobiography noted that O'Connor's nephew worked on Reagan's 1984 campaign. In Ferraro's opinion, the Catholic archbishop's monolithic focus on abortion unfairly ignored other moral issues—such as the nuclear arms race and U.S. complacency about world hunger—that might embarrass the Republican administration. Ferraro also criticized the "Church's increasingly conservative and militantly moralistic attitude."[39] According to Ferraro, Catholic institutional leaders and Republicans increasingly shared ideological goals.

Ferraro and others explained Catholic opposition to her candidacy as gender bias characteristic of a church that excluded women from its leadership. According to Ferraro, the Catholic clergy particularly feared women who favored legal abortion. A man might tolerate abortion as an abstract concept, but a woman could personally choose the procedure.[40] Author, journalist, and former priest James Carroll characterized Roman Catholic clergy as threatened by "uppity women."[41] According to scholar Mary Segers, the Catholic Church's male-dominated structure conditioned clerics to oppose women's full political status. Since Catholic men determined the religion's institutional decisions, these individuals would logically question a woman's ability to determine government policy.[42] In this interpretation, such fundamental flaws in Catholicism's basic structure prevented compromise between church teaching and Catholic women's political goals.

While Ferraro and the Democrats battled conservative Catholic clerics, President Reagan successfully courted American Catholics in 1984. Philadelphia's John Cardinal Krol publicly praised Reagan's endorsement of federal aid for parochial schools. In a Polish American neighborhood, President Reagan claimed to have consulted Pope John Paul II "on several occasions."[43] Political analysts credit Reagan's firm anticommunism with attracting Catholic supporters. Having denounced the Soviet Union as an "evil empire," Reagan initiated a missile defense system that the Soviets, and some Democrats, feared would extend the nuclear arms race into outer space. Reagan also promised to restrict abortions, appointed Catholics to federal offices, and reinstated an official U.S. ambassador to the Vatican.[44] While Reagan actively cultivated Catholics, Democratic presidential nominee Walter Mondale canceled a speaking engagement at the New York Archdiocese's annual Alfred E. Smith Memorial Dinner only days before the election. Mondale's decision further alienated this religious group. In the final result, 55 percent of Catholics endorsed Reagan, an improvement upon Nixon's record Republican success among this constituency in 1972.[45] Despite the nomination of a Catholic vice-presidential candidate, Democrats failed to attract American Catholics. In this year, the Republicans appealed to Catholic ambitions better than the Democrats did.

Prior to John Kerry's nomination in 2004, no Catholic had headed a major party ticket since 1960, but substantial speculation surrounded Mario Cuomo in 1988 and 1992. In a fashion similar to Eugene McCarthy, Cuomo often linked religious belief and a "progressive social philosophy." Instead of imitating John Kennedy's absolute distinctions between religion and politics, Cuomo used Christian language to justify public policies, such as government aid to the disadvantaged. Rather than distancing himself from spiritual discourse, Cuomo criticized conservatives for promoting "condemnatory Christianity." Having attended Catholic schools, Cuomo linked his ideas for political reform to his sincere, firm religious commitment. In historian Robert S. McElvaine's interpretation, such strong belief guaranteed Cuomo's respect for, and among, the working class: "The religious basis of Mario Cuomo's liberal values makes him the first politician since Robert Kennedy who has a realistic chance of restoring the Democratic coalition."[46] Cuomo's religious, rather than secular, liberalism offered a potential bridge between Democrats and Catholics.

In McElvaine's opinion, however, religion also explained Cuomo's unwillingness to lead the construction of that bridge. A more secular Catholic, such as John Kennedy, would not harbor the same internal doubt, humility, and selflessness about pursuing the nation's highest office. Cuomo even employed theological language to explain his ambivalence about the presidency: "The worst sin would be going [for the presidency] because I need it: 'Look Mama!'"[47] The same religious devotion that rooted Cuomo's commitment to social justice, McElvaine believed, discouraged this Catholic politician from manipulating public power to achieve this goal.

Both political parties consciously courted Catholic voters in the 1990s. Conservative evangelicals recruited Catholics by appealing to this group's traditional morality. This "Religious Right" identified particular issues—such as abortion and federal aid to private schools—as common ground with the Catholic community.[48] In 1996, Republican nominee Robert Dole vigorously pursued Catholics although the GOP's evangelical base alienated some Catholic voters. New Deal Catholics recalled evangelical opposition to Catholic political participation. Younger, more secular-minded Catholics often opposed the evangelicals' resistance to legal abortion. At the Republican National Convention, Dole chose New York Congresswoman Susan Molinari—young, pro-abortion rights, and Catholic—to deliver the keynote address, and even considered a Catholic vice-presidential candidate, such as Michigan Governor John Engler or Wisconsin Governor Tommy Thompson.[49] Although Dole declined to nominate a Catholic, a Republican Party publication confirmed Catholic voters' critical role in national elections.[50]

Democrats pursued Catholics in 1996 more effectively than did Republicans. President William J. Clinton's concentration on Irish,

Polish, and Mexican international affairs secured some ethnic Catholic support.[51] Democrats' portrayal of the religious right's goals as theocratic and reactionary further frightened New Deal Catholics. In the general election, 53 percent of Catholics supported Clinton. Since the same percentage of Catholic voters supported Republican congressional candidates in the 1994 midterm elections, this Democratic success proved particularly significant.[52] Although neither party nominated Catholics for the national ticket, Catholic voters enjoyed a powerful potential to "swing" the political balance of power.

Since John Kennedy's election, American Catholics have encountered decreasing electoral opposition from non-Catholics on purely religious grounds. Events from 1961 to 1972 undermined U.S. perceptions of a Catholic monolith. In the early 1960s, the nation's first Catholic president thwarted attempts to aid Catholic schools with federal funds. Pope John XXIII opened discussion of Catholicism's diversity, and thus encouraged some Catholics and non-Catholics to recognize common beliefs. In 1968, Catholic presidential candidates Eugene McCarthy and Robert Kennedy undermined Catholicism's image as militantly anticommunist by opposing U.S. military action in Vietnam. During this period, many Catholic voters gravitated to Republican President Nixon, who supported Catholicism's bid for federal aid to parochial schools and a national ban on abortion. These policy positions attracted a majority of Catholics despite the nomination of a Catholic to run for vice president on the Democratic ticket in 1968 and 1972.

From 1973 to 1988, abortion and anticommunism increasingly fractured American Catholics. Pope John Paul II and the U.S. Catholic bishops publicly denounced legal abortion, but polling data revealed divisions among the Catholic laity on this issue. In 1984, some Catholic prelates publicly chastised the Democratic ticket's Catholic vice-presidential nominee, Geraldine Ferraro, for endorsing legal abortion. Catholics' conflicting opinions on such controversial issues inhibited any unified bloc support from co-religionists. Conservative Republican Ronald Reagan received substantial support, however, from those Catholics who heeded the pope's aggressive anticommunism and opposition to abortion.

Since 1989, both political parties have recognized Catholic voters as potentially decisive in presidential elections. John Kerry has become the first Catholic nominated for president by a major party since John Kennedy. The absence of public skepticism about Kerry's Catholicism suggests that Catholics have fully assimilated to American political culture in the minds of most non-Catholics. Conservative Catholics and some members of the clerical hierarchy have raised doubts about Kerry, however, based on the Catholic candidate's staunch defense of abortion as a constitutional right.

More than forty years after John Kennedy's election as the nation's first Catholic president, U.S. Catholics continue to face special challenges when pursuing the presidency. As head of state, the president represents all Americans. Since the executive office remains a national symbol, a Catholic American needs to demonstrate his or her religion's compatibility with a nation-state traditionally guided by a Protestant elite. Yet Catholics also want a Catholic president who shares their faith, and thus proudly fulfills religious obligations. Kennedy's model—maintaining independence from clerical pressures without alienating Catholics—proved critical to his election. In 1960, America's respect for diversity and fear of communism allowed Catholics and non-Catholics to discover areas of agreement. Since that year, however, complex culture wars have created new suspicions of Catholicism's traditions. Resistance to government partnership with institutional religion has generated further animosity between the sacred and the secular. In the twenty-first century, a Catholic president may serve to reconcile these two, equally American, views of modern life.

Notes

Introduction

1. Richard M. Nixon, *Six Crises* (Garden City, NY: Doubleday and Company, Inc., 1962), 392–393, 366–367.
2. Richard Nixon, *RN: The Memoirs of Richard Nixon* (New York: Grosset and Dunlap, 1978), 226.
3. Theodore C. Sorensen, *The Kennedy Legacy* (New York: The Macmillan Company, 1969), 97.
4. Sorensen, *The Kennedy Legacy*, 64.
5. Sorensen, *The Kennedy Legacy*, 218–219.
6. Robert Dallek, *An Unfinished Life: John F. Kennedy, 1917–1963* (Boston: Little, Brown, and Co., 2003), 701–702.
7. Robert Wuthnow, "Understanding Religion and Politics," *Daedalus* 120 (summer 1991): 1–20.
8. Richard Polenberg, *One Nation Divisible: Class, Race, and Ethnicity in the United States Since 1938* (New York: J. B. Lippincott Company, 1980), 165–168.
9. Philip Gleason, *Keeping the Faith: American Catholicism Past and Present* (Notre Dame: University of Notre Dame Press, 1987), 32.
10. James Hennesey, *American Catholics: A History of the Roman Catholic Community in the United States* (New York: Oxford University Press, 1981), 308–309.
11. Charles R. Morris, *American Catholic: The Saints and Sinners Who Built America's Most Powerful Church* (New York: Vintage Books, 1997), 319, 281.
12. Thomas Maier, *The Kennedys: America's Emerald Kings: A Five-Generation History of the Ultimate Irish-Catholic Family* (New York: Basic Books, 2003), 519.
13. Maier, *The Kennedys*, 348.
14. Quoted originally by journalist Arthur Krock, but also appeared in Garry Wills, *The Kennedy Imprisonment: A Meditation on Power* (Boston: Little, Brown, and Co., 1981), 61. See also James S. Wolfe, "The Religion of and about John F. Kennedy," in *John F. Kennedy: The Promise Revisited,* ed. Paul Harper and Joann P. Krieg (New York: Greenwood Press, 1988), 287.
15. John T. McGreevy, *Catholicism and American Freedom: A History* (New York: W. W. Norton, 2003), esp. 166–188.
16. Mark S. Massa, S. J., *Catholics and American Culture: Fulton Sheen, Dorothy Day, and the Notre Dame Football Team* (New York: Crossroad, 1999), 131. Emphasis in original.
17. Mark S. Massa, S. J., *Anti-Catholicism in America: The Last Acceptable Prejudice* (New York: Crossroad, 2003), 99.
18. E.g., Philip Jenkins, *The New Anti-Catholicism: The Last Acceptable Prejudice* (Oxford: Oxford University Press, 2003); Robert P. Lockwood, ed., *Anti-Catholicism in American Culture* (Huntington, IN: Our Sunday Visitor, 2000); William A.

Donohue, *The Deepest Bias: Anti-Catholicism in American Life*, one-hour-videocassette (New York: Catholic League, 1996); Andrew Greeley, *An Ugly Little Secret: Anti-Catholicism in North America* (Kansas City, MO: Andrews McMeel, 1977).
19. Samuel P. Huntington, "The Hispanic Challenge," *Foreign Policy* (March/April 2004); Samuel P. Huntington, *Who Are We? The Challenges to America's National Identity* (New York: Simon and Schuster, 2004).

Chapter One

1. Arthur M. Schlesinger, Jr., *A Thousand Days: John F. Kennedy in the White House* (Boston: Houghton Mifflin, 1965), 20.
2. Mark S. Massa, S. J. *Anti-Catholicism in America: The Last Acceptable Prejudice* (New York: Crossroad, 2003), 7.
3. John Higham, *Strangers in the Land: Patterns of American Nativism, 1860–1925* (New Brunswick, NJ: Rutgers University Press, 1988), 79.
4. Philip Jenkins, *The New Anti-Catholicism: The Last Acceptable Prejudice* (Oxford: Oxford University Press, 2003), 25. Raymond D. Tumbleson, *Catholicism in the English Protestant Imagination: Nationalism, Religion, and Literature, 1660–1745* (Cambridge: Cambridge University Press, 1998).
5. David H. Bennett, *The Party of Fear: From Nativist Movements to the New Right in American History* (Chapel Hill: The University of North Carolina Press, 1988), 17.
6. Massa, *Anti-Catholicism in America*, 19. Mark Nicholls, *Investigating the Gunpowder Plot* (Manchester, UK: Manchester University Press, 1991).
7. Ray A. Billington, *The Origins of Nativism in the United States, 1800–1844* (New York: Arno Press, 1974), 1–4.
8. Massa, *Anti-Catholicism in America*, 19.
9. Jenkins, *New Anti-Catholicism*, 25.
10. Kevin P. Philips, *Cousins Wars: Religion, Politics, and the Triumph of Anglo-America* (New York: Basic Books, 1999).
11. Billington, *Origins of Nativism*, 1–29. See also, Ray A. Billington, *The Protestant Crusade 1800–1860: A Study in the Origins of American Nativism* (Chicago: Quadrangle, 1938), 1–25.
12. Bennett, *Party of Fear*, 19.
13. Bennett, *Party of Fear*, 19–20.
14. Bennett, *Party of Fear*, 21.
15. Billington, *Origins of Nativism*, 34–42.
16. Jay P. Dolan, *In Search of an American Catholicism: A History of Religion and Culture in Tension* (Oxford: Oxford University Press, 2002), 24, 20, 15–20.
17. Dale T. Knobel, *"America for the Americans": The Nativist Movement in the United States* (New York: Twayne Publishers, 1996), 34–38.
18. Nancy Lusignan Schultz, *Fire and Roses: The Burning of the Charlestown Convent, 1834* (New York: The Free Press, 2000), 165–166.
19. Massa, *Anti-Catholicism in America*, 24–25.
20. Philip Hamburger, *Separation of Church and State* (Cambridge, MA: Harvard University Press, 2002), 212.
21. Billington, *The Protestant Crusade*, 99–137.
22. Massa, *Anti-Catholicism*, 22–23. Billington, *The Protestant Crusade*, 99–137.

23. Theodore S. Hamerow, "The Two Worlds of the Forty-Eighters," in *The German Forty-Eighters in the United States*, Charlotte L. Brancaforte, ed. (New York: P. Lang, 1989), 33.
24. Knobel, *"America for the Americans,"* 48.
25. The name derived from members' response to queries about the organization: "I know nothing."
26. Bennett, *Party of Fear*, 129–130.
27. John T. McGreevy, *Catholicism and American Freedom: A History* (New York: W. W. Norton, 2003), 29, 58–59.
28. Bennett, *Party of Fear*, 153, 155. A. James Reichley, *Religion in American Public Life* (Washington, D.C.: Brookings Institution, 1985), 188.
29. The names of the two Catholics who participated in Lincoln's assassination are John and Mary Surratt. Knobel, *"America for the Americans,"* 162–163.
30. Mark W. Summers, *Rum, Romanism, and Rebellion* (Chapel Hill: University of North Carolina Press, 2000). Bruce L. Felknor, *Dirty Politics* (New York: W. W. Norton, 1966), 30–31.
31. Although Catholic Roger Taney had served as the Supreme Court's Chief Justice, Cleveland's subsequent nomination of a Catholic for the nation's highest court exacerbated nativist suspicions of a papal conspiracy behind the election. Knobel, *"America for the Americans,"* 202–203. Blaine, who had a Catholic mother, later claimed not to have heard the reverend's comment. Lawrence H. Fuchs, *John F. Kennedy and American Catholicism* (New York: Meredith Press, 1967), 59, 65.
32. Joseph P. O'Grady, *How the Irish Became Americans* (New York: Twayne Publishers, 1973), 69–73, 109.
33. Bennett, *Party of Fear*, 172.
34. Christopher Kauffman, *Faith and Fraternalism: The History of the Knights of Columbus, 1882–1982* (Cambridge: Harper and Row, 1982).
35. Bennett, *Party of Fear*, 160.
36. James Hennesey, S. J., *American Catholics: A History of the Roman Catholic Community in the United States* (New York: Oxford University Press, 1981), 177. Bennett, *Party of Fear*, 172.
37. Knobel, *"America for the Americans,"* 213.
38. Fuchs, *John F. Kennedy*, 60.
39. Knobel, *"America for the Americans,"* 191.
40. Bennett, *Party of Fear*, 181.
41. James Hennesey, *American Catholics*, 236–246.
42. Knobel, *"America for the Americans,"* 264.
43. James Hennesey, *American Catholics*, 226–228.
44. John E. Haynes, *Red Scare or Red Menace? American Communism and Anticommunism in the Cold War Era* (Chicago: Ivan R. Dee, 1996), 92.
45. John Haynes estimates that Lenin's orders resulted in 14,000 to 20,000 deaths. Haynes, *Red Scare or Red Menace?*, 89. Historian Peter Filene claimed that contemporaries figured that the Cheka murdered anywhere from 9,000 to 1.8 million. The Soviet government's suppression of Russia's Catholic churches never inspired the same outrage among Protestant sects, which had little established organization in that nation. A 1923 execution of Monsignor Buchkavich, vicar-general of the Roman Catholic Church in Russia, particularly inspired strident anticommunism among American Catholics. A Boston Methodist publication, however, accepted the Soviet justification that Monsignor Buschkavich's engagement in counterrevolutionary activity justified his punishment. Methodists and

Quakers, for example, "were convinced that the government did not seek to kill religion, but to liberate it from state control." Peter G. Filene, *Americans and the Soviet Experiment, 1917–1933* (Cambridge, MA: Harvard University Press, 1967), 82–84.
46. James M. O'Toole, *Militant and Triumphant: William Henry O'Connell and the Catholic Church in Boston, 1859–1944* (Notre Dame, IN: University of Notre Dame Press, 1992), 132–136. Hennesey, *American Catholics*, 233.
47. Bennett, *Party of Fear*, 214–216.
48. Horace M. Kallen, *Culture and Democracy in the United States: Studies in the Group Psychology of the American Peoples* (New York: Boni and Liveright, 1924).
49. Christopher M. Finan, *Alfred E. Smith: The Happy Warrior* (New York: Hill and Wang, 2002), 191.
50. Robert A. Slayton, *Empire Statesman: The Rise and Redemption of Al Smith* (New York: The Free Press, 2001), 206–207.
51. Slayton, *Empire Statesman*, 216.
52. J. Leonard Bates, *Senator Thomas J. Walsh of Montana: Law and Public Affairs, From TR to FDR* (Urbana: University of Illinois Press, 1999), 234, 237.
53. Finan, *Alfred E. Smith*, 180.
54. Bates, *Senator Thomas J. Walsh*, 236.
55. Robert K. Murray, *The 103rd Ballot: Democrats, Madison Square Garden, and the Politics of Disaster* (New York: Harper and Row, 1976), 180–200, 207–208, 214.
56. Murray, *The 103rd Ballot*, 180–200, 207–208, 214.

Chapter Two

1. Thomas Maier, *The Kennedys: America's Emerald Kings: A Five-Generation History of the Ultimate Irish-Catholic Family* (New York: Basic Books, 2003), 320.
2. Fletcher Knebel, "Democratic Forecast: A Catholic in 1960," *Look*, March 3, 1959.
3. Maier, *The Kennedys*, 317–320.
4. Robert A. Slayton, "The Great Smith-Roosevelt Feud," in *FDR, the Vatican, and the Roman Catholic Church in America, 1933–1945*, ed. David B. Woolner and Richard G. Kurial (New York: Palgrave, 2003), 59.
5. Robert A. Slayton, *Empire Statesman: The Rise and Redemption of Al Smith* (New York: The Free Press, 2001), 309.
6. Slayton, *Empire Statesman*, 319.
7. Slayton, *Empire Statesman*, 311. Edmund A. Moore, *A Catholic Runs for President: The Campaign of 1928* (New York: Ronald Press, 1956), 154, 25, 46, 109, 161.
8. Christopher M. Finan, *Alfred E. Smith: The Happy Warrior* (New York: Hill and Wang, 2002), 211.
9. Slayton, *Empire Statesman*, 246–247.
10. Slayton, *Empire Statesman*, 285, 287.
11. Finan, *Alfred E. Smith*, 210, 198.
12. David Burner, *The Politics of Provincialism: The Democratic Party in Transition, 1918–1932* (New York: Knopf, 1968), 208–216. See also, David Burner, *Herbert Hoover: The Public Life* (New York: Knopf, 1979), 204.
13. Robert Slayton, *Empire Statesman*, 260–262.

14. Moore, *A Catholic Runs for President*, vii.
15. Moore, *A Catholic Runs for President*, 164.
16. Slayton, *Empire Statesman*, x.
17. Slayton, *Empire Statesman*, 194.
18. Finan, *Alfred E. Smith*, 205.
19. Moore, *A Catholic Runs for President*, 169.
20. Slayton, *Empire Statesman*, 307.
21. Mabel Walker Willebrandt to Herbert Work, Republican National Committee Chairman, September 27, 1928. Herbert C. Hoover Campaign and Transition Papers, Box 72, Hebert C. Hoover Presidential Library, West Branch, IA.
22. Moore, *A Catholic Runs for President*, 146–147.
23. Slayton, *Empire Statesman*, 306, 321.
24. "A Test for Governor Smith," *New Republic*, April 6, 1927, p. 183; "More about Catholicism and the Presidency," *New Republic*, May 11, 1927, pp. 315–316. Walter Lippman to Al Smith, March 21, 1927 in *Public Philosopher: Selected Letters of Walter Lippmann*, ed. John Morton Blum (New York: Ticknor and Fields, 1985), 201–202. John T. McGreevy, *Catholicism and American Freedom: A History* (New York: W. W. Norton, 2003), 171. Moore, *A Catholic Runs for President*, 91.
25. Slayton, *Empire Statesman*, 302.
26. Ronald Steel, *Walter Lippmann and the American Century* (New York: Little, Brown, and Co., 1980), 245–246.
27. Slayton, *Empire Statesman*, 295.
28. Jay P. Dolan, *In Search of an American Catholicism: A History of Religion and Culture in Tension* (Oxford: Oxford University Press, 2002), 163.
29. Slayton, *Empire Statesman*, 295.
30. "Mrs. Sanger Calls Catholics Bigots," *New York Times*, April 25, 1928, p. 14. Quoted in McGreevy, *Catholicism and American Freedom*, 160.
31. Slayton, *Empire Statesman*, 311–312.
32. McGreevy, *Catholicism and American Freedom*, 148.
33. J. Leonard Bates, *Senator Thomas J. Walsh of Montana: Law and Public Affairs, From TR to FDR* (Urbana: University of Illinois Press, 1999), 282.
34. Bates, *Senator Thomas J. Walsh*, p. 282.
35. Quoted in Paul Carter, "The Other Catholic Candidate," *Pacific Northwest Quarterly* 55 (January 1964): 4. See also, Paul Carter, *Politics, Religion, and Rockets: Essays in Twentieth Century American History* (Tuscon: University of Arizona Press, 1991), 41–42.
36. Callahan to John Kohn, January 23, 1928. Thomas J. Walsh Papers, Library of Congress, Washington, D.C. (hereafter referred to as TWP), Container 179.
37. J. T. Carroll to Walsh, May 2, 1928. TWP, Container 179.
38. Thomas Lynch to Thomas Walsh, n.d., TWP, Container 181.
39. Western Union Telegram from P. W. Corake to Thomas Walsh, May 3, 1928. TWP, Container 179.
40. E.g. James P. Slattery, Columbus, Ohio, to Thomas Walsh. TWP, Container 182. J. T. O'Connor to Thomas Walsh, n.d., TWP, Container 181. Anonymous to Thomas Walsh, March 9, 1928, TWP, Container 179.
41. Slayton, *Empire Statesman*, 289, 296, 325.
42. Quoted in Maier, *The Kennedys*, 96.
43. Slayton, *Empire Statesman*, 326.
44. Maier, *The Kennedys*, 96, 99–100.

45. Maier, *The Kennedys*, 111–112.
46. Maier, *The Kennedys*, 100.
47. Maier, *The Kennedys*, 286.
48. George Q. Flynn, *American Catholics and the Roosevelt Presidency, 1932–1936* (Lexington: University of Kentucky Press, 1968), 15–25.
49. James Hennesey, *American Catholics: A History of the Roman Catholic Community in the United States* (New York: Oxford University Press, 1981), 260.
50. Slayton, *Empire Statesman*, 380–381, 387–388.
51. Charles R. Morris, *American Catholic: The Saints and Sinners Who Built America's Most Powerful Church* (New York: Vintage Books, 1997), 147.
52. Maier, *The Kennedys*, 137.
53. Maier, *The Kennedys*, 106–107.
54. Gerald P. Fogarty, S. J., "Roosevelt and the American Catholic Hierarchy," in *FDR, the Vatican, and the Roman Catholic Church in America, 1933–1945*, ed. David B. Woolner and Richard G. Kurial (New York: Palgrave, 2003), 18. See also, Edward Kantowicz, "Cardinal Mundelein of Chicago and the Shaping of Twentieth Century American Catholicism," *Journal of American History* 68 (June 1981): 52–68.
55. Philip Chen, "Religious Liberty in American Foreign Policy, 1933–41: Aspects of Public Argument Between FDR and American Roman Catholics," in *FDR, the Vatican, and the Roman Catholic Church*, 129–131.
56. Maier, *The Kennedys*, 130–134.
57. *Washington Post*, March 4, 1940, p. 1.
58. James A. Farley, *Jim Farley's Story: The Roosevelt Years* (New York: McGraw-Hill, 1948), 225–229.
59. Farley, *Jim Farley's Story*, 174–178.
60. Farley, *Jim Farley's Story*, 166.
61. *New York Times* July 17, 1940, p. 2.
62. Maier, *The Kennedys*, 128, 134.
63. McGreevy, *Catholicism and American Freedom*, 164–170.
64. Jay Dolan, *In Search of an American Catholicism*, 167; McGreevy, *Catholicism and American Freedom*, 164–165, 183, 166–167.
65. Maier, *The Kennedys*, 303–4.
66. Maier, *The Kennedys*, 306, 303.
67. Patrick Allitt, *Catholic Intellectuals and Conservative Politics in America, 1950–1985* (Ithaca, NY: Cornell University Press, 1993), 20.
68. Morris, *American Catholic*, 245, 248–249.
69. "The Catholic Vote in 1952 and 1956" (spring 1956) John F. Kennedy Pre-Presidential Papers (hereafter referred to as JFK PPP), John F. Kennedy Library, Boston, MA, Box 810.
70. Maier, *The Kennedys*, 283.
71. Sorensen, *Kennedy*, 83.
72. Memorandum printed in *Congressional Quarterly*, August 7, 1956, p. 1. JFK PPP, Box 810.
73. Maier, *The Kennedys*, 302.
74. "Drive On for Catholic Vice-President," *Christian Century*, August 15, 1956, p. 940–941. Italics added.
75. Arthur M. Schlesinger, Jr., *A Thousand Days: John F. Kennedy in the White House* (Boston: Houghton Mifflin, 1965), 6–7. Maier, *The Kennedys*, 280–281.
76. Maier, *The Kennedys*, 282–90.

77. Maier, *The Kennedys*, 322–323.

Chapter Three

1. William C. Martin, *With God on Our Side: The Rise of the Religious Right in America* (New York: Broadway Books, 1996), 54.
2. "Dr. Graham hails Kennedy victory," *New York Times*, January 17, 1960, p. 24.
3. Billy Graham, *Just As I Am: The Autobiography of Billy Graham* (San Francisco: Harper, 1997), 394–396.
4. Carol V. R. George, *God's Salesman: Norman Vincent Peale and the Power of Positive Thinking* (New York: Oxford University Press, 1993), 129.
5. A. James Reichley, *Religion in American Public Life* (Washington, D.C.: Brookings Institution, 1985), 185.
6. Mark D. Hisch, "Election of 1884," in *History of American Presidential Elections: 1789–1968*, ed. Arthur M. Schlesinger, Jr., vol. 1 (New York: Chelsea House, 1978).
7. Chapter Two of this book discusses Smith's campaign in greater detail.
8. Michael H. Carter, "Diplomacy's Detractors: American Protestant Reaction to FDR's 'Personal Representative' at the Vatican," in *FDR, the Vatican, and the Roman Catholic Church in America, 1933–1945*, ed. David B. Woolner and Richard G. Kurial (New York: Palgrave, 2003); George Q. Flynn, *American Catholics and the Roosevelt Presidency, 1932–1936* (Lexington: University of Kentucky Press, 1968).
9. Anne C. Loveland, *American Evangelicals and the U.S. Military, 1942–1993* (Baton Rouge: Louisiana University Press, 1996), 5–8.
10. David H. Watt, *A Transforming Faith: Explorations of Twentieth-Century Evangelicalism* (New Brunswick, NJ: Rutgers University Press, 1991), 64.
11. Mark Silk, *Spiritual Politics: Religion and America Since World War II* (New York: Simon and Schuster, 1988).
12. George, *God's Salesman*, 61, 64.
13. Donald Meyer, *The Positive Thinkers: Popular Religious Psychology from Mary Baker Eddy to Norman Vincent Peale and Ronald Reagan* (Middletown, CT: Wesleyan University Press, 1988); Silk, *Spiritual Politics*.
14. Norman Vincent Peale, *A Guide to Confident Living* (Englewood Cliffs, NJ: Macmillan, 1948).
15. George, *God's Salesman*, 136.
16. Meyer, *The Positive Thinkers*, 262. George, *God's Salesman*, 137–138.
17. Martin, *With God on Our Side*, 39–40.
18. Grant Wacker, "'Charles Atlas With a Halo': America's Billy Graham," *Christian Century* 109 (April 1, 1992): 336–341.
19. Richard V. Pierard, "Billy Graham and the U.S. Presidency," *Journal of Church and State* 22 (winter 1980): 119.
20. Silk, *Spiritual Politics*, 68.
21. Silk, *Spiritual Politics*, 40.
22. John M. Fenton, *In Your Opinion . . . The Managing Editor of the Gallup Poll Looks At Polls, Politics, and the People From 1945–1960* (Boston: Little, Brown, and Co., 1960), 198–199.
23. George, *God's Salesman*, 192–193, 182, 79–80.

24. George, *God's Salesman*, 195–196.
25. Pierre Salinger, *With Kennedy* (New York: Doubleday, 1966), 34–35; Pierre Salinger *P.S.: A Memoir* (New York: St. Martin's Griffin, 1996), 74–75.
26. Theodore C. Sorensen, *Kennedy* (New York: Harper and Row, 1965), 143.
27. Graham, *Just As I Am*, 389.
28. George, *God's Salesman*, 196.
29. Stephen E. Ambrose, *Nixon: The Education of a Politician, 1913–1962* (New York: Simon and Schuster, 1987), 546–547. Emphasis in original.
30. Ambrose, *Nixon*, 546–547.
31. Despite discouraging Graham to avoid public support for the Republican ticket, Nixon received the evangelical minister's political advice regarding the campaign's religious issue. Nixon told Graham, "Your ministry is more important than my getting elected President." John Pollock, *Billy Graham: The Authorized Biography* (New York: McGraw-Hill, 1966), 218. Anticipating the "southern strategy" that helped Nixon win presidential elections in 1968 and 1972, Graham highlighted Nixon's potential to win support among Protestants in the South.
32. William C. Martin, *A Prophet With Honor: The Billy Graham Story* (New York: W. Morrow and Co., 1991), 273.
33. Martin, *A Prophet With Honor*, 274.
34. Martin, *A Prophet With Honor*, 275.
35. Martin, *A Prophet With Honor*, 52. Graham, *Just As I Am*, 391.
36. George, *God's Salesman*, 198.
37. Graham, *Just As I Am*, 391. Martin, *With God on Our Side*, 52.
38. Martin, *With God on Our Side*, 53.
39. The *New York Times* printed this statement, September 8, 1960, p. 25. A corresponding statement issued by Protestants and Other Americans United for Separation of Church and State (POAU) included liberal skepticism toward a Catholic president. Chapter Four will address this organization's role in the 1960 election.
40. "The Campaign: The Power of Negative Thinking," *Time*, September 19, 1960, p. 21.
41. "Priest Sees Bias as Bad as in 1928," *New York Times*, September 10, 1960, p. 8.
42. "Clergy and Scholars Fight Religious Pleas to Voters," *New York Times*, September 12, 1960, p. 1.
43. "The Campaign," *Time*, p. 21.
44. John F. Kennedy Pre-Presidential Papers (hereafter referred to as JFK PPP), Box 1003. Cartoon published in the *San Francisco Chronicle*, September 12, 1960.
45. Mark S. Massa, S. J., *Anti-Catholicism in America: The Last Acceptable Prejudice* (New York: Crossroad, 2003), 81.
46. Reprinted in Theodore H. White, *The Making of the President 1960* (New York: Atheneum, 1961), 427–430. See also, "John F. Kennedy: Address to the Greater Houston Ministerial Association," available at http://www.americanrhetoric.com/speeches/johnfkennedyhoustonministerialspeech.html.
47. Porter McKeeves, *Adlai Stevenson: His Life and Legacy* (New York: Morrow, 1989), 469.
48. George, *God's Salesman*, 203.
49. *New York Times*, September 16, 1960, p. 18.
50. Norman V. Peale to "Friends," September 15, 1960. JFK PPP, Box 1003.
51. *New York Times*, September 19, 1960, p. 39.

Notes 181

52. *New York Times*, October 31, 1960, p. 1.
53. JFK PPP, Box 1021.
54. *Minneapolis Tribune* advertisement, November 6, 1960, p. 8.
55. *New York Times*, November 6, 1960, p. 25.
56. Richard V. Pierard, "Billy Graham and the U.S. Presidency," *Journal of Church and State* 22 (winter 1980): 120.
57. Pollock, *Billy Graham*, 219–220. Graham, *Just As I Am*, 392–393.
58. Martin, *Prophet with Honor*, 269.
59. George, *God's Salesman*, 208.

Chapter Four

1. James A. Michener, *Report of the Country Chairman* (New York: Bantam Books, 1961), 26–31.
2. Michener, *Report of the Country Chairman*, 29.
3. Michener, *Report of the Country Chairman*, 32
4. Dale T. Knobel, *"America for the Americans": The Nativist Movement in the United States* (New York: Twayne Publishers, 1996); John Higham, *Strangers in the Land: Patterns of American Nativism, 1860–1925* (New Brunswick, NJ: Rutgers University Press, 1988); Ray Allen Billington, *The Origins of Nativism in the United States, 1800–1844* (New York: Arno Press, 1974); *Between the Times: The Travail of the Protestant Establishment in America, 1900–1960* William R. Hutchinson, ed. (Cambridge, UK: Cambridge University Press, 1989); T. J. Jackson Leers, *No Place of Grace: Antimodernism and the Transformation of American Culture, 1880–1920* (New York: Pantheon, 1981).
5. Robert Moats Miller, *Bishop G. Bromley Oxnam: Paladin of Liberal Protestantism* (Nashville, TN: Abingdon Press, 1990), 399.
6. Peter Viereck, *Shame and Glory of the Intellectuals: Babbit Jr. vs. the Rediscovery of Values* (Boston: Beacon Press, 1953), 45.
7. John T. McGreevy, *Catholicism and American Freedom: A History* (New York: W. W. Norton, 2003), 166–188. John T. McGreevy, "Thinking on One's Own: Catholicism in the American Imagination, 1928–1960," *Journal of American History* 84 (June 1997): 97–130.
8. Allida Black, *Casting Her Own Shadow: Eleanor Roosevelt and the Shaping of Postwar Liberalism* (New York: Columbia University Press, 1996).
9. Harry S. Truman Post-Presidential Files, *Mr. Citizen* file, September 11, 1959, pp. 5–7, and October 21, 1959, pp. 29–31, Harry S. Truman Library, Independence, MO (hereafter HST); see also Alonzo Hamby, *Man of the People: A Life of Harry S. Truman* (New York: Oxford University Press, 1995); and James Giglio, "Harry S. Truman and the Multifarious Ex-Presidency," *Presidential Studies Quarterly* 12 (spring 1982): 241–242.
10. American Civil Liberties Union Papers (hereafter ACLU), boxes 770, 776, 1142, Seeley G. Mudd Manuscript Library, Princeton University.
11. McGreevy, *Catholics and American Freedom*, 183–185. Lawrence P. Creedon and William D. Falcon, *United for Separation: An Analysis of the POAU Assaults on Catholicism* (Milwaukee: Bruce, 1959), 15–17.
12. Samuel Walker, *In Defense of American Liberties: A History of the ACLU* (New York: Oxford University Press, 1990), 220–222; Daniel F. Rice, *Reinhold Niebuhr*

and John Dewey: An American Odyssey (Albany: State University of New York Press, 1993), 185–214.
13. George Q. Flynn, *American Catholics and the Roosevelt Presidency, 1932–1936* (Lexington: University of Kentucky Press, 1968).
14. John Cogley, *Catholic America: Two Centuries of American Life* (New York: The Dial Press, 1973); Jay P. Dolan, *The American Catholic Experience: A History from Colonial Times to the Present* (Garden City, NY: Image Books, 1985), 421–422; James Hennesey, *American Catholics: A History of the Roman Catholic Community in the United States* (New York: Oxford University Press, 1981); Charles R. Morris, *American Catholic: The Saints and Sinners Who Built America's Most Powerful Church* (New York: Vintage Books, 1997), ix, 280–281, 319.
15. John Courtney Murray, "Paul Blanshard and the New Nativism," *Month* 191 (April 1951): 214–225. On Murray's use of "PU," see Mark S. Massa, S. J., *Anti-Catholicism in America: The Last Acceptable Prejudice* (New York: Crossroad, 2003), 73.
16. Arthur M. Schlesinger Jr., *A Thousand Days: John F. Kennedy in the White House* (Boston: Houghton Mifflin, 1965), 14.
17. John Kenneth Galbraith, *A Life In Our Times: Memoirs* (New York: Houghton Mifflin, 1981), 386.
18. David Halberstam, *The Best and the Brightest* (New York: Random House, 1969), 13.
19. James MacGregor Burns, *John Kennedy: A Political Profile* (New York: Harcourt, Brace, and Company, 1959), 86–88.
20. Paul Blanshard, *American Freedom and Catholic Power* (Boston: Beacon Press, 1949); Paul Blanshard, *Communism, Democracy, and Catholic Power* (Boston: Beacon Press, 1951); Paul Blanshard, *The Irish and Catholic Power: An American Interpretation* (Boston: Beacon Press, 1953); Paul Blanshard, *American Freedom and Catholic Power*, 2d ed. (Boston: Beacon Press, 1958); see also Paul Blanshard, *Democracy and Empire in the Caribbean: A Contemporary Review* (New York: Beacon Press, 1947); and Paul Blanshard, *Right to Read: The Battle Against Censorship* (Boston: Beacon Press, 1955).
21. "POAU Publishes Challenge to Catholic Candidates," *Church and State,* February 1958, p. 1; Glenn L. Archer and Albert J. Menendez, *The Dream Lives On: The Story of Glenn L. Archer and Americans United* (Washington: R.B. Luce, 1982), 144–145.
22. "Senator Kennedy Pleads 'Sixth Amendment,'" *Church and State,* April 1958, 1, 3.
23. Vincent A. Carrafiello, Fairfield University ACLU member, to "Dear Sirs," April 10, 1959, box 1191, ACLU.
24. Alan Reitman to Vincent Carrafiello, April 20, 1959, box 1191, ACLU.
25. Quoted in "Jack, the Front Runner," *Time,* March 16, 1959, p. 24.
26. Archer and Menendez, *Dream Lives On,* 147–148.
27. Robert McAfee Brown, "Senator Kennedy's Statement," *Christianity and Crisis,* March 16, 1959, p. 25.
28. Handwritten notes. Box 7, folder 7–11, Paul B. Blanshard Papers (hereafter PBB), Bentley Historical Library, University of Michigan, Ann Arbor.
29. Paul Blanshard, *Personal and Controversial: An Autobiography by Paul Blanshard* (Boston: Beacon Press, 1973), 240.
30. Blanshard, *American Freedom and Catholic Power,* 59.
31. Blanshard, *God and Man,* 10–11.

32. E.g., Metropolitan Memorial Methodist Church Bulletin, 10.2.60, John F. Kennedy Pre-Presidential Papers (hereafter JFK PPP), box 1021, John F. Kennedy Library, Boston (hereafter JFKL).
33. Handwritten marginalia, PBB, box 5; John A. Mackay to Glenn [Archer], May 10, 1960, box 5, Americans United for Separation of Church and State Papers (hereafter referred to as AU), Seeley G. Mudd Manuscript Library, Princeton University, Princeton, NJ; Paul B. Blanshard to Ed [Darling, director, Beacon Press], February 13, 1960, box 3, folder 3–44, PBB.
34. Theodore Sorensen to Paul Blanshard, March 14, 1960, box 3, folder 3–45, PBB.
35. "Catholics in America," *New Republic*, March 21, 1960, p. 14.
36. "Catholics in America," p. 13.
37. Gilbert A. Harrison to Arthur Schlesinger Jr., Arthur M. Schlesinger Papers, box W-35, JFKL.
38. "The Religion Issue (cont'd.)," *Time*, May 2, 1960, 13.
39. Paul Blanshard's column, "Kennedy Speaks Out," *Humanist*, July-August 1960, 230, box 5, PBB.
40. "Religion Becomes Conspicuous Issue in Presidential Race," *Church and State*, June 1960, 6.
41. C. Stanley Lowell to Paul B. Blanshard, June 30, 1960, box 3, folder 3–47, PBB.
42. Lowell to Blanshard, June 30, 1960.
43. *Church-State News* 1 (1), box 20, folder 20–20, PBB.
44. Paul Blanshard to Glenn A. Archer and C. Stanley Lowell, July 7, 1960, PBB, box 3, folder 3–47.
45. Paul Blanshard to Edwin J. Lukas, American Jewish Committee, July 19, 1960, box 3, folder 3–46, PBB.
46. John M. Fenton, *In Your Opinion . . . The Managing Editor of the Gallup Poll Looks at Polls, Politics, and the People From 1945 to 1960* (Boston: Little, Brown, and Co., 1960), 194–216.
47. Samuel Lubell press release, March 23, 1960, box 27, Samuel Lubell Papers, Thomas Dodd Archives, University of Connecticut, Storrs, CT (hereafter Lubell Papers).
48. Samuel Lubell press release, May 2, 1960, box 5, Lubell Papers.
49. Harold R. Gordon, Esq., Chicago, to Joseph L. Rauh, Esq., June 10, 1960; Violet Gunther, undated memo to Samuel Beer attached, Samuel Beer Papers, box 1, JFKL.
50. Harry S. Truman Post-Presidential Files, *Mr. Citizen* File, September 11, 1959, pp. 5–7, and October 21, 1959, pp. 29–31, HST; *Washington Post*, January 22, 1960, vertical file, HST.
51. E.g., David and Sylvia Bader of Great Neck, NY, to President Harry Truman, Harry S. Truman Post-Presidential Files, political file, 1960 Presidential Campaign (1) box 701, HST.
52. Malin's August 14 statement appeared in "ACLU Says Religious Test for President Unconstitutional, Voters Can Query Candidates On Religious Ties Affecting Government Policies," ACLU Weekly Bulletin #2056, September 5, 1960, box 1191, ACLU.
53. ADA National Board Meeting Minutes, August 27, 1960, *Americans for Democratic Action Papers, 1932–1965* (Sanford, NC, 1978), series 2, reel 46.
54. Damon Stetson, "Truman Accuses G.O.P. of Bigotry," *New York Times*, September 6, 1960, p. A26.
55. Carol V. R. George, *God's Salesman: Norman Vincent Peale and the Power of Positive Thinking* (New York: Oxford University Press, 1993).

56. Minutes, Board of Trustees Meeting, Protestants and Other Americans United for Separation of Church and State, September 6, 1960, box 3, AU.
57. "Protestant Groups' Statements," *New York Times,* September 8, 1960, p. A25.
58. "Text of Statement on Religious Issue," *New York Times,* September 16, 1960, p. A18.
59. John C. Bennett, "The Roman Catholic 'Issue' Again," *Christianity and Crisis,* September 19, 1960, p. 126.
60. "Religious Smoke Screen," *Christian Century,* September 21, 1960, pp. 1075–1077.
61. "Text of Statement by Churchmen and Scholars on Religion and Politics"; see also Mrs. George W. Pieksen to Paul Blanshard, September 14, 1960, and Paul Blanshard to Mrs. [George W.] Pieksen, September 18, 1960, box 3, folder 3–49, PBB.
62. Edward Darling to Paul Blanshard, September 19, 1960, box 3, folder 3–49, PBB. Underline in original.
63. Paul Blanshard to Glenn Archer and C. Stanley Lowell, September 26, 1960, box 3, folder 3–49, PBB.
64. Bobbie Forster, "Catholic Church Is Charged With 'Clerical Tyranny,'" (Little Rock) *Arkansas Democrat,* October 4, 1960, p. 1; "Broadside Is Fired at Catholic Church: Dr. Glenn Archer Speaks At Baptist Meeting," (Memphis) *Commercial Appeal,* October 21, 1960, p. 1; Frank Harwell, "Speaker Urges 'Church Liberty': POAU Head Attacks Clerical Imperialism," *Birmingham Post-Herald,* October 26, 1960, pp. 1–2; Glenn Archer speech copy, "A Study of the Religious Issue," September 20, 1960, p. 14, box 4, AU; "Speaker Warns Against Church Try For Power," *Fresno Bee,* October 23, 1960, p. 1; Nathan Miller, "Rabbi Raps Rally Timing: Says Kennedy Makes Church-State Stand Clear," *Baltimore Sun,* October 29, 1960, box 4, AU.
65. "Reformation and Election," *Christian Century,* October 26, 1960, p. 1236.
66. Richard Scammon, "How the Negroes Voted," *New Republic,* November 21, 1960, pp. 8–9.
67. V. O. Key Jr., *The Responsible Electorate: Rationality in Presidential Voting, 1936–1960* (Cambridge, MA: Belknap Press, 1966), 118.
68. Samuel Lubell press release, "Religious Issue Helps Kennedy," November 9, 1960, Lubell Papers.
69. Michener, *Report of the Country Chairman,* 35–38, 108.

Chapter Five

1. Emanuel Perlmutter, "Powell Attacks Clergy of South," *New York Times,* September 26, 1960, p. 28.
2. Victor Lasky, *JFK: The Man and the Myth* (New York: The MacMillan Company, 1963), 486–487.
3. Nat S. Finney, "Butler Says It's Impossible To Block Kennedy Now," *Buffalo Evening News,* June 23, 1960, Charles P. Taft Papers (hereafter referred to as CPT), Box 260, Library of Congress, Washington, D.C.
4. "Paul Butler's Remarks Hit By Democrat," *Buffalo Evening News,* June 25, 1960, CPT, Box 260.
5. "How to Win in July and Lose in November," *Christian Century,* July 13, 1960, p. 820, CPT, Box 260.

6. Claude Robinson, Inc., *A Study Concerning the Influence of Religion on the Public's Presidential and Vice Presidential Preference in Reference to the 1960 Elections* (January 1960), Research Park, Princeton, NJ, James P. Mitchell Papers, Box 192, Dwight D. Eisenhower Presidential Library, Abilene, KA (hereafter referred to as DDE).
7. Theodore C. Sorensen, *The Kennedy Legacy* (New York: The Macmillan Company, 1969), 60, 82.
8. *New York Times,* January 3, 1960, p. 1.
9. Wayne Morse to Mrs. Emilie Papez Kirk, February 5, 1960, Wayne Morse Papers (hereafter referred to as WM), Box A112, University of Oregon, Eugene, OR.
10. *Anti-Defamation League Bulletin* (April 1960): 2.
11. Hubert Humphrey to Arthur M. Schlesinger, Jr., April 18, 1960, Joseph L. Rauh, Jr. papers, Box 18, Library of Congress, Washington, D.C.
12. This paper's masthead boasted "Largest Circulation in Phelps County," *Rolla Daily News* (Missouri), June 30, 1960, p. 1, Harry S. Truman Post-Presidential Files, Political File, Box 701, Harry S. Truman Presidential Library, Independence, MO (hereafter referred to as HST).
13. Harry S. Truman Post-Presidential Files, *Mr. Citizen* File, September 11, 1959, pp. 5–7, HST. See also, Harry S. Truman, Post-Presidential Files, *Mr. Citizen* File, October 21, 1959, pp. 29–31, HST.
14. E.g., Milton J. Schlesinger, Detroit MI, to Harry S. Truman, July 2, 1960; Pearl L. Bell, Fortville, IN, to Harry S. Truman, July 4, 1960, Harry S. Truman Post-Presidential Files, Political File, Box 701, HST.
15. "Press Conference," July 2, 1960, Harry S. Truman Post Presidential Files, Name File, Box 63, HST; Edward Keether, Coeur d'Alene, IO, to Harry S. Truman, July 3, 1960, Harry S. Truman Post-Presidential Files, Political File, Box 701, HST.
16. Harry S. Truman Post-Presidential Files, Political File, Boxes 701–707, passim, HST; David H. Stowe Papers, 1960 Presidential Campaign File, Box 23, HST.
17. Drew Pearson reported Luce's name in the *Tampa Tribune,* May 6, 1959, Box K2, WM. Ann C. Whitman Diary, July 29, 1959, DDE. Referenced in Stephen E. Ambrose, *Nixon: The Education of a Politician, 1913–1962* (New York: Simon and Schuster, 1987), 546.
18. Claude Robinson, Inc., *A Study Concerning the Influence of Religion on the Public's Presidential and Vice Presidential Preference in Reference to the 1960 Elections* (January 1960) Research Park, Princeton, NJ, James P. Mitchell Papers, Box 192, DDE.
19. Robert H. Finch Oral History, June 19, 1967, p. 31, Columbia University Oral History Research Office, DDE.
20. April 23, 1960, Washington, D.C. remarks quoted in Confidential Memorandum, August 16, 1960, James P. Mitchell Papers, Box 193, DDE.
21. Dwight D. Eisenhower, Presidential Papers, Press Conference Series, Box 10, DDE.
22. *New York Times,* June 28, 1960; *London Herald Tribune,* July 19, 1960, p. 1; *Passaic Citizen* (New Jersey), July 21, 1960, James P. Mitchell Papers, Box 192, DDE.
23. Edward J. Zahn, Jr., to James P. Mitchell, July 8, 1960, James P. Mitchell Papers, Box 192, DDE. Claude Jasper was the Wisconsin Republican chairman.
24. "Memorandum on the Religious Issue," John F. Kennedy, Pre-Presidential Papers, Box 1015, John F. Kennedy Library. Underline in original.
25. Leonard W. Hall and Robert H. Finch, "Confidential Memorandum," August 16, 1960, James P. Mitchell Papers, Box 193, DDE.

26. Press Conference, August 24, 1960, p. 9, Press Conference Series, Box 10, Dwight D. Eisenhower, Papers as President of the United States (Ann Whitman File), DDE.
27. With the nomination of a Catholic presidential candidate, Democrats selected Jackson to become the first non-Catholic Democratic national chairman since 1928; Anthony Lewis, "Nixon Seeks Date to End All Talk of Religious Issue," *New York Times*, September 12, 1960, p. 1; Nixon spoke on the National Broadcast Corporation's "Meet the Press" program.
28. Tom Wicker, "Jackson Urges a Press Inquiry On 'Organized' Hate Campaign," *New York Times*, September 15, 1960, p. 28.
29. "Expedience Seen In Nixon Tactics," September 29, 1960, Box 213, CPT.
30. Murphy worked both as special counsel to the president, and under secretary of agriculture during the Truman administration. David Lloyd served both as an administrative assistant to the president, and personal assistant to Truman.
31. Charles S. Murphy to "Boss," September 29, 1960, Charles S. Murphy Papers, Box 21, HST.
32. Harry S. Truman to Dean, October 9, 1960, Dean Acheson Papers, Box 180, HST.
33. Press Release, October 11, 1960, p. 3–4, Harry S. Truman Post-Presidential Files, Speech Files, Box 731, HST. Underline in original.
34. "Truman Stands on Speeches; Rebuffs Texas Baptist Pastors," *New York Times*, October 13, 1960, p. 25.
35. Carl M. Brauer, *John F. Kennedy and the Second Reconstruction* (New York: Columbia University Press, 1977), 51.
36. Quoted in Thomas Maier, *The Kennedys: America's Emerald Kings: A Five-Generation History of the Ultimate Irish-Catholic Family* (New York: Basic Books, 2003), 413.
37. Harris Wofford, *Of Kennedys and Kings: Making Sense of the Sixties* (New York: Farrar, Strauss, Giroux, 1980), 12.
38. Layhmond Robinson, "Democrats Hold A City's Negroes," *New York Times*, October 9, 1960, p. 64.
39. James Q. Wilson, "How Will the Negroes Vote?" *Reporter*, October 13, 1960, 34–36.
40. Taylor Branch, *Parting the Waters: America in the King Years, 1954–1963* (New York: Simon and Schuster, 1988), 350; See also, Harris Wofford, *Of Kennedys and Kings*, 12–13.
41. *New York Times*, October 5, 1960.
42. Branch, *Parting the Waters*, 343.
43. Lasky, *JFK*, 486–487.
44. Branch, *Parting the Waters*, 351–359.
45. Brauer, *John F. Kennedy*, 46–48.
46. John F. Kennedy Pre-Presidential Papers, Box 1016, JFKL; Wofford, *Of Kennedys and Kings*, 28, 22–24.
47. John Kenneth Galbraith, *A Life in Our Times: Memoirs* (New York: Houghton Mifflin, 1981), 386.
48. Charles S. Murphy to "Boss," October 31, 1960, Charles S. Murphy Papers, Box 21 (also in Box 72), HST.
49. "Mitchell Hits Religious Issue," *Washington Post*, September 9, 1960, CPT, Box 260.
50. Laurence F. Mills, "A Catholic," to Secretary James P. Mitchell, October 7, 1960, James P. Mitchell Papers, Box 193, DDE.
51. Secretary of Labor to Laurence F. Mills, [October 31, 1960?], unsent, attachment, James P. Mitchell to Laurence F. Mills, November 30, 1960, James P. Mitchell Papers, Box 193, DDE.

52. Undated, unsent letter from Secretary of Labor to Reverend James Rizer, Norfolk, VA, James P. Mitchell Papers, Box 193, DDE.
53. Anonymous, [September 20–October 10, 1960?], "Memorandum on the Religious Issue," Fred Seaton Papers, Republican Party Series, 1960 Campaign Subseries, Box 6, DDE.
54. Research Division, Republican National Committee, "Press References to Religion in the 1960 Campaign," October 18, 1960, Fred Seaton Papers, Republican Party Series, 1960 Campaign Subseries, Box 6, DDE.
55. Mary Cobb Lewis to James Mitchell, November 7, 1960, James P. Mitchell Papers, Box 193, DDE. All caps in original.
56. Dwight D. Eisenhower, Papers as President, 1953–1961, Ann Whitman File, DDE Diary Series, Box 54, DDE.
57. Richard M. Nixon, *Six Crises* (Garden City, NY: Doubleday and Company, Inc., 1962), 367–368.
58. Richard Scammon, "How Negroes Voted" in *New Republic,* November 21, 1960.
59. V. O. Key, Jr., *The Responsible Electorate: Rationality in Presidential Voting, 1936–1960* (Cambridge, MA: Belknap Press, 1966), 118.
60. Samuel Lubell Press Release, "Religious Issue Helps Kennedy," November 9, 1960, SL.
61. Maier, *The Kennedys,* 284.
62. Dwight D. Eisenhower, "Nationalities for Nixon," September 19, 1960, Dwight D. Eisenhower, Papers as President of the United States (Ann Whitman File), Speech Series, Box 3, DDE.
63. Dwight D. Eisenhower, Waging Peace, 1956–1961 (Garden City, NY: Doubleday, 1965), 590–603.

Chapter 6

1. *Wall Street Journal,* March 7, 1960.
2. Gerald W. Johnson, *New Republic,* May 30, 1960, p. 10.
3. John Chamberlain, "The Chameleon Image of JFK," *National Review,* April 23, 1960, pp. 261–63. Quoted in Patrick Allitt, *Catholic Intellectuals and Conservative Politics in America, 1950–1985* (Ithaca, NY: Cornell University Press, 1993), 89.
4. Robert Dallek, *An Unfinished Life: John F. Kennedy, 1917–1963* (New York: Little, Brown, and Co., 2003), 159–163.
5. W. J. Rorabaugh, *Kennedy and the Promise of the Sixties* (Cambridge, UK: Cambridge University Press, 2002), 10–11; see also David M. Oshinsky, *A Conspiracy So Immense: The World of Joe McCarthy* (New York: The Free Press, 1983), 33; and James MacGregor Burns, *John Kennedy: A Political Profile* (New York: Harcourt, Brace, and Company, 1959), 149–154.
6. Robert Amoroy, Jr., Oral History. Quoted in Dallek, *Unfinished Life,* 162.
7. Peter Collier and David Horowitz, *The Kennedys: An American Drama* (New York: Summit Books, 1984), 299–300.
8. Al Smith Dinner Speech, October 22, 1959, John F. Kennedy Pre-Presidential Papers (hereafter referred to as JFK PPP), Box 1029, John F. Kennedy Presidential Library, Boston, MA.
9. "Texts on Kennedy's Stand," *New York Times,* April 18, 1960, p. 23.

10. "Kennedy Again Supports Church-State Separation: Air Force Manual Decried," *New York Times,* April 18, 1960, p. 1.
11. "Texts," *New York Times,* April 18, 1960, p. 23.
12. *New York Times,* March 9, 1960.
13. "'Distortion' of Cardinal Laid to Press," *Baltimore Sun,* March 12, 1960, p. 4; *New York Times,* March 12, 1960.
14. Michael R. Beschloss, *Mayday: Eisenhower, Khrushchev and the U-2 Affair* (New York: Harper and Row, 1986), 318–319.
15. Allitt, *Catholic Intellectuals,* 30.
16. Anthony Trawick Bouscaren to editor, *Brooklyn Tablet,* July 2, 1960, p. 6. Uncatalogued Papers, Richard M. Nixon Library, Yorba Linda, CA (hereafter referred to as RMN).
17. Juniper Carol, "Kennedy for President? A Catholic Priest Says 'No.'" *Human Events,* July 28, 1960, pp. 313–314. JFK PPP, Box 1020.
18. Joseph F. Murray to editor, *Brooklyn Tablet,* July 23, 1960, p. 6. Uncatalogued Papers, RMN.
19. "Kennedy's Marxist Record: His Record in Question—Not His Religion," *Common Sense: The Nation's Anti-Communist Newspaper,* No. 345, June 15, 1960, Paul B. Blanshard Papers, Box 20, Bentley Historical Library (hereafter referred to as PBB).
20. "Is Kennedy a Catholic?" *The Cross and The Flag,* August 1960, p. 4. Richard M. Nixon General Correspondence File, Box 705, National Archives and Records Administration—Pacific Southwest Division, Laguna Niguel, CA (hereafter referred to as NARA).
21. Manion served as professor of Constitutional Law for twenty years, and dean from 1941 to 1952. *New York Times,* July 29, 1979, p. 36.
22. "Suicide in Los Angeles," *The Cross and The Flag,* August 1960, p. 28. Richard M. Nixon General Correspondence Files, Box 705, NARA.
23. "Osservatore," *New York Times,* June 4, 1960, Charles P. Taft Papers, Box 260, Library of Congress, Washington, D.C.
24. Cronin learned of Hiss' Communist Party affiliation while preparing a report on communism for the American Catholic Bishops. Stephen E. Ambrose, *Nixon: The Education of a Politician, 1913–1962* (New York: Simon and Schuster, 1987), 144–146.
25. Helen Gahagan Douglas, *A Full Life* (Garden City, NY: Doubleday, 1982), 322–323.
26. Greg Mitchell, *Tricky Dick and The Pink Lady: Richard Nixon vs. Helen Gahagan Douglas—Sexual Politics and the Red Scare, 1950* (New York: Random House, 1998), 177–178, 229.
27. *Newsweek,* July 9, 1956, p. 29.
28. Thomas Maier, *The Kennedys: America's Emerald Kings: A Five-Generation History of the Ultimate Irish Catholic Family* (New York: Basic Books, 2003), 283; Another study estimated that the Republican ticket won 44 percent of Catholic voters in 1952 and 49 percent in 1956. Nelson W. Polsby and Aaron Wildavsky, *Presidential Elections: Contemporary Strategies of American Electoral Politics* (New York: Free Press, 1988), 303.
29. Samuel Lubell, *Future of American Politics* (New York: Doubleday, 1956), 238, 236.
30. Jonathan Aitken, *Nixon: A Life* (Washington: Regnery Pub., 1993), 251–254.
31. *America,* vol. CI, no. 19, Richard M. Nixon General Correspondence Files, Box 30, NARA.

Notes 189

32. Congressional Record, Appendix, August 11, 1959, p. A 6892. Richard M. Nixon General Correspondence Files, Box 197, NARA.
33. The Notre Dame seniors selected Nixon, from five nominees, by an overwhelming majority. John Kennedy received this award in 1956. Charles Tausche, "Nixon Voted 'Patriot of the Year,'" January 15, 1960, Richard M. Nixon General Correspondence Files, Box 138, NARA.
34. Mary Halligan, Indianapolis, IN, to James P. Mitchell, September 14, 1960, James P. Mitchell Papers, Box 193, Dwight D. Eisenhower Presidential Library, Abilene, KA.
35. John H. Hoeppel, editor, *National Defense* (Arcadia, CA), past commander, American Legion. JFK PPP, Box 1014. See also, Isidor Schaffer to Peale, n.d., JFK PPP, Box 1012.
36. Donald D. Van Marter, Detroit, MI, to Norman Vincent Peale, September 9, 1960, JFK PPP Box 1012.
37. David Kenney and Robert E. Hartley, *An Uncertain Tradition: U.S. Senators from Illinois, 1818–2003* (Carbondale: Southern Illinois University Press, 2003), 175.
38. "Charles Percy Memo," September 26, 1960, Uncatalogued Papers, RMN. Nixon Campaign Director Robert Finch requested this memorandum from Percy, who attempted to connect Nixon's refusal to exploit anti-Catholicism with President Abraham Lincoln's defense of the Declaration of Independence's pronouncement "all men are created equal." Percy's speech draft for Nixon even quoted Lincoln's refusal to tolerate the Know-Nothing Party's discrimination against Catholics: "When it comes to this, I should prefer emigrating to some country where they make no pretense of loving liberty—to Russia, for instance, where despotism can be taken pure without the base alloy of hypocrisy." While no communist systems existed during Lincoln's presidency, Percy implied that all authoritarian governments limited religious freedom and oppressed minority religions.
39. Samuel Lubell press release, "Catholics and Young Voters Could Win New York for Kennedy," October 18, 1960, No. 17, Lubell Papers, Box 5.
40. Samuel Lubell press release, October 28, 1960, Lubell Papers, Box 21.
41. Samuel Lubell press release, October 18, 1960 Lubell Papers, Box 5.
42. Samuel Lubell press release, "Catholics and Young Voters Could Win New York for Kennedy," October 18, 1960, No. 17, Lubell Papers, Box 5.
43. Samuel Lubell press release, October 20, 1960, Lubell Papers, Box 21.
44. Richard M. Nixon General Correspondence File, Box 519, NARA.
45. All caps in original. "YES, THERE IS A 'CATHOLIC BLOC' VOTE—UNITED AGAINST COMMUNISM." Uncatalogued Papers, RMN. This pamphlet invoked a Catholic theme by encouraging voters to "examine their conscience"—a phrase used to describe Catholic preparation for sacramental confession. A handwritten "Communism" replaced the typed original, "Mr. K." These last words were printed in all caps. The Roman Catholic Church used the phrase "examination of conscience" to counsel believers on preparing for the sacrament of confession. Although the original type read "examine *our* conscience" (emphasis added), someone replaced "our" with "their" in pencil.
46. "WHY CATHOLICS SHOULD VOTE FOR NIXON: *The Real Issue is Atheistic Communism,*" Uncatalogued Papers, RMN. Underline in original.
47. Advertisement, "An Open Letter to American Catholics: 'There IS a "Catholic" Issue,'" *New York Times*, October 20, 1960, PBB, Box 20.
48. *New York Times*, October 20, 1960, PBB, Box 20.
49. Interview with author, December 19, 1998.

50. Aiken, *Nixon*, 280.
51. Seymour Hersh, *The Dark Side of Camelot* (New York: Little, Brown, and Co., 1997), 178.
52. Dallek, *Unfinished Life*, 288–289.
53. Hersh, *Dark Side of Camelot*, 180.
54. Samuel Lubell press release, "Confusion Tabs '60 As the 'Election Without Mandate,'" November 4, 1960, Lubell Papers, Box 5.
55. *Time*, November 16, 1960.

Chapter Seven

1. *U.S. News and World Report* republished "The Bailey Memo" in the August 1, 1960, edition; see Dave Powers Papers, Box 29, John F. Kennedy Library (hereafter referred to as JFKL). A copy of this memo, titled "Catholic Voters and the Democratic National Ticket—*An Analysis of Available Data and Polls*," was also found in Richard M. Nixon Papers, General Correspondence, Box 138, National Archives and Records Administration—Pacific Southwest Division, Laguna Niguel. The context of the memo's creation is discussed in Theodore C. Sorensen, *Kennedy* (New York: Harper and Row, 1965).
2. In 1952, Democratic presidential candidate Adlai Stevenson secured more of New York's heavily Catholic regions than the state's 1950 Democratic gubernatorial nominee, a Roman Catholic. Michigan's 1952 Catholic, Democratic senatorial candidate trailed Protestant Democrat G. Mennen Williams' gubernatorial returns in Catholic regions. "More About 'Catholic Vote' In U.S. Elections," *U.S. News and World Report*, August 17, 1956, pp. 42–46, 132–135.
3. Louis Harris and Associates, "A Survey of the Race for President in the State of California," March 1958, John F. Kennedy Pre-Presidential Papers (hereafter referred to as JFK PPP), Box 815, JFKL.
4. Louis Harris and Associates, "An Analysis of Presidential Preferences in Michigan, January, 1960," JFK PPP Box 816.
5. Theodore H. White, *The Making of the President 1960* (New York: Atheneum, 1961), 165–167; "The Professor's New Course," *Time*, October 24, 1960, pp. 29–32.
6. Louis Harris and Associates, "A Study of the 1960 Presidential Election in New York State," September 19, 1960, JFK PPP, Box 816, pp. 1–19.
7. Louis Harris and Associates, "The Key Groups In Georgia," [October 1960?], Richard M. Scammon Papers # 900, Box 1, JFKL.
8. "Religious Affiliations of Members of 86th Congress," *Congressional Quarterly Weekly Report*, January 8, 1960, pp. 61, 63. JFK PPP Box 1015.
9. John M. Allswang, *California Initiatives and Referendums: A Survey and Guide to Research* (Los Angeles: Edmund G. "Pat" Brown Institute of Public Affairs, California State University, Los Angeles, 1991).
10. Louis Harris and Associates, "A Survey of the Race for President in the State of California," March 1958, JFK PPP, Box 815.
11. E.g., *Ripsaw*, South Bend, IN, Edmund G. Brown Papers (hereafter referred to as Brown Papers), Carton 432, Bancroft Library, University of California at Berkeley.
12. Charles P. Taft and Bruce L. Felknor, *Prejudice and Politics* (New York: Anti-Defamation League of B'nai B'rith, 1960), 44–46.

13. Greg Mitchell, *Tricky Dick and the Pink Lady: Richard Nixon vs. Helen Gahagan Douglas—Sexual Politics and the Red Scare, 1950* (New York: Random House, 1998), 178–179, 99–101, 256.
14. Edmund G. Brown, Sr., *Years of Growth, 1939–1966: Law Enforcement, Politics, and the Governor's Office* (Berkeley, CA: Regents of the University of California, 1982), 221; Frederick G. Dutton, *Democratic Campaigns and Controversies, 1954–1966* (Berkeley, CA: Regents of the University of California, 1981), 64.
15. Richard Graves to Frederick G. Dutton, Executive Secretary, Governor's Office, July 30, 1959, Brown Papers, Carton 429.
16. Richard Graves to Frederick G. Dutton, Executive Secretary, Governor's Office, August 20, 1959, Brown Papers, Carton 429.
17. Brown, *Years of Growth*, 400–401, 458. Polling data revealed Kennedy's ability to defeat Brown in the California primary. If Kennedy could win the New Hampshire, Wisconsin, and West Virginia primaries, Brown pledged his endorsement at the national convention. See Robert Dallek, *An Unfinished Life: John F. Kennedy, 1917–1963* (Boston: Little, Brown, and Co., 2003), 247. Powers Papers, Box 26, JFKL.
18. E.g., Wesley Humphrey of Beverly Hills, CA, to Brown, May 6, 1960, Brown Papers, Carton 429.
19. Alexander H. Pope to Wesley Humphrey, May 12, 1960, Brown Papers, Carton 431.
20. E.g., Edmund G. Brown to J. Arthur David, June 10, 1960, Brown Papers, Carton 432.
21. *Presidential Preview*, June 7, 1960, p. 2, James P. Mitchell Papers, Dwight D. Eisenhower Library, Abilene, KA (hereafter referred to as Mitchell Papers), Box 193.
22. "Brown's Victory May Be Costly: The Democratic Split," *San Diego Union*, June 22, 1960, p. b-2, Brown Papers, Carton 429.
23. Dallek, *Unfinished Life*, 247.
24. White, *Making of the President*, 176–177.
25. "Brown Supports Kennedy," *Kennedy Convention Bulletin*, July 11, 1960, p. 1, William F. Knowland Papers, Bancroft Library, University of California, Berkeley, Carton 295.
26. Dallek, *Unfinished Life*, 263.
27. Thomas Lynch, *A Career In Politics and the Attorney General's Office* (Berkeley: Regents of the University of California, 1982), 124.
28. Stanley Mosk, *Attorney General's Office and Political Campaigns, 1958–1966* (Berkeley: Regents of the University of California, 1980), 40.
29. Brown, *Years of Growth*, 399.
30. C. P. Stevens, Secretary, Democrats for Rockefeller, to "Delegates to the Republican Convention," July 16, 1960, Brown Papers, Box 274.
31. Stevens, "Delegates to the Republican Convention."
32. James A. Michener, *Report of the County Chairman* (New York: Bantam Books, 1961), 108.
33. Carey McWilliams, "The Kennedys Take Over," *The Nation*, July 23, 1960, Brown Papers, Carton 432.
34. Rev. Dan Gilbert, D.D., LL.D., "The True, Inside Story of the Rigging and 'Fixing' of the Democrat Convention in Los Angeles," *Inside Election Report, No. 3*, Brown Papers, Carton 432.
35. Garvin W. Hale of San Jose, CA, to Senator John Kennedy, September 6, 1960, JFK PPP Box 977.

36. *New York Times,* September 14, 1960, p. 1.
37. "Issue Seen in A Glass Darkly," *San Francisco Chronicle,* September 9, 1960, p. 28; "Religious Bias," *San Francisco Chronicle,* September 9, 1960, p. 28.
38. "Religion Is Not An Issue: One Nation Under God," *San Diego Union,* September 14, 1960, p. b-2.
39. "Foundation For Freedom," *San Diego Union,* September 14, 1960, p. b-2.
40. "Confidential Report, GMW's Campaign Swing Through California," September 30, 1960, Margaret Price Papers, Bentley Historical Library, University of Michigan, Ann Arbor, MI, Box 4.
41. Democratic National Chairman Henry M. Jackson received letters from the Richmond County Chair, October 10, 1960; Onondaga County Chair, October 3, 1960; San Joaquin County Chair, October 4, 1960; Orange County Chair, September 29, 1960; and Riverside County Chair, October 3, 1960. Henry M. Jackson Papers, University of Washington, Seattle, Box 18, Accession No. 3560–12.
42. Samuel Lubell press release, "Kennedy Seen Gaining Religious Spite Vote," October 13, 1960, No. 6, Samuel Lubell Papers, Thomas Dodd Archives Center, University of Connecticut, Storrs, CT, (hereafter referred to as Lubell Papers), Box 5.
43. Herbert S. Parmet, *Richard Nixon and His America* (Boston: Little, Brown, and Co., 1990), 198–201; Mitchell, *Tricky Dick and The Pink Lady.*
44. Samuel Lubell press release, "Kennedy Seen Gaining Religious Spite Vote."
45. White, *Making of the President,* 16.
46. White, *Making of the President,* 461.
47. "Breakdown of Votes Cast in Metropolitan Areas, 1960 Presidential Campaign," Patrick Hillings, GOP Central Committee of Los Angeles, to Tom Kuchel, November 23, 1960, Thomas H. Kuchel Papers, Bancroft Library, University of California, Berkeley, Carton 262.
48. Michael Barone, *Our Country: The Shaping of America From Roosevelt to Reagan* (New York: Free Press, 1990), 333–334.
49. Kevin P. Phillips, *The Emerging Republican Majority* (New Rochelle, NY: Arlington House, 1969), 455–458, 71–72.
50. Morrie Ryskind, "Pat Brown's Phony Alibi Won't Wash; Nixon Won on His Merits," *Los Angeles Times,* November 23, 1960, Part III, p. 5. Brown Papers, Carton 429.
51. Tom Quimby to Governor Williams, February 25, 1960, Memorandum, G. Mennen Williams Papers (hereafter referred to as GMW), Box 501, Bentley Historical Library, University of Michigan, Ann Arbor, MI.
52. "Religious Affiliations of Members of 86th Congress," *Congressional Quarterly Weekly Report,* January 8, 1960, pp. 61, 63. JFK PPP Box 1015.
53. John M. Fenton, *In Your Opinion . . . The Managing Editor of the Gallup Polls, Politics, and the People From 1945 to 1960* (Boston: Little, Brown, and Co., 1960), 209; Ray Moseley, "Many Catholics Would Bolt Party," Detroit Free Press, September 11, 1960, p. C-3.
54. Leslie W. Tentler, *Seasons of Grace: A History of the Catholic Archdiocese of Detroit* (Detroit: Wayne State University Press, 1990).
55. White, *Making of the President,* 165–167; "The Professor's New Course," *Time,* October 24, 1960, pp. 29–32.
56. E.g., W.H. Parks, of Romeo, MI, to G. Mennen Williams, January 11, 1960, GMW Box 501.
57. G. Mennen Williams to Parks, February 15, 1960, GMW Box 501.

58. Detroit News, February 17, 1960, p. 10A, JFK PPP Box 949.
59. Detroit Times, March 24, 1960, "Kennedy Offers Williams Cabinet Job in Deal," p. 8, GMW Box 501.
60. April 17, 1960, GMW Box 502.
61. N.d., GMW Box 502.
62. Neil Staebler to Mr. Harold C. McKinney, Jr., May 4, 1960, Neil Staebler Papers, Bentley Historical Library, University of Michigan, Ann Arbor, MI, Box 77.
63. White, *Making of the President*, 151–152.
64. *Presidential Preview*, June 7, 1960, p. 2, Mitchell Papers, Box 193.
65. Neil Staebler Memorandum to County Chairmen, September 1960, Staebler Papers, Box 76.
66. Neil Staebler to "Democratic Leader," September 16, 1960, Michigan State Central Committee Papers, Bentley Historical Library, University of Michigan, Ann Arbor, MI, Box 3.
67. Hiley H. Ward, "Critics of Peale Too Extreme," *Detroit Free Press*, September 10, 1960, p. 9.
68. James Robinson, "State Church Body Hits Religion Issue," *Detroit Free Press*, September 10, 1960, p. 3.
69. "A Hurricane Named 'Hate'," *Detroit Free Press*, September 13, 1960, p. 6.
70. *Detroit News*, September 14, 1960, p. 12-B.
71. "Political Notes—Who's for Whom," *Time*, October 10, 1960, p. 26.
72. Joseph C. Ingraham, "President Decries 'Evil Propaganda' in Election," *New York Times*, October 18, 1960, p. 26.
73. White, *Making of the President*, 377.
74. Barone, *Our Country*, 333–334.
75. Dallek, *Unfinished Life*, 320.
76. Richard Scammon, *America Votes* (New York: Macmillan, 1961), 271; "Religious Affiliations of Members of 86th Congress," *Congressional Quarterly Weekly Report*, January 8, 1960, 61, 63. JFK PPP Box 1015.
77. "New York: Anatomy of a Key State," *Time*, October 31, 1960, p. 14.
78. White, *Making of the President*, 153.
79. White, *Making of the President*, 165–169.
80. James Q. Wilson, *The Amateur Democrat: Club Politics in Three Cities* (Chicago: University of Chicago Press, 1962), 55; Louis Harris and Associates, "A Study of Presidential Primaries in New York City," April 1959, JFK PPP Box 816.
81. Louis Harris and Associates, "A Study of Presidential Primaries."
82. Eleanor Roosevelt to G. Mennen Williams, May 25, 1960, GMW Box 501.
83. E.g., Annamay Jones to Mrs. Franklin Roosevelt, March 28, 1960, Harry S. Truman Post-Presidential Papers, General File, Box 370, Harry S. Truman Library, Independence, MO (hereafter referred to as HSTL).
84. White, *Making of the President*, 152–154.
85. Peter Blake, of New York City, to Pierre E. G. Salinger, March 31, 1960, JFK PPP Box 1040.
86. Allida Black, *Casting Her Own Shadow: Eleanor Roosevelt and the Shaping of Postwar Liberalism* (New York: Columbia University Press, 1996), 248.
87. Burner, *John F. Kennedy*, 45.
88. Peter Collier and David Horowitz, *The Kennedys: An American Drama* (New York: Summit Books, 1984), 299–300.
89. Dallek, *Unfinished Life*, 233.

90. David Burner, *John F. Kennedy and a New Generation* (New York: Harper Collins, 1988), 45.
91. Wagner received some New York delegates' support for the vice presidency in 1956, but Kennedy eventually appeared as a stronger candidate, and the state shifted loyalty. *Presidential Preview,* June 21, 1960, p. 5, Mitchell Papers, Box 193.
92. White, *Making of the President,* 153–154.
93. Dallek, *Unfinished Life,* 235
94. White, *Making of the President,* 154.
95. Underline in original. *Presidential Preview,* June 28, 1960, pp. 5–7. Mitchell Papers, Box 193.
96. *Presidential Preview,* June 28, 1960, pp. 4–5, Mitchell Papers, Box 193.
97. FDR, Jr., had two brothers who attended the convention. California delegate James Roosevelt and Colorado delegate Elliott Roosevelt both supported Kennedy. Brother John Roosevelt, a Republican, supported Nixon. *Presidential Preview,* July 11, 1960, p. 3, Mitchell Papers, Box 193.
98. Collier and Horowitz, *Kennedys,* 296.
99. *Presidential Preview,* June 28, 1960, pp. 4–5, Mitchell Papers, Box 193.
100. "New York: Anatomy of a Key State," *Time,* October 31, 1960, p. 14.
101. Samuel Lubell press release, "Catholics and Young Voters Could Win N.Y. for Kennedy," October 18, 1960, No. 17, Lubell Papers, Box 5.
102. "New York: Anatomy of a Key State," *Time,* October 31, 1960, p. 14.
103. Samuel Lubell press release, "Catholics and Young Voters," Lubell Papers, Box 5.
104. Barone, *Our Country,* 333–334.
105. Fenton, *In Your Opinion,* 203, 213.
106. John A. Goldsmith, *Colleagues: Richard B. Russell and His Apprentice, Lyndon B. Johnson* (Washington, D.C.: Seven Locks Press, 1993), 75–81.
107. T. David Lisle, "Southern Baptists and the Issue of Catholic Autonomy in the 1960 Presidential Campaign," in *John F. Kennedy: The Promise Revisited,* ed. Paul Harper and Johann P. Krieg, 273–276. Please see Chapter Three for further discussion of this difference.
108. Samuel Lubell, "South Inclined to Favor Nixon," *Washington Daily News,* March 1, 1960, p. 2, Lubell Papers, Box 27.
109. Phil Farkas, Albany, GA, to Senator John F. Kennedy, January 19, 1958, JFK PPP Box 998.
110. Mrs. Mary F. (C.G.) McCay, Decatur, GA, to John F. Kennedy, February 14, 1958, JFK PPP Box 998. Kennedy's reply suggested that "the pluralistic society which has developed under our Constitution," allowed "diverse opinions [to] exist side by side." John F. Kennedy to Mrs. Mary F. (C.G.) McCay, Decatur, GA, March 21, 1958, JFK PPP Box 998.
111. Mrs. Mary F. (C.G.) McCay, Decatur, GA, to Honorable Harry S. Truman, April 20, 1960, Harry S. Truman Post-Presidential Papers, Political File (hereafter referred to as HST PF), Box 370, HSTL.
112. Melvin J. Wise, "Can A Loyal Catholic Be A Good President of the United States?" Druid Hills Church of Christ, Atlanta, GA, HST PF Box 703.
113. Samuel Lubell press release, "Religious Issue Seen Overstressed in West Virginia," May 2, 1960, Lubell Papers, Box 5; Samuel Lubell, "Check Shows Huge Kennedy Victory," *Washington Daily News,* May 14, 1960, Lubell Papers, Box 21.
114. Dallek, *Unfinished Life,* 265.
115. *Presidential Preview,* July 11, 1960, p. 4, Mitchell Papers, Box 193.

116. *Presidential Preview,* July 19, 1960, p. 5, Mitchell Papers, Box 193.
117. *Presidential Preview,* July 19, 1960, p. 5, Mitchell Papers, Box 193. Most analysts failed to report this attitude, however, since many liberals voiced opposition to a southerner, such as Johnson, on civil rights grounds.
118. Charles Pou, "Fortson Accuses GOP of Anti-Catholic Smut: Al Smith-Type Campaign Aims at Kennedy, He Says," *Atlanta Journal,* September 7, 1960, p. 1.
119. Charles Pou, "State GOP Hotly Denies Anti-Catholic Charge," *Atlanta Journal,* September 8, 1960, p. 5.
120. *Savannah Morning News,* September 9, 1960, p. 9-A.
121. "The Big Meeting," *Atlanta Journal,* September 9, 1960, p. 12.
122. "Fiery Cross Put in Yard of Church," *Atlanta Constitution,* September 10, 1960, p. 5.
123. William S. White, "Kennedy Jolted By Georgia Vote," *Atlanta Constitution,* September 17, 1960, p. 4.
124. National Media Analysis, Reports 22–25, Robert Merriam Papers, Dwight D. Eisenhower Library, Abilene, KA.
125. *Atlanta Constitution,* September 8, 1960, p. 4.
126. "Baptists and Catholics Both Deserve Better," *Atlanta Constitution,* September 10, 1960, p. 4. Vandiver neglected to endorse Kennedy explicitly, but attended a conference of five southern state party leaders who supported the Democratic ticket. Frank Wells, "Leaders of 5 States Fight for Kennedy," *Atlanta Constitution,* September 9, 1960, p. 1.
127. Sally Sanford, "Pastor's Opinions on Catholic Issue," *Atlanta Journal,* October 2, 1960, JFK PPP Box 1016.
128. Scammon Papers #900, Box 1, pp. 4, 8–10, JFKL.
129. Goldsmith, *Colleagues,* 80–81.
130. Scammon Papers #900, Box 1, pp. 4, 8–10, JFKL.
131. "Where The Power Lies," *Time,* October 10, 1960, pp. 24–25.
132. White, *Making of the President,* 321, 461.
133. Philip E. Converse, Angus Campbell, Warren E. Miller, Donald E. Stokes, "Stability and Change in 1960: A Reinstating Election" in *Elections and the Political Order,* ed. Campbell, et al. (New York: Wiley, 1966), 84–93.
134. Ithiel de Sola Pool, Robert P. Abelson, Samuel L. Popkin, *Candidates, Issues, and Strategies: A Computer Simulation of the 1960 Presidential Election* (Cambridge, MA: The M.I.T. Press, 1964), 115–117.
135. V. O. Key, Jr., "Interpreting the Election Results," in *The Presidential Election and Transition, 1960–1961,* ed. Paul T. David (Washington, D.C.: Brookings Institution, 1961), 155–175.
136. Pool, et al. *Candidates, Issues, and Strategies,* 117–118.

Epilogue

1. Lawrence J. McAndrews, "Beyond Appearances: Kennedy, Congress, Religion, and Federal Aid to Education," *Presidential Studies Quarterly* 21 (summer 1991), 545–557.
2. Paul Blanshard to Ed Wilson, March 8, 1961, Paul B. Blanshard Papers (hereafter referred to as PBB), Box 3, Bentley Historical Library, University of Michigan, Ann Arbor.

3. PBB, Box 3. Although 75 percent of Catholics voted for Kennedy in 1960, the new president received criticism from the Jesuit publication *America* for refusing to receive Catholic dignitaries. *America,* January 13, 1962.
4. *Christian Century,* January 24, 1962, PBB, Box 20.
5. Herbert S. Parmet, *JFK: The Presidency of John F. Kennedy* (New York: Dial Press, 1983).
6. Julia M. Corbett, *Religion in America,* 3rd ed. (Upper Saddle River, NJ: Prentice-Hall, 1997), 94.
7. Paul B. Blanshard, *Paul Blanshard on Vatican II* (Boston: Beacon Press, 1966).
8. Garry Wills, *The Kennedy Imprisonment* (New York: Little, Brown, and Co., 1983). Garry Wills, *Bare Ruined Choirs: Doubt, Prophecy, and Radical Religion* (New York: Doubleday and Co., 1972).
9. Theodore H. White, *Making of the President 1964* (New York: Atheneum, 1965), 320–323.
10. James D. Fairbanks and John Francis Burke, "Religious Periodicals and Presidential Elections, 1960–1988," *Presidential Studies Quarterly* 22 (winter 1992), 98–99.
11. Research Staff, Republican National Committee, *1960 Elections: A Summary Report With Supporting Tables* (April 1961), Dwight D. Eisenhower, Presidential Papers, Campaign Series, Box 4 (1960 Elections), Dwight D. Eisenhower Presidential Library, Abilene, KA.
12. Barry M. Goldwater, *Goldwater* (New York: St. Martin's Press, 1988), 157.
13. White, *Making of the President 1964,* 464–466.
14. *America,* December 16, 1967, p. 735.
15. Fairbanks and Burke, "Religious Periodicals in Presidential Elections," 100; Original quotation in "A Candidate Ill-Served," *Commonweal* 88 (May 10, 1968), 221.
16. Eugene McCarthy, "Religion in Politics, Midwest Variety," in *Once a Catholic: Prominent Catholics and Ex-Catholics Discuss the Influence of the Church on Their Lives and Work,* ed. Peter Occhigrosso (Boston: Houghton Mifflin, 1987), 283, 275.
17. Theo Lippman, Jr., *Muskie* (New York: W. W. Norton, 1971), 39.
18. Louis H. Bean, "More About 'Catholic Vote' In U.S. Elections," *U.S. News and World Report,* August 17, 1956, pp. 42–46, 132–135. See Chapter Seven.
19. Louis H. Bean, *How to Predict the 1972 Election* (New York: Quadrangle Books, 1972), 84–85.
20. Bean, *How to Predict the 1972 Election.*
21. Shriver mentioned only one potentially scandalous incident. The *National Enquirer* printed a Paris nightclub photograph of Shriver dancing with "a beautiful young lady in hot pants." McGovern accepted Shriver's assurance that the woman was a family friend, and proceeded with the nomination. Theodore H. White, *Making of the President 1972* (New York: Bantam Books, 1973), 209–210.
22. White, *Making of the President 1972,* 229–230.
23. White, *Making of the President 1972,* 229–230.
24. Timothy A. Byrnes and Mary C. Segers, "Introduction," in *The Catholic Church and the Politics of Abortion: A View from the States,* ed. Timothy A. Byrnes and Mary C. Segers (Boulder, CO: Westview Press, 1992), 4–5; *Time,* September 24, 1984, p. 20.
25. White, *Making of the President 1972,* 229–230.
26. White, *Making of the President 1972,* 344.
27. David C. Leege, "The Catholic Vote in '96: Can it be found in church?" *Commonweal,* September 27, 1996, pp. 11–18.

28. Leo P. Ribuffo, *Right, Center, Left: Essays in American History* (New Brunswick, NJ: Rutgers University Press, 1992), 217, 220.
29. Gerald M. Pomper, "The Nominating Contests," in *The Election of 1980: Reports and Interpretations,* ed. Gerald M. Pomper (Chatham, NJ: Chatham House Publishers, 1980), 28–29.
30. Ribuffo, *Right, Center, Left,* 241–242.
31. Henry A. Plotkin, "Issues in the Presidential Campaign," in *Election of 1980,* 51–55.
32. Carl Bernstein and Marco Politi, *His Holiness: John Paul II and the Hidden History of Our Time* (New York, 1996), 355–361.
33. Gerald M. Pomper, "The Presidential Election," *Election of 1980,* 71–73.
34. Wilson Carey McWilliams, "The Meaning of the Election," in *Election of 1980,* 178–180.
35. Ed Magnuson, "Pressing the Abortion Issue," *Time,* September 24, 1984, pp. 18–20. All caps in original.
36. Melinda Beck, "More Debate on Abortion," *Newsweek,* September 24, 1984, pp. 18–20, 27.
37. Ed Magnuson, "Pressing the Abortion Issue," *Time,* September 24, 1984, pp. 18–20.
38. Wilson Carey McWilliams, "The Meaning of the Election," in *The Election of 1984: Reports and Interpretations,* ed. Gerald M. Pomper (Chatham, NJ: Chatham House Publishers, 1985), 172.
39. Geraldine Ferraro, *Ferraro: My Story* (New York, 1985), 239.
40. Ferraro, *Ferraro,* 213, 215, 221. Segers, "Ferraro, the Bishops, and the 1984 Election," 155.
41. Mary C. Segers, "Ferraro, the Bishops, and the 1984 Election," in *Shaping New Vision: Gender and Values in American Culture,* ed. Clarrisa W. Atkinson (Ann Arbor, MI: UMI Research Press, 1987), 156; *Commonweal,* November 2–16, 1984, p. 604.
42. Segers, "Ferraro, the Bishops, and the 1984 Election," 161.
43. Ed Magnuson, "Pressing the Abortion Issue," *Time,* September 24, 1984, pp. 18–20.
44. Gerald M. Pomper, "The Presidential Election," in *The Election of 1984,* 68.
45. McWilliams, "Meaning of the Election," in *The Election of 1984,* 172.
46. Robert S. McElvaine, *Mario Cuomo: A Biography* (New York: Scribner's, 1988), 61–89.
47. McElvaine, *Mario Cuomo,* 88–89, 97.
48. George W. Gerner, "Catholics and The 'Religious Right': We Are Being Wooed." *Commonweal,* May 5, 1995, pp. 15–20.
49. David C. Leege, "The Catholic Vote in '96."
50. James T. McHugh, "Catholics and the 1996 Election," *First Things,* February 1997, pp. 15–17.
51. Lee Walczak and Richard S. Dunham, "Can Clinton Keep Catholics In His Fold?" *Business Week,* April 15, 1996, p. 55.
52. Thomas J. Reese, "An Election Footnote: Catholics Come Home to the Democratic Party," *America,* December 7, 1996.

Selected Bibliography

Manuscript Collections

Bancroft Library, University of California at Berkeley. Edmund G. Brown Papers. Thomas H. Kuchel Papers. William F. Knowland Papers.
Bentley Historical Library, University of Michigan, Ann Arbor. Carl McIntire Papers. Democratic Party, Michigan State Central Committee Papers. G. Mennen Williams Papers. Gerald L. K. Smith Papers. Margaret Price Papers. Neil Staebler Papers. Paul B. Blanshard Papers.
Brown University, John Hay Library, Providence, RI. Hall-Hoag Collection of Extremist Pamphlets and Literature.
Brown University, Rockefeller Library, Providence, RI. Americans for Democratic Action Papers (microfilm edition).
Charles P. Taft Papers, Library of Congress, Washington, D.C.
Dwight D. Eisenhower Library, Abilene, KA. Arthur Summerfield Papers. Dwight D. Eisenhower, Papers as President of the United States (Ann Whitman File). Fred Seaton Papers. Frederick Fox Papers. James C. Hagerty Papers. James P. Mitchell Papers. Republican National Committee Papers. Leonard W. Hall Papers. White House Central Files. Robert H. Finch Oral History, June 19, 1967.
Gerald R. Ford Library Archives, Ann Arbor, MI. Gerald R. Ford Congressional Papers.
Harry S. Truman Library, Independence, MO. Harry S. Truman Post-Presidential Files. Charles S. Murphy Papers. David H. Stowe Papers. Dean Acheson Papers.
Herbert C. Hoover Library, West Branch, IA. Herbert C. Hoover Papers. Bourke Hickenlooper Papers.
John F. Kennedy Library, Boston. John F. Kennedy Pre-Presidential Papers. Arthur M. Schlesinger, Jr. Papers. Democratic National Committee Papers. Samuel H. Beer Papers. John Kenneth Galbraith Papers. Richard M. Scammon Papers. Robert F. Kennedy Pre-Administration Papers. Theodore C. Sorensen Papers.
Library of Congress, Washington, D.C. Charles P. Taft Papers. G. Bromley Oxnam Papers. Joseph L. Rauh, Jr. Papers. Thomas J. Walsh Papers.
National Archives Pacific Southwest Division, Laguna Niguel, CA. Records of the Richard M. Nixon Pre-Presidential Papers.
New York Public Library, New York City. Norman Thomas Papers.
New York State Library, Albany. Alfred E. Smith Personal Papers. Alfred E. Smith Public Papers.
Richard M. Nixon Library Archives, Yorba Linda, CA. Uncatalogued Papers.
Seeley G. Mudd Library, Princeton University, Princeton, NJ. Adlai Stevenson Papers. American Civil Liberties Union Papers. Americans United for Separation of Church and State Papers.
Thomas J. Dodd Research Archives, University of Connecticut, Storrs. Samuel Lubell Papers.
University of Oregon Special Collections, Eugene. Wayne S. Morse Papers.
University of Washington Special Collections, Seattle. Henry M. Jackson Papers. Warren G. Magnuson Papers.

Published Oral History

Brown, Edmund G., Sr. *Years of Growth, 1939–1966: Law Enforcement, Politics, and the Governor's Office*. Berkeley, CA: Regents of the University of California, 1982.
Dutton, Frederick G. *Democratic Campaigns and Controversies, 1954–1966*. Berkeley, CA: Regents of the University of California, 1981.
Lynch, Thomas. *A Career In Politics and The Attorney General's Office*. Berkeley, CA: Regents of the University of California, 1982.
Mosk, Stanley. *Attorney General's Office and Political Campaigns, 1958–1966*. Berkeley, CA: Regents of the University of California, 1980.

Secondary Sources

Aitken, Jonathan. *Nixon: A Life*. Washington: Regnery Pub., 1993.
Allitt, Patrick. *Catholic Intellectuals and Conservative Politics in America, 1950–1985*. Ithaca, NY: Cornell University Press, 1993.
Allswang, John M. *California Initiatives and Referendums: A Survey and Guide to Research*. Los Angeles: Edmund G. "Pat" Brown Institute of Public Affairs, California State University, Los Angeles, 1991.
Alsop, Joseph W. *"I've Seen the Best of It": Memoirs*. New York: W. W. Norton, 1992.
Ambrose, Stephen E. *Nixon: The Education of a Politician, 1913–1962*. New York: Simon and Schuster, 1987.
Appleby, Joyce. *Capitalism and a New Social Order: The Republican Vision of the 1790s*. New York: New York University Press, 1984.
Archer, Glenn L. and Albert J. Menendez. *The Dream Lives On: The Story of Glenn L. Archer and Americans United*. Washington: R.B. Luce, 1982.
Asher, Herbert B. *Presidential Elections and American Politics: Voters, Candidates, and Campaigns Since 1952*. 3d ed. Homewood, IL: Dorsey Press, 1984.
Barber, James David. *The Presidential Character: Predicting Performance in the White House*. 2d ed. Englewood Cliffs, NJ: Prentice-Hall, Inc., 1977.
Barone, Michael. *Our Country: The Shaping of America From Roosevelt to Reagan*. New York: Free Press, 1990.
Barrett, Patricia. *Religious Liberty and the American Presidency: A Study in Church-State Relations*. New York: Herder, 1963.
Bates, J. Leonard. *Senator Thomas J. Walsh of Montana: Law and Public Affairs, from TR to FDR*. Urbana: University of Illinois Press, 1999.
Bean, Louis H. *How to Predict the 1972 Election*. New York: Quadrangle Books, 1972.
Beck, Melinda. "More Debate on Abortion." *Newsweek* (1984): 18–20, 27.
Bell, Daniel., ed. *The Radical Right*. Garden City, NY: Doubleday, 1964.
Bennett, David H. *The Party of Fear: From Nativist Movements to the New Right in American History*. Chapel Hill: The University of North Carolina Press, 1988.
Bernstein, Carl and Marco Politi, *His Holiness: John Paul II and the Hidden History of Our Time*. New York: Doubleday, 1996.
Bianci, Eugene C. *John XXIII and American Protestants*. Washington: Corpus Books, 1968.
Billington, Ray A. *The Protestant Crusade 1800–1860: A Study in the Origins of American Nativism*. Chicago: Quadrangle, 1938.

Selected Bibliography

Billington, Ray A. *The Origins of Nativism in the United States, 1800–1844.* New York: Arno Press, 1974.

Black, Allida. *Casting Her Own Shadow: Eleanor Roosevelt and the Shaping of Postwar Liberalism.* New York: Columbia University Press, 1996.

Blanshard, Paul B. *American Freedom and Catholic Power.* Boston: Beacon Press, 1949.

Blanshard, Paul B. *Communism, Democracy, and Catholic Power.* Boston: Beacon Press, 1951.

Blanshard, Paul B. *The Irish and Catholic Power: An American Interpretation.* Boston: Beacon Press, 1953.

Blanshard, Paul B. *American Freedom and Catholic Power.* 2d ed. Boston: Beacon Press, 1958.

Blanshard, Paul B. *God and Man in Washington.* Boston: Beacon Press, 1960.

Blanshard, Paul B. *Freedom and Catholic Power in Spain and Portugal: An American Interpretation.* Boston: Beacon Press, 1962.

Blanshard, Paul B. *Paul Blanshard on Vatican II.* Boston: Beacon Press, 1966.

Blanshard, Paul B. *Personal and Controversial: An Autobiography.* Boston: Beacon Press, 1973.

Boller, Paul F. *Presidential Campaigns.* New York: Oxford University Press, 1984.

Bowden, Henry W. *Dictionary of American Religious Biography.* Westport, CT: Greenwood Press, 1993.

Branch, Taylor. *Parting the Waters: American in the King Years, 1954–1963.* New York: Simon and Schuster, 1988.

Brauer, Carl M. *John F. Kennedy and the Second Reconstruction.* New York: Columbia University Press, 1977.

Brinkley, Alan. *Voices of Protest: Huey Long, Father Coughlin, and the Great Depression.* New York: Vintage Books, 1982.

Burner, David. *The Politics of Provincialism: The Democratic Party in Transition, 1918–1932.* New York: Knopf, 1968.

Burner, David. *Hebert Hoover: The Public Life.* New York: Knopf, 1979.

Burner, David. *John F. Kennedy and a New Generation.* New York: Harper Collins, 1988.

Burns, James MacGregor. *John Kennedy: A Political Profile.* New York: Harcourt, Brace, and Company, 1959.

Burns, Richard D. *Herbert Hoover: A Bibliography of His Times and Presidency.* Wilmington, DE: Scholarly Resources, Inc., 1991.

Byrnes, Timothy A., and Mary C. Segers. "Introduction." In *The Catholic Church and the Politics of Abortion: A View from the States.* Timothy A. Byrnes and Mary C. Segers, ed. Boulder, CO: Westview Press, 1992.

Campbell, Angus, et al. *The American Voter: An Abridgment.* New York: John Wiley and Sons, 1964.

Campbell, Angus, et al. *Elections and the Political Order.* New York: John Wiley and Sons, 1966.

Carter, Paul. "The Campaign of 1928 Re-Examined: A Study in Political Folklore." *Wisconsin Magazine of History* 46 (1963): 263–272.

Carter, Paul "The Other Catholic Candidate: The 1928 Presidential Bid of Thomas J. Walsh." *Pacific Northwest Quarterly* 55 (1964): 1–8.

Carter, Paul. Politics, *Religion, and Rockets: Essays in Twentieth Century American History.* Tuscon: University of Arizona Press, 1991.

Chalmers, David M. *Hooded Americanism: The First Century of the Ku Klux Klan, 1865–1965.* Garden City, NY: Doubleday, 1965.

Coben, Stanley "A Study in Nativism: The American Red Scare of 1919–1920." *Political Science Quarterly* 79 (1964): 52–75.
Cogley, John. *Catholic America: Two Centuries of American Life.* New York: The Dial Press, 1973.
Converse, Philip E. "Stability and Change in 1960: A Reinstating Election." *American Political Science Review* 55 (1961).
Cooney, John. *The American Pope: The Life and Times of Francis Cardinal Spellman.* New York: Times Books, 1984.
Creedon Lawrence P., and William D. Falcon. *United for Separation: An Analysis of the POAU Assaults on Catholicism.* Milwaukee: Bruce, 1959.
Crosby, Donald F. *God, Church, and Flag: Senator Joseph R. McCarthy and the Catholic Church, 1950–1957.* Chapel Hill: University of North Carolina Press, 1978.
Dallek, Robert. *An Unfinished Life: John F. Kennedy, 1917–1963.* Boston: Little, Brown, and Co., 2003.
David, Paul T., ed. *The Presidential Election and Transition, 1960–1961.* Washington, D.C.: Brookings Institution, 1961.
Davis, Lawrence B. *Immigrants, Baptists, and the Protestant Mind in America.* Urbana: University of Illinois Press, 1985.
Dick, Bernard F. *The Star-Spangled Screen: The American World War II Film.* Lexington: University Press of Kentucky, 1985.
Doherty, Thomas Patrick. *Projections of War: Hollywood, American Culture, and World War II.* New York: Columbia University Press, 1993.
Dolan, Jay P. *The American Catholic Experience: A History from Colonial Times to the Present.* Garden City, NY: Image Books, 1985.
Dolan, Jay P. *In Search of An American Catholicism: A History of Religion and Culture in Tension.* Oxford: Oxford University Press, 2002.
Douglas, Emily Taft. *Margaret Sanger: Pioneer of the Future.* New York: Holt, Rinehart and Winston, 1970.
Douglas, Helen Gahagan. *A Full Life.* Garden City, NY: Doubleday, 1982.
Drinan, Robert F. *The Fractured Dream: America's Divisive Moral Choices.* New York: Crossroad, 1991.
Dulce, Barton and Edward J. Richter. *Religion and the Presidency, A Recurring American Problem.* New York: Macmillan, 1962.
Ellis, John T., and Robert Trisco. *A Guide to American Catholic History.* 2d ed. Santa Barbara, CA: ABC-Clio, 1982.
Evans, Hiram W. "The Klan's Fight for Americanism." *North American Review* CCXXIII, 8 (March 1926): 33–63.
Faber, Harold, ed. *The Kennedy Years.* New York: The Viking Press, 1964.
Fairlie, Henry. *The Kennedy Promise: The Politics of Expectation.* Garden City, NY: Doubleday and Company, 1973.
Farley, James A. *Behind the Ballots: The Personal History of a Politician.* New York: Harcourt, Brace, and Company, 1938.
Farley, James A. *Jim Farley's Story: The Roosevelt Years.* New York: McGraw-Hill, 1948.
Farley, James A., and James C. G. Conniff. *Governor Al Smith.* New York: Vision Books, 1959.
Felknor, Bruce L. *Dirty Politics.* New York: W. W. Norton, 1966.
Fenton, John M. *In Your Opinion . . . The Managing Editor of the Gallup Poll Looks At Polls, Politics, and the People From 1945–1960.* Boston: Little, Brown, and Co., 1960.
Ferraro, Geraldine. *Ferraro: My Story.* Toronto: Bantam Books, 1985.

Filene, Peter G. *Americans and the Soviet Experiment, 1917–1933*. Cambridge, MA: Harvard University Press, 1967.
Finan, Christopher M. *Alfred E. Smith: The Happy Warrior*. New York: Hill and Wang, 2002.
Fisher, James Terence. *The Catholic Counterculture in America, 1933–1962*. Chapel Hill: University of North Carolina Press, 1989.
Flynn, Edward J. *You're the Boss*. New York: Viking Press, 1947.
Flynn, George Q. *American Catholics and the Roosevelt Presidency, 1932–1936*. Lexington: University of Kentucky Press, 1968.
Flynn, George Q. *Roosevelt and Romanism: Catholics and American Diplomacy, 1937–1945*. Westport, CT: Greenwood Press, 1976.
Forster, Arnold and Benjamin R. Epstein. *ADL Report on the Ku Klux Klan*. New York, 1962.
Franchot, Jenny. *Roads to Rome: The Antebellum Protestant Encounter with Catholicism*. Berkeley: University of California Press, 1994.
Fried, Richard M. *Nightmare In Red: The McCarthy Era in Perspective*. New York: Oxford University Press, 1990.
Fuchs, Lawrence H. "The Senator and the Lady." *American Heritage* 25 (1964): 57–61.
Fuchs, Lawrence H. *John F. Kennedy and American Catholicism*. New York: Meredith Press, 1967.
Fuchs, Lawrence H. "Election of 1928." In *History of American Presidential Elections, 1979–1968*. Vol. III. Arthur M. Schlesinger, Jr., ed. New York: Chelsea House Publishers, 1971.
Gallup, George, Jr., and Jim Castelli. *The American Catholic People: Their Beliefs, Practices, and Values*. Garden City, NY: Doubleday, 1987.
Gallup, Dr. George H. *Gallup Poll, Public Opinion, 1935–1971*. Vol. 3, 1959–1971. New York: Random House, 1972.
George, Carol V. R. *God's Salesman: Norman Vincent Peale and the Power of Positive Thinking*. New York: Oxford University Press, 1993.
Gerner, George W. "Catholics and The 'Religious Right': We Are Being Wooed." *Commonweal* (1995): 15–20.
Giglio, James N. *The Presidency of John F. Kennedy*. Lawrence: University Press of Kansas, 1991.
Giglio, James N. *John F. Kennedy: A Bibliography*. Westport, CT: Greenwood Press, 1995.
Gillon, Steven M. *Politics and Vision: The ADA and American Liberalism, 1947–1985*. New York: Oxford University Press, 1987.
Glazer, Nathan, and Daniel Patrick Moynihan. *Beyond the Melting Pot: The Negroes, Puerto Ricans, Jews, Italians, and Irish of New York City*. Cambridge, MA: The M.I.T. Press, 1963.
Gleason, Philip. *Keeping the Faith: American Catholicism Past and Present*. Notre Dame, IN: University of Notre Dame Press, 1987.
Gleason, Philip. *Speaking of Diversity: Language and Ethnicity in Twentieth Century America*. Baltimore: John Hopkins University Press, 1992.
Goldsmith, John A. *Colleagues: Richard B. Russell and His Apprentice, Lyndon B. Johnson*. Washington, D.C.: Seven Locks Press, 1993.
Goldwater, Barry M. *Goldwater*. New York: St. Martin's Press, 1988.
Goodwin, Doris Kearns. *The Fitzgeralds and the Kennedys*. New York: Simon and Schuster, 1987.
Graham, Billy. *Just As I Am: The Autobiography of Billy Graham*. San Francisco: Harper, 1997.

Graham, Frank. *Al Smith American: An Informal Biography*. New York: G.P. Putnam's Sons, 1945.
Greeley, Andrew M. *The Church and the Suburbs*. New York: Paulist Press, 1963.
Greeley, Andrew M. *The Catholic Experience: An Interpretation of the History of American Catholicism*. Garden City, NY: Doubleday, 1969.
Greeley, Andrew M. *An Ugly Little Secret: Anti-Catholicism in North America*. Kansas City, MO: Andrews McMeel, 1977.
Guth, James L., and John C. Green, ed. *The Bible and the Ballot Box: Religion and Politics in the 1988 Election*. Boulder, CO: Westview Press, 1991.
Halberstam, David. *The Unfinished Odyssey of Robert Kennedy*. New York: Random House, 1968.
Halberstam, David. *The Best and the Brightest*. New York: Random House, 1969.
Halberstam, David. *The Fifties*. New York: Villard Books, 1993.
Hamburger, Philip. *Separation of Church and State*. Cambridge, MA: Harvard University Press, 2002.
Hamby, Alonzo L. *The Imperial Years: The United States Since 1939*. New York: Weybright and Talley, 1976.
Hamby, Alonzo L. *Man of the People: A Life of Harry S Truman*. New York: Oxford University Press, 1995.
Hamerow, Theodore S. "The Two Worlds of the Forty-Eighters." In *The German Forty-Eighters in the United States*. Charlotte L. Brancaforte, ed. New York: P. Lang, 1989.
Hamilton, Charles V. *Adam Clayton Powell, Jr.: The Political Biography of an American Dilemma*. New York: Atheneum, 1991.
Hamilton, Nigel. *JFK: Reckless Youth*. New York: Random House, 1992.
Handlin, Oscar. *Al Smith and His America*. Boston: Little, Brown, and Co., 1958.
Harper, Paul, and Joann P. Krieg, eds. *John F. Kennedy: The Promise Revisited*. New York: Greenwood Press, 1988.
Haynes, John E. *Red Scare or Red Menace? American Communism and Anticommunism in the Cold War Era*. Chicago: Ivan R. Dee, 1996.
Hellmann, John. *The Kennedy Obsession: The American Myth of JFK*. New York: Columbia University Press, 1997.
Hennesey, James. *American Catholics: A History of the Roman Catholic Community in the United States*. New York: Oxford University Press, 1981.
Hennessey, James. "Roman Catholicism and American Politics, 1900–1960." In *Religion and American Politics: From the Colonial Period to the 1980s*. Mark Noll, ed. New York: Oxford University Press, 1990.
Herberg, William. *Protestant, Catholic, Jew: An Essay in American Religious Sociology*. 2d ed. Garden City, NY: Anchor Books, 1960.
Hickey, Neil, and Ed Edwin. *Adam Clayton Powell and the Politics of Race*. New York: Fleet Publishing, 1965.
Higham, John. *Strangers in the Land: Patterns of American Nativism, 1860–1925*. New Brunswick, NJ: Rutgers University Press, 1988.
Hirsch, Mark D. "Election of 1884." In *History of American Presidential Elections: 1789–1968*. Vol. 1. Arthur M. Schlesinger, Jr., ed. New York: McGraw-Hill, 1971.
Hofstadter, Richard. "Could a Protestant Have Beaten Hoover in 1928?" *Reporter* 22 (1960): 31–33.
Hofstadter, Richard. "The Paranoid Style in American Politics." *Harper's Magazine* 229 (1964): 77–82.
Hunter, James Davison. *Culture Wars: The Struggle to Define America*. New York: Basic Books, 1991.

Selected Bibliography 205

Hutcheson, Richard G. *God in the White House: How Religion Has Changed the Modern Presidency.* New York: McMillan Publishing Company, 1988.

Ignatiev, Noel. *How the Irish Became White.* New York: Routledge, 1995.

Jaffe, Julian F. *Crusade Against Radicalism: New York During the Red Scare, 1914–1924.* Port Washington, N.Y.: Kennikat Press, 1972.

Jenkins, Philip. *The New Anti-Catholicism: The Last Acceptable Prejudice.* Oxford: Oxford University Press, 2003.

Jorstad, Erling. *The Politics of Doomsday: Fundamentalists of the Far Right.* Nashville: Abingdon Press, 1970.

Josephson, Matthew, and Hannah Josephson. *Al Smith: Hero of the Cities: A Political Portrait Drawing on the Papers of Frances Perkins.* Boston: Houghton Mifflin Company, 1969.

Kallen, Horace M. *Culture and Democracy in the United States: Studies in the Group Psychology of the American Peoples.* New York: Boni and Liveright, 1924.

Kallen, Horace M. *Secularism is the Will of God.* New York: Twayne, 1954.

Kauffman, Christopher J. *Faith and Fraternalism: The History of the Knights of Columbus, 1882–1982.* Cambridge: Harper and Row, 1982.

Kelsey, George D. *Social Ethics Among Southern Baptists, 1917–1969.* Metuchen, NJ: Scarecrow Press, 1973.

Key, V. O., Jr. *The Responsible Electorate: Rationality in Presidential Voting, 1936–1960.* Cambridge, MA: Belknap Press, 1966.

Knobel, Dale T. *"America for the Americans": The Nativist Movement in the United States.* New York: Twayne Publishers, 1996.

Koppes, Clayton R. *Hollywood Goes To War: How Politics, Profits, and Propaganda Shaped World War II Movies.* New York: Collier Macmillan, 1987.

Lally, Francis J. *The Catholic Church in a Changing America.* Boston: Little, Brown, and Co., 1962.

Lasky, Victor. *JFK: The Man and the Myth.* New York: The MacMillan Company, 1963.

Lee, Robert, and Martin E. Marty, ed. *Religion and Social Conflict.* New York: Oxford University Press, 1964.

Leege, David C. "The Catholic Vote in '96: Can it be found in church?" *Commonweal* 27 (1996): 11–18.

Leffler, Melvyn P. *The Specter of Communism: The United States and the Origins of the Cold War, 1917–1953.* London: Allen Lane: 1994.

Levy, Mark K., and Michael S. Kramer. *The Ethnic Factor: How America's Minorities Decide Elections.* New York: Simon and Schuster, 1972.

Lewis, David. *King: A Critical Biography.* Baltimore: Penguin Books, 1970.

Lichtmann, Allan J. *Prejudice and the Old Politics: The Presidential Election of 1928.* Chapel Hill: University of North Carolina Press, 1979.

Lippman, Theo, Jr. *Muskie.* New York: W. W. Norton, 1971.

Lipset, Seymour Martin, and Earl Raab. *The Politics of Unreason: Right-Wing Extremism in America, 1790–1970.* New York: Harper and Row, 1970.

Lisle, T. David. "Southern Baptists and the Issue of Catholic Autonomy in the 1960 Presidential Campaign." In *John F. Kennedy: The Promise Revisited.* Paul Harper and Joann P. Krieg, eds. New York: Greenwood Press, 1988.

Loveland, Anne C. *American Evangelicals and the U.S. Military, 1942–1993.* Baton Rouge: Louisiana University Press, 1996.

Lubell, Samuel. *The Future of American Politics.* 2d ed. New York: Doubleday, 1956.

Magnuson, Ed. "Pressing the Abortion Issue." *Time* (1984): 18–20.

Maier, Thomas. *The Kennedys: America's Emerald Kings: A Five-Generation History of the Ultimate Irish-Catholic Family.* New York: Basic Books, 2003.

Manchester, William. *One Brief Shining Moment.* Boston: Little, Brown, and Company, 1983.

Marsden, George M. "Afterword: Religion, Politics, and the Search for an American Consensus." In *Religion and American Politics: From the Colonial Period to the 1980s.* Mark A. Noll, ed. New York: Oxford University Press, 1990.

Marshall, Charles C. "An Open Letter to the Honorable Alfred E. Smith." *Atlantic Monthly* 139 (1927): 540–549.

Marshall, Charles C. *Governor Smith's American Catholicism.* New York, 1928.

Martin, Ralph G. *Seeds of Destruction: Joe Kennedy and His Sons.* New York: G.P. Putnam's Sons, 1995.

Martin, William C. *A Prophet With Honor: The Billy Graham Story.* New York: W. Morrow and Co., 1991.

Martin, William C. *With God on Our Side: The Rise of the Religious Right in America.* New York: Broadway Books, 1996.

Massa, Mark Steven. *Catholics and American Culture : Fulton Sheen, Dorothy Day, and the Notre Dame Football Team.* New York: Crossroad, 1999.

Massa, Mark Steven. *Anti-Catholicism in America: The Last Acceptable Prejudice.* New York: Crossroad, 2003.

Matthews, Christopher. *Kennedy and Nixon: The Rivalry That Shaped Postwar America.* New York: Simon and Schuster, 1996.

Matusow, Allen J. *The Unraveling of America: A History of Liberalism in the 1960s.* New York: Harper and Row, 1984.

McAndrews, Lawrence J. "Beyond Appearances: Kennedy, Congress, Religion, and Federal Aid to Education." *Presidential Studies Quarterly* (1991): 545–57.

McCarthy, Eugene. "Religion in Politics, Midwest Variety." In *Once a Catholic: Prominent Catholics and Ex-Catholics Discuss the Influence of the Church on Their Lives and Work.* Peter Occhigrosso, ed. Boston: Houghton Mifflin, 1987.

McElvaine, Robert S. *Mario Cuomo: A Biography.* New York: Scribner's, 1988.

McGreevy, John T. "Thinking on One's Own: Catholicism in the American Intellectual Imagination, 1928–1960." *Journal of American History* 84 (June 1997).

McGreevy, John T. *Catholicism and American Freedom: A History.* New York: W. W. Norton, 2003.

McHugh, James T. "Catholics and the 1996 Election." *First Things* 70 (1997): 15–17.

McWilliams, Wilson Carey. "The Meaning of the Election." In *The Election of 1980: Reports and Interpretations.* Gerald M. Pomper, ed. Chatham, NJ: Chatham House Publishers, 1980.

McWilliams, Wilson Carey. "The Meaning of the Election." In *The Election of 1984: Reports and Interpretations.* Gerald M. Pomper, ed. Chatham, NJ: Chatham House Publishers, 1985.

Menendez, Albert J. *Religion At The Polls.* Philadelphia: Westminster Press, 1977.

Menendez, Albert J. *John F. Kennedy: Catholic and Humanist.* Buffalo, NY: Prometheus Books, 1978.

Meyer, Donald. *The Positive Thinkers: Popular Religious Psychology from Mary Baker Eddy to Norman Vincent Peale and Ronald Reagan.* 2d ed. Middletown, CT: Wesleyan University Press, 1988.

Michener, James A. *Report of the County Chairman.* New York: Bantam Books, 1961.

Miller, Robert Moats. *Bishop G. Bromley Oxnam: Paladin of Liberal Protestantism.* Nashville, TN: Abingdon Press, 1990.

Mitchell, Greg. *Tricky Dick and the Pink Lady: Richard Nixon vs. Helen Gahagan Douglas—Sexual Politics and the Red Scare, 1950.* New York: Random House, 1998.
Moore, Edmund A. *A Catholic Runs for President: The Campaign of 1928.* New York: Ronald Press, 1956.
Morris, Charles R. *American Catholic: The Saints and Sinners Who Built America's Most Powerful Church.* New York: Vintage Books, 1997.
Murray, Robert K. *Red Scare: A Study in National Hysteria, 1919–1920.* Minneapolis: University of Minnesota Press, 1955.
Murray, Robert K. *The 103rd Ballot: Democrats and the Disaster in Madison Square Garden.* New York: Harper and Row, 1976.
Murrin, John M. "Religion and Politics in America from the First Settlements to the Civil War." In *Religion and American Politics: From the Colonial Period to the 1980s.* Mark A. Noll, ed. New York: Oxford University Press, 1990.
Nash, George H. *The Conservative Intellectual Movement in America, Since 1945.* New York: Basic Books, 1976.
Neal, Donn C. *The World Beyond the Hudson: Alfred E. Smith and National Politics, 1918–1928.* New York: Garland Publishing, 1983.
Nixon, Richard M. *Six Crises.* Garden City, NY: Doubleday and Company, Inc., 1962.
Nixon, Richard. *RN: The Memoirs of Richard Nixon.* New York: Grosset and Dunlap, 1978.
O'Connor, Richard. *The First Hurrah: A Biography of Alfred E. Smith.* New York: C.P. Putnam's Sons, 1970.
O'Donnell, Kenneth P., and David F. Powers. *"Johny We Hardly Knew Ye": Memories of John Fitzgerald Kennedy.* New York: Little, Brown, and Co., 1972.
O'Grady, Joseph P. *How the Irish Became Americans.* New York: Twayne Publishers, 1973.
Oshinsky, David M. *A Conspiracy So Immense: The World of Joe McCarthy.* New York: The Free Press, 1983.
O'Toole, James M. *Militant and Triumphant: William Henry O'Connell and the Catholic Church in Boston, 1859–1944.* Notre Dame, IN: University of Notre Dame Press, 1992.
Parmet, Herbert S. *JFK: The Presidency of John F. Kennedy.* New York: Dial Press, 1983.
Parmet, Herbert S. *Richard Nixon and His America.* Boston: Little, Brown, and Co., 1990.
Paterson, Thomas G. *Contesting Castro: The United States and the Triumph of the Cuban Revolution.* New York: Oxford University Press, 1994.
Peale, Norman Vincent. *A Guide to Confident Living.* Englewood Cliffs, NJ: Macmillan, 1948.
Peale, Norman Vincent. *The Power of Positive Thinking.* New York: Prentice-Hall, 1952.
Peel, Roy V., and Thomas C. Donnelly. *The 1928 Campaign: An Analysis.* Westport, CT: Greenwood Press, 1931.
Pelotte, Donald E. *John Courtney Murray: Theologian in Conflict.* New York: Paulist Press, 1975.
Petersen, Svend. *A Statistical History of the American Presidential Elections.* Westport, CT: Greenwood Press, 1981.
Phillips, Kevin P. *The Emerging Republican Majority.* New Rochelle, NY: Arlington House, 1969.
Pierard, Richard V. "Billy Graham and the U.S. Presidency." *Journal of Church and State* 22 (1980).
Pike, James A. *A Roman Catholic in the White House.* Westport, CT: Greenwood Press, 1960.

Plotkin, Henry A. "Issues in the Presidential Campaign." In *Election of 1980: Reports and Interpretations*. Gerald M. Pomper, ed. Chatham, NJ: Chatham House Publishers, 1980.

Polenberg, Richard. *War and Society: The United States, 1941–1945*. New York: J. B. Lippincott Company, 1972.

Polenberg, Richard. *One Nation Divisible: Race, Class, and Ethnicity in the United States Since 1938*. New York: Viking Press, 1980.

Poling, Daniel A. *Mine Eyes Have Seen*. New York: McGraw-Hill, 1959.

Pollock, John. *Billy Graham: The Authorized Biography*. New York: McGraw-Hill, 1966.

Pomper, Gerald M. "The Nominating Contests." In *The Election of 1980: Reports and Interpretations*. Gerald M. Pomper, ed. Chatham, NJ: Chatham House Publishers, 1980.

Pomper, Gerald M. "The Presidential Election." In *The Election of 1980: Reports and Interpretations*. Gerald M. Pomper, ed. Chatham, NJ: Chatham House Publishers, 1980.

Pool, Ithiel de Sola, Robert P. Abelson, and Samuel L. Popkin. *Candidates, Issues, and Strategies: A Computer Simulation of the 1960 Presidential Election*. Cambridge, MA: The M.I.T. Press, 1964.

Reese, Thomas J. "An Election Footnote: Catholics Come Home to the Democratic Party." *America*, December 7, 1996.

Reeves, Richard. *President Kennedy: Profile of Power*. New York: Simon and Schuster, 1993.

Reichley, A. James. *Religion in American Public Life*. Washington: Brookings Institution, 1985.

Ribuffo, Leo P. *Right, Center, Left: Essays in American History*. New Brunswick, NJ: Rutgers University Press, 1992.

Rice, Arnold S. *The Ku Klux Klan in American Politics*. Washington: Public Affairs Press, 1962.

Rice, Daniel F. *Reinhold Niebuhr and John Dewey: An American Odyssey*. Albany, NY: State University of New York Press, 1993.

Richter, Edward J., and Berton Dulce. *Religion and the Presidency: A Recurring American Problem*. New York: Macmillan, 1962.

Riordon, William L., ed. *Plunkitt of Tammany Hall*. New York: Alfred A. Knopf, 1948.

Rogin, Michael P. *The Intellectuals and McCarthy: The Radical Spectre*. Cambridge, MA: M.I.T. Press, 1967.

Rorabaugh, W. J. *Kennedy and the Promise of the Sixties*. Cambridge, UK: Cambridge University Press, 2002.

Roseboom, Eugene H. *A History of Presidential Elections: From George Washington to Jimmy Carter*. 4th ed. New York: Macmillan, 1979.

Rossiter, Clinton. *The American Presidency: The Powers and Practices, the Personalities and Problems of the Most Important Office on Earth*. 2d ed. New York: Harcourt, Brace, and World, Inc., 1960.

Russell, Francis. *The President Makers: From Mark Hanna to Joseph P. Kennedy*. Boston: Little, Brown, and Co., 1976.

Salinger, Pierre. *With Kennedy*. New York: Doubleday, 1966.

Salinger, Pierre. *P.S. A Memoir*. New York: St. Martin's Griffin, 1997.

Scammon, Richard M., and Ben J. Wattenberg. *The Real Majority*. New York: Coward, McCann and Geohegan, Inc., 1970.

Schlesinger, Arthur M., Jr. *The Vital Center: the Politics of Freedom*. Boston: Houghton Mifflin, 1949.

Schlesinger, Arthur M., Jr. *A Thousand Days: John F. Kennedy in the White House.* Boston: Houghton Mifflin, 1965.

Schlesinger, Arthur M. Jr. *Robert Kennedy and His Times.* Boston: Houghton Mifflin, 1978.

Schultz, Nancy L. *Fire and Roses: The Burning of the Charlestown Convent, 1834.* New York: The Free Press, 2000.

Segers, Mary C. "Ferraro, the Bishops, and the 1984 Election." In *Shaping New Vision: Gender and Values in American Culture.* Clarrisa W. Atkinson, ed. Ann Arbor, MI: UMI Research Press, 1987.

Silk, Mark. *Spiritual Politics: Religion and America Since World War II.* New York: Simon and Schuster, 1988.

Slayton, Robert A. *Empire Statesman: The Rise and Redemption of Al Smith.* New York: The Free Press, 2001.

Smith, Alfred E. "Governor Smith's Reply." *Atlantic Monthly* 139 (April, 1927).

Smith, Alfred E. *Up to Now: An Autobiography.* New York: The Viking Press, 1929.

Sorensen, Theodore C. *Kennedy.* New York: Harper and Row, 1965.

Sorensen, Theodore C. *The Kennedy Legacy.* New York: The Macmillan Company, 1969.

Sorensen, Theodore C. "Election of 1960." *History of American Presidential Elections, 1789–1968.* Vol. IV. Arthur M. Schlesinger, Jr., ed. New York: Chelsea House Publishers, 1971.

Spector, Ronald. *Admiral of the New Empire: The Life and Career of George Dewey.* Baton Rouge: Louisiana State University Press, 1974.

Sullivan, Mark. *Our Times: The United States, 1900–1925.* Vol. 1. New York: Charles Scribner's Sons, 1937.

Summers, Mark W. *Rum, Romanism, and Rebellion: The Making of a President, 1884.* Chapel Hill: University of North Carolina Press, 2000.

Taft, Charles P., and Bruce L. Felknor. *Prejudice and Politics.* New York: Anti-Defamation League of B'nai B'rith, 1960.

Viereck, Peter. *Shame and Glory of the Intellectuals: Babbit Jr. vs. the Rediscovery of Values.* Boston: Beacon Press, 1953.

Wacker, Grant. "'Charles Atlas With a Halo': America's Billy Graham." *Christian Century* 109 (1992).

Wade, Wyn Craig. *The Fiery Cross: The Ku Klux Klan in America.* New York: Simon and Schuster, 1987.

Walczak, Lee and Richard S. Dunham. "Can Clinton Keep Catholics In His Fold?" *Business Week* (1996): 55.

Walker, Samuel. *In Defense of American Liberties: A History of the ACLU.* New York: Oxford University Press, 1990.

Wang, Peter H. *Legislating "Normalcy": The Immigration Act of 1924.* San Francisco: R and E Research Associates, 1975.

Warner, Emily Smith with Daniel Hawthorne. *The Happy Warrior: A Biography of My Father, Alfred E. Smith.* Garden City, NY: Doubleday, 1956.

Watt, David H. *A Transforming Faith: Explorations of Twentieth-Century Evangelicalism.* New Brunswick, NJ: Rutgers University Press, 1991.

Welch, Richard E., Jr. *The Presidencies of Grover Cleveland.* Lawrence: University Press of Kansas, 1988.

White, John Kenneth and William D'Antonio. "The Catholic Vote in Election '96." *The Public Perspective* (June/July 1992).

White, Theodore H. *The Making of the President 1960.* New York: Atheneum, 1961.

White, Theodore H. *The Making of the President 1964.* New York: Atheneum, 1965.

White, Theodore H. *The Making of the President 1972.* New York: Bantam Books, 1973.

White, Theodore H. *America in Search of Itself: The Making of the President, 1956–1980.* New York: Harper and Row, 1982.
Whitfield, Stephen J. *Culture of the Cold War.* Baltimore: Johns Hopkins University Press, 1991.
Wills, Garry. *Nixon Agonistes: The Crisis of the Self-Made Man.* Boston: Houghton Mifflin, 1970.
Wills, Garry. *Bare Ruined Choirs: Doubt, Prophecy, and Radical Religion.* Garden City, NY: Doubleday and Co., 1972.
Wills, Garry. *The Kennedy Imprisonment: A Meditation on Power.* Boston: Little, Brown, and Co., 1982.
Wilson, James Q. *The Amateur Democrat: Club Politics in Three Cities.* Chicago: University of Chicago Press, 1962.
Wofford, Harris. *Of Kennedys and Kings: Making Sense of the Sixties.* New York: Farrar, Strauss, Giroux, 1980.
Wolfe, James S. "The Religion of and about John F. Kennedy." In *John F. Kennedy: The Promise Revisited.* Paul Harper and Joann P. Kreig, eds. New York: Greenwood Press, 1988.
Wolfinger, Raymond E. *The Politics of Progress.* Englewood Cliffs, NJ: Prentice-Hall, Inc., 1974.
Woolner, David B. and Richard G. Kurial, ed. *FDR, the Vatican, and the Roman Catholic Church in America, 1933–1945.* New York: Palgrave, 2003.

Dissertations and Theses

Hughes, Melvin E., Jr. "The 1928 Presidential Election in Florida." Ph.D. diss., Florida State University, 1976.
Lisle, Teddy David. "The Canonical Impediment: John F. Kennedy and the Religious Issue During the 1960 Presidential Campaign." Ph.D. diss., University of Kentucky, 1982.
McGreevy, John T. "American Catholics and the African-American Migration, 1919–1970." Ph.D. diss., Stanford University, 1992.
Reagan, Hugh D. "The Presidential Campaign of 1928 in Alabama." Ph.D. diss., University of Texas, 1961.
Rosen, Roberta. "A Roman Catholic Runs for President: A Comparison of the Anti-Catholic Literature in the Nineteenth Century, and in the Presidential Campaigns of 1928 and 1960." Master's thesis, Smith College, 1961.
Sarbaugh, Timothy Jerome. "John Fitzgerald Kennedy, The Catholic Issue, and Presidential Politics, 1959–1960." Ph.D. diss., Loyola University of Chicago, 1988.
Smith, John Sword Hunter. "Al Smith and the 1928 Presidential Campaign in Idaho, Nevada, Utah, and Wyoming: A Media Perspective." Ph.D. diss., University of Utah, 1976.

Index

Abortion, 9–10, 82, 97, 160, 164–172
Abram, Morris, 92
Adams, Charles Francis, 37
Africa, 14, 119, 145
African Americans, 8, 12, 17–18, 20–21, 23, 29, 36, 46, 75, 81–84, 90–93, 95, 97, 137, 154–156
Allitt, Patrick, 43
American Civil Liberties Union (ACLU), 69, 72, 78
Americans for Democratic Action, 75, 78–79
Americans United for Separation of Church and State, see Protestants and Other Americans United for Separation of Church and State
Anticommunism, 7–9, 28, 43, 46, 167, 171; see also Communism
Archer, Glenn, 69, 76, 79, 80–81
Bailey, John, 44, 148
Bailey Memorandum, 44, 85, 93–94, 163; assessment of "Bailey thesis," 129–157
Barton, Arthur J., 32
Beacon Press, 80
Bean, Louis H., 44, 129, 163–164
Beecher, Lyman, 12, 15–16, 19, 30, 99
Bennett, David H., 13–14
Bennett, John C., 8, 69, 74, 80
Bernardin, Archbishop Joseph, 166
Bilbo, Theodore, 29–30
Billington, Ray A., 13
Birth control, 33, 69–70, 74, 76, 163
Black, Allida, 147
Blake, Eugene Carson, 74
Blake, Peter, 147
Blanshard, Paul B., 7, 42, 69–77, 80–81, 159, 161
Bob Jones College, 53
Boggs, Hale, 85
Bonzano, Giovanni, 31
Bouscaren, Anthony, 117
Bowles, Chester, 149

Branch, Taylor, 92
Brauer, Carl, 91
Brown, Edmund G. "Pat," 3, 9, 87, 110, 130–141, 148, 157, 161
Brown, Jerry, 9
Brown, Robert McAfee, 69, 72
Buchanan, Patrick J., 9, 160, 165
Buckley, Charles A., 146, 148
Buckley, James L., 114, 124–125
Buckley, William F., 8, 57, 113
Burchard, Samuel D., 18–19, 51
Burner, David, 30–31, 148
Bushnell, Horace, 51
Butler, Paul, 78, 84–86
Byrnes, James F., 40
Caldwell, Willie W., 32
California, 3, 9–10, 35–36, 87, 110, 114, 120, 129–141, 148, 153, 156–157, 161, 163, 166–167, 191n, 194n
Cannon, James, 32
Carey, Mathew, 15
Carol, Juniper, 117
Carrafiello, Vincent, 72
Carroll, Charles, 15
Carroll, James, 169
Carroll, John, 15
Carroll, J. T., 35
Carter, James E., 110, 166–167
Carter, Paul, 35
Catholic Church, 5, 7, 8, 12–19, 21–22, 33–34, 39, 42, 45–46, 51, 54, 56–60, 65, 68–71, 73, 80–81, 99–100, 113–114, 118–121, 124–126, 131, 136, 148, 150–151, 154, 160, 162–163, 169; Pope(s), 3, 6, 13, 18, 22, 28, 30, 40, 43, 52, 55, 75, 86, 99, 100, 108, 122, 152, 167; Pope Day, see Guy Fawkes Day; see also individual popes; Priest(s), 3–4, 16, 18, 21, 30, 33, 39, 50–51, 60–61, 67, 70, 94, 117, 120, 132, 166, 169; Cardinal(s), 8, 21, 31, 38–40, 43, 46,

74, 111, 115, 122, 165–166, 168–169; see also individual names; see also Vatican
Cerf, Bennett, 67, 71
Chamberlain, John, 113
China, 8, 56, 96, 113–114, 117, 124, 126
church-state separation, 3, 5, 7, 27, 29, 33, 42, 46, 66, 67–82 (passim), 84, 93, 100, 116, 143, 148, 159, 161, 168; see also separation of church and state
Clinton, William J., 170–171
Collier, Peter, 148
Colombia, 51, 60
Colson, Charles, 165
Communism, 6–9, 21–22, 28, 39, 42–43, 46, 57, 71, 82, 166–167, 169, 171–172
Cooke, Terence Cardinal, 165
Coolidge, Calvin, 31
Corake, P. W., 36
Coughlin, Charles, 28, 38–39, 41
Cronin, Father John, 120, 188n
Crotty, Peter, 148
Cuba, 20, 126
Cuomo, Mario, 9, 160, 169–170
Curley, Archbishop Michael J., 21
Cushing, Richard Cardinal, 46, 74, 102–103, 121–122
Daley, Richard J., 133, 153
Dallek, Robert, 2
Darling, Edward, 80
Davis, John W., 24
Del Sesto, Christopher, 84, 88
Democratic National Committee (DNC), 31, 41, 78, 86, 89–90, 143, 146
DeSapio, Carmine, 131, 146, 148
Dewey, John, 29, 34, 42
Diem, Ngo Dinh, 160
Dilling, Elizabeth, 118
Dole, Robert, 170
Douglas, Helen Gahagan, 114, 120, 132, 135, 139
Douglass, Frederick, 17
Drinan, Robert, 166
Dutton, Frederick, 132–133
Eagleton, Thomas, 160, 164
Einstein, Albert, 42
Eisenhower, Dwight D., 8, 44, 50, 53–54, 56–57, 64–65, 84, 86–87, 89, 91, 94–96, 114, 116–118, 120–126, 139–140, 145, 147, 150, 156
Engler, John 170

Fadiman, Clifton, 67–68
Farley, James, 6–7, 25, 27–28, 37–41, 45–46, 101
Fawkes, Guy, see Guy Fawkes Day
Ferraro, Geraldine, 9, 160, 167–169, 171
Fillmore, Millard, 17
Finch, Robert, 87–88, 189n
Finletter, Thomas K., 146
Finnegan, James, 45
First Amendment, 14, 69, 72, 116, 159
Fitzgerald, John F., 37
Flanigan, Peter, 125
Ford Foundation, 125
Frankfurter, Felix, 34
Gainey, Dan, 95
Gaither, H. Rowan, Jr., 125
Galbraith, John Kenneth, 70, 93
Garvey, Marcus, 36
Georgia, 9, 20, 29, 92, 129–131, 151–157
Gilbert, Dan, 138
Glass, Carter, 41
Gleason, Philip, 4
Goldman, Ralph M., 129
Goldwater, Barry, 121–122, 161–162
Graham, William "Billy," 7, 49–58, 64–65, 89, 105
Graves, Richard, 133–134, 136
Greater Houston Ministerial Association, see Kennedy, John F. speech to Houston's Ministers
Greeley, Andrew, 4
Green, William J., 133
Gruenther, Alfred M., 86
Gunther, Violet M., 78
Guy Fawkes Day, 13–14, 28
Hall, Leonard W., 88
Hargis, Billy James, 116
Harriman, Averell, 83, 93, 149
Harris, Louis, 130–131, 147, 155; see also Harris Poll
Harris Poll, 164
Harrison, Gilbert A., 75, 78
Hayes, Cardinal Patrick, 31
Hays, Paul, 149
Heflin, J. Thomas, 29–30, 35, 64
Hennessey, James, 4
Higham, John, 11
Hogan, Frank S., 147
Holy See, 6–7, 16, 21–22, 27, 31, 42, 58, 119, 162; see also Vatican, Vatican II
Hoover, Herbert C., 29–32, 37, 96, 108
Hoover, Lou, 32–33, 37

Horowitz, David, 148
Houston Ministerial Association, see Kennedy, John F. speech to Houston's Ministers
Howe, Louis, 31
Humanae Vitae ("On Human Life"), 163
Humphrey, Hubert H., 44, 55, 77, 84–86, 132, 142–143, 162–163
Huntington, Samuel P., 10
Ickes, Harold, 40
Immigration, 10, 12, 16–19, 46, 51–52, 99, 209
Irish Americans, 10, 15–20, 27, 30, 32, 36, 43–44, 46, 51, 55, 67, 71, 99–100, 137, 140, 146, 167, 170
Jackson, Andrew, 19
Jackson, Donald, 117
Jackson, Henry M., 89–90, 94, 139, 186n, 192n
Javits, Jacob K., 147
Jefferson, Thomas, 19, 41
Jenkins, Philip, 13
Jewish Americans, 1, 6, 8–9, 12, 22–23, 29, 36, 38–40, 46, 52, 61, 70, 74, 77–78, 81–84, 88, 91, 93, 95–96, 118, 137, 147, 166
Johnson, Gerald W., 113
Johnson, Lyndon B., 57, 116, 151, 153, 155, 161–162; as part of "Truman-Kennedy-Johnson Team," 124; Vietnam Policy, 163
Jones, Bob, 51
Judd, Walter H., 56
Judeo-Christian, 53, 96, 108, 122–123, 125
Kallen, Horace, 22
Keating, Kenneth B., 147
Kempton, Murray, 4
Kennedy, Edward, 164, 166, 168
Kennedy, Jacqueline, 4
Kennedy, Jean, 115
Kennedy, John F., ix-x, 1–10, 24, 27, 38, 41–47, 102–111; and nativism, 49–50, 53–66; and church-state separation, 67–82, 159–160; and pluralism, 83–98; and communism, 113–127; and Bailey thesis, 129–157; as president, 159–161, 164, 170; speech to Houston's Ministers, 5, 7, 61, 90, 138–139, 144, 150–151
Kennedy, Joseph P., 24, 27–28, 37–41, 45–47, 49
Kennedy, Joseph P., Jr., 41
Kennedy, Patricia, 115
Kennedy, Robert F., 2, 4, 92–93, 95, 115, 161–163, 170
Kennedy, Rose, 45
Keogh, Eugene J., 148
Kerry, John F., 3, 9–10, 160, 169, 171–172
Key, V. O. Jr., 2, 157
Keyes, Alan, 9
Khrushchev, Nikita, 121
King, Coretta Scott, 92–93
King, Martin Luther, Jr., 8, 84, 91–92, 155–156
King, Martin Luther, Sr., 8, 84, 91–93, 155
Knights of Columbus, ix, 19, 33, 70
Krol, John Cardinal, 169
Ku Klux Klan, 6, 12, 18, 20–24, 28–30, 33, 36, 51–52, 64, 70, 83, 91–92, 142, 145
Latin America, 10, 20, 46, 151; see also individual countries, South America
Lawrence, David, 46, 102
Lehman, Herbert H., 83, 146–147
Lindeman, E. C., 34
Lindley, Ernest K., 40
Lippmann, Walter, 22, 29, 33, 126
Lloyd, David, 90, 186n
Lodge, Henry Cabot, 57, 123
L' Osservatore Romano, see *Osservatore Romano*
Lowell, C. Stanley, 69, 76–77, 79–80
Lubell, Samuel, 44, 77, 82, 95, 120, 122–123, 126, 139, 150–152
Luce, Clare Booth, 86
Luce, Henry, 64
Lukas, Edwin, 77
MacArthur, Douglas, 54
Maier, Thomas, 5, 37
Malin, Patrick Murphy, 69, 78
Manion, Clarence E., 118, 188n
Marshall, Charles, 29, 33, 43
Martin, William, 64
Marty, Martin, 72
Massa, Mark, 5
McAdoo, William G., 23–24, 35–36
McCarran, Patrick A., 114
McCarthy, Eugene, 4, 86, 90, 159, 161–163, 169, 171
McCarthy, Joseph R., 8, 28, 41, 43, 113–115, 118, 148; see also McCarthyism
McCarthyism, 143
McCormack, John W., 45, 53, 58, 77
McElvaine, Robert S., 170
McGinley, Conde, 118

McGovern, George, 164–165, 196n
McGreevy, John, 5
McIntyre, Archbishop J. Francis, 120, 132
McKinney, Frank, 45
McKinney, Harold C., 143–144
McWilliams, Carey, 137–138
McWilliams, Wilson Carey, 167
Medieros, Humberto Cardinal, 166
Michener, James A., 67–68, 70, 82, 137
Michigan, x, 9, 109, 129–131, 134, 139, 141–147, 156–157, 170
Miller, William E., 123, 161–162
Miller, Robert Moats, 68
Mitchell, James P., 56, 76, 84, 88, 93–95, 121
Molinari, Susan, 170
Mondale, Walter, 166, 169
Moore, Edmund, 31
Morris, Charles, 4–5
Morse, Samuel F. B., 12, 15–16, 19, 99
Morse, Wayne, 84–85
Mosk, Stanley, 135–136
Mouzon, Edwin, 31–32
Moynihan, Daniel Patrick, 43
Muhammad, Elijah, 83
Mundelein, Cardinal George, 38–41
Murphy, Charles S., 90, 93, 186n
Murphy, Frank, 38
Murphy, James B., ix
Murray, John Courtney, 3, 50, 60–61, 70
Murray, Robert, 24
Muskie, Edmund, 160–161, 163–164
Mussolini, Benito, 22
National Association of Evangelicals (NAE), 58, 63–64, 79–81
National Conference of Citizens for Religious Freedom (NCCRF), 59–63, 65, 79–80; see also Peale, Norman Vincent
National Council of Churches (NCC), 114, 116
Niebuhr, Reinhold, 7, 34, 50, 69, 80, 150
Nixon, Richard M., ix, 1–2, 8–9, 54–58, 64–66, 70, 79, 83–84, 86–91, 93–96, 108, 111, 113–114, 119–127, 132, 135–137, 139–140, 145, 149–150, 152, 154, 156–157, 160, 164–166, 169–171
Novak, Robert D., 113
O'Connell, William Cardinal, 21–22, 39
O'Connor John Cardinal, 9, 168
O'Conor, Charles, 19

Osservatore Romano, 108, 119
Oxnam, G. Bromley, 74
Pacelli, Eugenio, 39
Peale, Norman Vincent, 7, 49–56, 58–63, 65, 121–122, 138–139, 144, 154
Pelikan, Jaroslav, 70, 75
People's Republic of China, see China
Percy, Charles, 122, 189n
Peru, ix-x, 120
Philippines, 45
Phillips, Kevin P., 140
Poland 117, 124; see also Polish Americans
Polenberg, Richard, 3
Poling, Daniel, 63
Polish Americans, 167, 169, 171
Pope, Alexander H., 134
Pope John XXIII, 159–161, 171
Pope John Paul II, 167, 169, 171
Pope Paul VI, 163
Powell, Adam Clayton, 83–84, 91–92
Prendergast, Michael H., 146–148
Protestants and Other Americans United for Separation of Church and State (POAU), 7, 42, 69–81, 180n
Racism, 84, 91, 155–156
Raskob, John J., 31, 38
Reagan, Ronald W., 167–169, 171
Reed, Marshall R., 144
Reitman, Alan, 69, 72
Religious Right, 170–171
Republican National Committee (RNC), 32, 94, 123, 154
Reuther, Walter, 118, 140–141, 143, 145
Richardson, Bill, 10
Roche, John, 79
Robinson, Claude, 87
Robinson, Joseph, 29–30
Rockefeller, Nelson, 136–137, 147
Roe v. Wade, 165; see also Abortion
Romani, John H., 129
Roosevelt, Eleanor, 8, 69, 83, 91, 115, 130, 146–148, 157
Roosevelt, Franklin D., 7, 25, 28–29, 31, 37–41, 46, 51, 54, 70, 116, 124, 167
Roosevelt, Franklin D., Jr., 149
Russell, Richard, 9, 151, 155
Rustin, Bayard, 36
Ryan, John A., 21–22
Sanger, Margaret, 33

Index

Sayre, Frank, 54
Schlesinger, Arthur M., Jr., 7, 11, 70, 75, 86, 93
Schwarzenegger, Arnold, 10
secular, secularism, secularization, 4, 5, 8, 33–34, 42–44, 66, 70, 72, 74–75, 82, 125, 159, 162, 167–168, 170
Shriver, R. Sargent, 9, 84, 92, 160–161, 164–165, 196n
Slayton, Robert, 36
Smathers, George A., 49
Smith, Alfred E., 6, 11–12, 21–25, 27–46, 51–53, 73, 81, 95–96, 101, 108, 111, 115–116, 123–124, 146–147, 151, 155, 169
Smith, Gerald L. K., 8, 114, 118–119, 122, 125
Sorensen, Theodore C., 2, 43–44, 54–55, 61, 74, 85, 88, 93–94, 129–131, 141, 146, 151, 156–157, 159, 163; see also Bailey Memorandum
South America, 120, 137
Soviet Union, 8, 21, 39, 96, 113–117, 121, 125–126, 143, 169, 175n
Spain, 6, 12–14, 17, 19, 39, 51, 54, 60
Spellman, Francis Cardinal, 8, 28, 39, 43, 69–70, 108, 111, 115–116, 121–122, 148
Staebler, Neil, 130, 141–145
Stevenson, Adlai E., 45, 62, 87, 110, 113–115, 117, 120, 133–135, 137–138, 147, 149, 156, 190n
Stowe, Harriett Beecher, 16–17
Switzerland, 58
Symington, Missouri Senator Stuart, 149
Talmadge, Herman E., 154
Tammany Hall, 18–19, 21, 31, 81, 146
Taney, Roger, 17, 175n
Taylor, Clyde, 58
Television, 1, 2, 89, 121, 164
Thompson, Tommy, 170
Timlin, Bishop James, 168

Tipton, Harold, 120
Truman, Harry S., 8, 51, 53, 69, 78–79, 81, 84, 86, 90, 93–94, 114, 124,
"Truman-Kennedy-Johnson Team," 126
Truman Administration, 152
Union of Soviet Socialist Republics, see Soviet Union
United Auto Workers (UAW), 109, 118, 140–141, 145
Vandiver, Ernest, 154, 195n
Vatican, 4, 7, 27, 30, 31, 39, 41, 44–45, 51, 59–60, 63–65, 67, 69, 71, 73–76, 81, 89, 93, 108, 119, 121, 124, 138, 144, 159–162, 169; see also Holy See
Vatican II, 161–162
Venezuela, 120
Vietnam, 160, 162–163, 165, 171
Wacker, Grant, 52–53
Wagner, Robert F., 131, 133, 147–148, 153, 161, 194n
Wallace, Walter C., 88, 94
Walsh, Thomas J., 6, 12, 21, 23–24, 28–29, 34–36, 38, 101
Washington, George, 14
Watson, Thomas, 20
West Virginia, 24, 55–56, 77, 85–87, 135, 143, 149, 152, 162, 191n
Wetzler, Ben, 148
White, Theodore H., 143, 147–148
White, William S., 154
Whitfield, George, 14
Willebrandt, Mabel Walker, 32
Williams, G. Mennen, 9, 109, 130, 139–143, 145–147, 157
Williams, Michael, 30
Williams, Roger, 13
Wisconsin, 55, 77, 85–88, 115, 119, 135, 142–143, 148, 166, 170, 185n, 191n
Wofford, Harris, 84, 91–92
Women, 6, 32, 46, 165, 169
Yugoslavia, 117, 124
Zahn, Edward J., Jr., 88
Ziffren, Paul, 132, 135